LIGHT UP THE DARKNESS

Xulon Press
2301 Lucien Way #415
Maitland, FL 32751
407.339.4217
www.xulonpress.com

Printed in the United States of America.

ISBN-13: 9781545623978

Acknowledgements

There are many pastors, teachers, and friends who have faithfully stood at their posts and impacted me on my life's Journey. Some of their names have been forgotten however the substance of their messages of God's amazing love and power are resident in my soul. We will find their names listed in God's Hall of Fame.

Special thanks to these men who have been on the front lines defending the faith and presenting the Gospel. Some had radio and tape ministries; some were preachers at local churches in towns that I drove through. They were spreading God's messages to whoever would listen on radio broadcasts. These were my companions teaching sound Biblical doctrines as I drove from place to place making business calls. Some, have impacted me on a personal basis. Some were my Pastors at my local church. They continue to touch lives today as they faithfully teach God's Word.

A.R. Bernard Sr., Pastor, Christian Cultural Center, Author and Speaker

James Dobson, PhD., Founder, Focus on the Family, Author

Tim Elmore, Founder, and President of "Growing Leaders," Author and Speaker

Toney Evans, Pastor-Teacher, Oak Cliff Bible Fellowship, featured speaker of "The Alternative" and Author

Chip Ingram, Pastor-Teacher, Venture Christian Church, featured speaker, of "Living On The Edge" and Author

David Jeremiah, Pastor-Teacher, Shadow Mountain Community Church, featured speaker of "Turning Point" and Author

D. James Kennedy (1930-2007), Senior Pastor, Coral Ridge Presbyterian Church, Founder of Evangelism Explosion Institute and Knox Theological Seminary

John MacArthur, Pastor-Teacher, Grace Community Church, Sun Valley, CA, and featured teacher of "Grace To You" Media Ministry

Josh McDowell, Speaker, and Author of more than 150 books including "More than a Carpenter"

J. Vernon McGee (1904-1988), Pastor of Church of the Open Door in Los Angeles, CA, Founder and featured speaker of "Through The Bible"

James Merritt, Pastor-Teacher, Cross Point Church, featured speaker of "Touching Lives," and Author

Adrian Rogers (1931-2005), Pastor, Bellevue Baptist Church, featured speaker, "Love Worth Finding."

Chuck Swindoll, Founding and Sr. Pastor, Stonebriar Community Church, Featured speaker of Insight for Living, Author, and past President of Dallas Theological Seminary

R. B. Thieme, Jr. (1918-2009), Pastor-Teacher, Berachah Church, Houston TX, Author

Ed Young, Sr. Pastor Second Baptist Church, Houston TX

Moody Bible Institute and Moody Radio

Salem and all Christian radio stations that are primarily teaching, training and encouraging Christians to walk closer to God.

Dedication

To you,

the reader

Table of Contents

THE PREMISE

We navigate a complicated world filled with social pressures and an unrelenting "push" to conform. All Christians should, but may not, know the power of timeless principles that help us speak truth to darkness. *Light Up The Darkness* is written to Christians to help them learn and remember who they are in Christ. It is a call to radical change in our lives and the lives of others. This change is based on understanding what God thinks, His will, and His purpose for our lives. It reminds us of why we are here.

We tend to be "creatures of the moment." Christians can attend church regularly and still have little training, knowledge or understanding of who God is and what He desires of us. We have been told over and over again by false prophets and the world that our purpose is to keep the "Ten Commandments." The purpose of the "Ten Commandments" was and still is to prove man could not keep God's standard. They were meant to point us to Jesus. They tell us how to relate with God and how to live in peace with humanity. Not all Christians know they have a Divine purpose or the provisions and Operating Assets God has provided for His children. We are reluctant to talk to strangers or friends about Jesus and the difference He has made in our lives. Our witness has been neutralized because we often spend most of our lives imitating the unbeliever. The path of least resistance tempts us, political correctness muzzles us. Stepping forward to live out our beliefs is consistently discouraged here and around the world.

The purpose of this book is to encourage Christians to remember all that God has done for them. It is a call to duty, for God has appointed us to be Ambassadors of His Kingdom. We are to represent Him, but how exactly do we do that effectively when faced with skepticism, agnosticism, censorship and "gaslighting" from nonbelievers and especially when we don't know what God thinks? It's important to know God's attitudes and insights—how He thinks and how He equips us for our mission, and we can understand all those things. We will explore only four of the Operating Assets which have been provided to aid us in our quest. The Bible, Prayer, Stall Recovery, and the Trust Factor.

1 Corinthians 2:16 and other passages promise that the Bible is the mind of Christ, so we can learn what God thinks as we study scripture. This level of knowledge is desperately needed as we strengthen our walk with God. It might even lead to a course correction for those who struggle to fulfill His purpose in their lives.

OVERVIEW

Light Up The Darkness is divided into seven distinct sections and twenty-two chapters. I've laid out the book in what seems to be a logical progression. However, each chapter stands independently of the others, so you have the freedom to start anywhere and read through it in a way that most interests you. My desire is that it will help you see and understand events in your life from God's view point, and that you that you recognize His appointments in your life. Also, that you will be better equipped to respond to life's situations in a way that glorifies our Lord.

Part I: The Purpose and Overview
Part II: God Exists
Part III. The Situation
Part IV. The Awakening
Part V God Does Intervene In History
Part VI. God Has A Plan For You And Has Equipped You For A Purpose
Part VII. History Is His Story

Part I: The Purpose and Overview

The three-pronged purpose is to provide necessary information for readers to develop confidence in what and why they believe so that they will be better equipped to defend the faith.

Humans, with three exceptions (Adam, Eve and Jesus), were born slaves to sin. Jesus has provided an escape to freedom for us if we will accept it. Those who have become members of His family have been appointed Ambassadors to represent His kingdom. We are beacons to reflect His light, yet most of us have failed. Our reflectors are smudged and filthy. *Light Up The Darkness* provides the necessary basic information for the restoration and maintenance of our mirrors to their proper operating condition.

Part II: God Exists

Based on several current religious surveys, six to eight percent of the world's population is either atheist or agnostic. The balance is either religious or claims no admitted view. These surveys reveal humanity is really baffled about who and what God is. At some point Christian leaders let Christianity be categorized as a religion. It is not! This assumption leads to even more confusion. Religion is man attempting to do what he can in an effort to please God. Christianity is God reaching down to man to save humanity and fellowship with him. Lacking knowledge of what the Bible teaches about God, and not having a solid foundation of God's wisdom, man will fall for anything. God reveals Himself as a Father, a Son, and the Holy Spirit; yet Christians say He is One. Which is He One or Three? This section explains the Trinity and details the function of each member of the Godhead, as well as the Oneness of His Essence.

Part III: The Situation

No perceptible difference exists in the lives of many Christians and unbelievers. We all are searching for happiness and find that it is elusive. For the Christian, happiness is the wrong goal. We should seek a holy lifestyle. But the moment we were rescued from the slave market of sin, Satan put his Operation Neutralization Plan into effect. If he can neutralize us, others will not see us as positive Christian witnesses. If the lost can't see a difference in the way we live, they will see no reason for God. Our lives are our opportunity to show our world that Jesus does make a hugh difference. Political correctness tears at the fabric of who we are in Christ and as a nation. It is imperative for us to remember what God has done and is doing in our lives.

Part IV: The Awakening

We and our children no longer speak the same language. We use the same words, but the words have different meanings or perceptions. The last command our Lord gave before returning to Heaven was to recruit disciples and teach them to obey His commandments. We have our marching orders! It is important to recognize the blessings God has provided. We do that by learning, remembering and acknowledging His grace gifts to us.

Part V: God Does Intervene In History

Five case studies reveal how God has intervened. Historical records of these events leave God out of the accounts. But God cares enough to take action. What Coach Lombardi did with the Green Bay Packers shows us what can happen when we make a mental adjustment. When mindsets are changed, outcomes can be improved. Examples of God intervening in history to change outcomes are meant to encourage and to train. *Light Up The Darkness* should help Christians change their mindset and encourage us to make the mental adjustments we must make if we are going to represent God well.

Part VI: God Has A Plan For You And Has Equipped You For that Purpose

All Christians need to know that God knew us and set a plan in action for our benefit before we were ever formed. PHASE

1 is Salvation, and all that word requires. At the moment of salvation, we become a new creation. We are changed, we are no longer what or who we were. Thirty-eight things happened to us that changed us, and they are documented with Scripture references. PHASE 2, The Believer In Time, begins at the moment of salvation and ends at the rapture or death. Ours is a mission impossible, but we have been equipped with at least one gift, maybe more and essential Operating Assets to enable us to complete our mission. We also have natural talents, which may or may not be utilized to achieve His purpose. PHASE 3 is The Believer in Eternity, beginning at death, the Rapture, or the second advent of Christ. It has no ending.

Part VII: History Is His Story

God is in control—always has been, always will be. From eternity past through all times and throughout eternity future. God has divided time into different segments. He deals with humanity differently in each segment. The intent is to show that neither society nor the environment is not man's problem…man's heart is.

INTRODUCTION

If you've never realized it before now, let me assure you that God has a sense of humor. The only proof I need is that He convinced me to write this book. Once I committed to writing it, I wanted to start at the beginning…but at which beginning should I start? There are so many beginnings! God was patient with me as I struggled with that question. Finally, He had enough, and in that small, still, voice forcibly said, "Just start; it doesn't matter where. Wherever you begin will not be the beginning anyway." So, I did, and He was right. He's always right!

Don't recoil at the idea that I heard God speak. I know that seems spooky. Maybe that's because a lot of scary things have been said and done in the name of God. In our human-centered world, we can lack the wisdom and knowledge to distinguish His voice from other voices. Sometimes our own authority doesn't seem to be enough, and we vainly invoke His name to appear to be speaking with a much higher authority. Neither of these examples is valid in this case. I may have only heard Him in my mind, I don't know, but I did hear Him. It was as real as if He was standing right next to me, and I am convinced that He wanted me to write this for you, and just as importantly, for me. As I resisted, He was consistent in expressing His desire; I could not escape His directive.

One of the fantastic benefits of being a Christian is that we are equipped to hear God's voice no matter how He speaks to us. Sometimes we can hear Him speak in our quiet moments and other times as we read His Word, the Bible. He may speak to us through our parents and friends, sometimes in that small soft voice, or perhaps a loud shout. He may talk as we wrestle with a situation that has enveloped us – sometimes it's in the trickle of a quiet stream of the rush or the mighty river, and sometimes it's in the birds chirping early in the morning. However, He chooses, God does speak to everyone who is listening! God has even created situations to cause those who are not listening to stop and hear Him. Trust in Him always! If we do not, we will not recognize the blessings of His appointments for us each day. The worse possible scenario would be to recognize that we missed one of His appointments, only realizing it after it had passed. No, the worse would be that we are so absorbed in our own agenda that we didn't even realize God was in what just happened.

May it be as meaningful to you as you read it, as it was to me to write.

CHAPTER ONE

The Purpose is to Equip the Saints

Many Jesus followers dream of going to the Holy lands and walking where Jesus walked. Some actually go and come home raving about their life changing experiences. Reading the accounts of the life of Jesus, the things He said and did, we can surmise that Jesus was a very upbeat, happy person. I love the picture of Him smiling and can hear Him laughing out loud. He was personable, and always helping people by solving their unsolvable problems. He didn't worry but instead carried His concerns and petitions to His Heavenly Father. Jesus was always communicating and teaching. He enjoyed being with people the conversations they had. Today, we would describe Him as a "People person." Jesus lived His life in the center of His Fathers Will.

He's always been a People Person. In the earliest preincarnate days Jesus enjoyed walking side-by-side with those who called Him friend. He walked and talked with Adam and Eve in the garden for an undetermined amount of time. Is there anything more enjoyable than walking and talking with a friend in a garden, or park, at the beach, or on a mountain trail?

God and Enoch had such a good time enjoying their fellowship that one day they just kept walking right into Paradise. Enoch didn't die; he just was no more. Abram's faith so delighted the Lord that God said, come on Abram, let's go for a long walk. Abram gathered what he could and off they went. God loved him so much that He changed his name to Abraham and they were constant companions. Abraham was not perfect; the Bible clearly reveals that but God loved him and he loved God, the Bible clearly explains that also. We are not perfect either, and God loves us anyway.

Long ago at another time, when interest rates on home loans soured to over 27%, I was trapped in a project building a house that was to be our dream home. I wasn't a builder and knew nothing about the building trades. What do you have to know? A lot, actually. I had taken wood working and electric shop in high school, but that didn't prepare me for the task before me. I found myself in a place where I had to take on this hugh project and was totally unprepared to handle it. I was given some excellent advice from the professionals, and it all came together. I was the cleanup man for the carpenters, the electrician's helper, the plumber's helper, the insulation installer, the landscape Architect, and crew. When other sub contactors were working, I was there with a clip board in hand trying to look knowledgeable, so they would think I knew what I was doing. I was on site alone a lot, just Jesus and me. My fondest memories of those days are of the fellowship Jesus and I had talking, singings and working. I can relate a little to the task before Noah. God was ever-present with Noah as he built the ark. What's rain? Noah hadn't ever seen rain. Had Noah ever even seen a boat? If he had he certainly had not seen one like the one God was having him build. God was able to communicate with Noah to design and build this escape module, known simply as the Ark. During the building process Noah was preaching to his friends and neighbors, but they didn't listen, they mocked and laughed at him, but God was there to comfort, fellowship and direct. The point is, God is the same today. He still enjoys communicating and fellowshipping with those who love Him, He is always available.

Every believer has a reason for being. We have a purpose. In our eyes, it may be a great or not so great purpose, but in God's eyes, each is necessary and great. God sees the big picture, and we sometimes can't see past our own noses.

Light Up The Darkness is written to provide information that will help us understand:

1. What we believe and why we believe it, therefore equipping us to defend the faith effectively.
2. Who God is, and who we are in Christ.
3. That we have been equipped with promises and Operating Assets so we can accomplish our purposes.

Knowing these things, we will not be able to stand and say, "I don't know enough about Jesus and what He means to me or why you should know Him." We will understand our call and will stand tall in our defense of the faith.

We are called to be the salt and the light of the world. We may become a lighthouse, protecting souls by drawing attention to the hazards and dangers that lurk all around us. We might be a spotlight, searching for the lost or lighting up the way. We might be like a lightning bug with a tiny light that thrills and delights little children, and the child in all of us. We might be a bolt of lightning illuminating the darkness in a soul. The brilliance of that moment is breathtakingly beautiful, and a soul is changed forever. Whatever light we have or may develop, it is not our light; it is His light. We are only mirrors reflecting His light, so let it shine.

These purposes will be accomplished if we become acutely aware of just how much God truly loves us and the multitude of ways He has always shown it. God has, from the beginning, continually intervened in history and will continue until His story (history) is completed. The Old Testament is full of historical interventions by God, and the New Testament includes the highlights of God's thirty-three-year intervention as Jesus as well as the Holy Spirit's motivation and direction and proclamations from the Father.

Archeologists are still confirming the Biblical accounts of ancient history—things once believed to be inaccurate because they could not be proven. But the real reason was and is unbelief. God continues to work in modern times the same way, but the natural man only sees the work as luck or misfortune, a capricious "Mother Nature," or merely unexplainable events. But history is His Story. Interestingly the believer, like the unbeliever will take the credit when the fortunes of life occur and quickly blame God when the misfortunes visit. God reveals His Sovereign right to rule, His Righteousness, His perfect Love, and His perfect plan for each of us—in His perfect timing.

Light Up The Darkness is written primarily, but not only, for people who have been Christians and faithful members of their church, since their youth, and still cannot articulate why they are Christians or what difference Jesus has made in their lives. It is also written for those who are seeking. We who are Christians owe these lost ones, whom we see almost every day, a profound apology for being too timid to speak and share the greatest gift ever given or to share the greatest story ever told. We likewise owe an apology to our Lord for disobeying His departing command.

Some have said God is so infinite that we mortals cannot possibly know and understand Him. That is true to some degree, I suppose. Even His Word says:

Isaiah 55: 8-9 (NIV)

"[8] For My thoughts are not your thoughts neither are your ways My ways," declares the Lord. [9] "As the heavens are higher than the earth, so are My ways higher".

But that cannot be the sum of it. God has recorded the contents of His heart and mind in His Word and protected it throughout all time from being diluted, changed or destroyed. God wants us to know Him in a very personal. intimate and profound way.

The Bible covers history from before the beginning of time and records events that will happen after the end of time. The Bible was written for three reasons: to lead the lost to God, to train the believers in God's ways, and so we can know, with assurance, His love for us and our destiny. The Holy Spirit will open our hearts and minds to the wonders, revelations, and mysteries it contains so we can know without a doubt. We have a destiny, a purpose, and is an integral part of His Story. Within this plan, every believer has a specific purpose for being. You and I are who we are today because we are the sum of our lineage that has gone on before us. It is no coincidence that we find ourselves here at this time and place in these particular circumstances. There is a considerable purpose for our being, and it has to do with the here and now.

If the Saints walk close to God; if we see and hear the things happening around us from His perspective instead of a secular worldview. If we can recognize His appointments in our lives, our decisions and our actions will bring glory to our Lord. If the Saints become courageous and fearless in our defense of the Gospel of Jesus Christ—then God will smile and say well done.

Over eighty percent of the world's population acknowledges the existence of a supernatural power. Even nature in all its splendor reveals it is the result of a master designer and that designer is the God of the universe.

Luke 19:40 (NIV)

40 *"I tell you," he (Jesus) replied, "if they (humans) keep quiet, the stones will cry out."*

Psalm 19:1-2 (NIV)

1 *The heavens declare the glory of God; the skies proclaim the work of his hands.*
2 *Day after day they pour forth speech; night after night they reveal knowledge.*

There is a master plan. The existence of a supernatural, super-powerful entity is inescapable to even the casual observer of nature. Sadly, many choose to worship the creation rather than the Creator. Still, others try to earn their way to a heavenly afterlife through good works or certain other behaviors. The belief that we must earn our way to a heavenly existence is so common that it has even wormed its heretical way into some of Christendom. God's Word has consistently renounced this concept from the earliest writings. Salvation is a free gift of God!

There are only two groups of people on Earth—the unbelievers and the believers.

A. There are three groups of unbelievers:
   1.) Those who refuse to believe in spite of the evidence before them.
   2.) Those who agree that there may be a God, but haven't seen any evidence of one. They say they are open to being convinced. They are not searching, but instead are sitting back with their eyes closed waiting for someone to convince them. They sit on the throne of their lives and see no need. Those who search find.

Many of our most prominent Apologists were once skeptics who honestly searched for the truth.

3.) Those lost in religion trying to earn their way to Heaven.
   a. They who worship the creation rather than the Creator.
   b. They who believe they must appease God by whatever means man can imagine.
   c. They who believe they can gain God's favor by keeping laws or customs.

B. Believers are saved by grace and believe God rather than man. Believers can be divided into two groups:
   1.) Christians who are in fellowship with God because God is on the throne of their lives.
   2.) Carnal Christians who are out of fellowship with God. They imitate the unbeliever; they sit on the throne of their lives. Since they are saved, their salvation is secure. They did nothing to earn it, and they can do nothing to lose it. This behavior does not surprise God. He was prepared for it and has provided a way for the fallen believer to recover and regain the lost fellowship. Stall Recovery is extremely important; it is the subject of Chapter 19.

The tricky part is that in a moment, the Lord of the Christian's life can change. We can be "in the Spirit" singing His praises one moment, and then something happens that causes us to slip back into our human habits of imitating the unbeliever. We become lord of our life and fall out of fellowship. We should recognize the change and execute the Stall Recovery technique immediately, agreeing with God that we are wrong, and ask for forgiveness.

Some of us falsely believe that Christians cannot sin. They are wrong and can't square that concept with scripture.

Many falsely believe that they can lose their salvation. They cannot. If they have it, they can't lose it. Because they think they can lose their salvation, they actually don't know if they are saved or not. When asked if they are going to heaven, their response will always be "I hope so," or "I think I am," or "I try to be good." If you ask, "how good do you have to be to go to heaven?" They don't know. The truth is, not one of us can be good enough. If it were possible for anyone to be good enough to go to heaven, Jesus went to the cross for nothing.

Christians should know they are going to heaven; they should answer with assurance, "Yes I am going to heaven. Jesus completely paid my debt on the cross and set me free. Jesus is my Lord and Savior, and I am heaven bound."

Some become very religious, doing as the Scribes and Pharisees did, becoming legalistic and trying to do what they cannot do—keep the Law.

Too many Christians believe that they are not equipped to talk intelligently about Jesus, and they are right. New Christians—knowing very little—are excited, enthusiastic and eager to tell others about the difference Jesus has made in their lives, and the Gospel spreads. If they aren't taught, they don't mature, and the enthusiasm wanes. There is so much to learn, and they realize they know so little and are eager to learn. If they aren't taught, they fall for one of Satan's best tricks; they become afraid that they will not represent their Lord well, so they fail their primary mission to make disciples and train them. Or worse, they fall away from Jesus completely.

When God called us, He changed us and provided the necessary assets for us to fulfill His purpose for our lives. Our primary objective is to know God and to know Him well enough to introduce Him to those who do not. We are to be His light. No matter what our spiritual gifts, talents, or purpose, our primary mission is to light up the darkness with His love. To be effective, we desperately need to know Jesus better.

C. There remains one other group of people we see today; they call themselves "nones" and we are seeing more and more of them. I'll call them the "disengaged people." The disengaged people just seem to hang out. Nothing seems to bother or excite them. They are here, but not here at the same time. Nothing seems to be real to them. They don't seem to have the capability to think, plan, or execute. They seem just to exist, mechanically going through necessary motions void of feeling or emotion. Their entire vocabulary seems to be "whatever," "like," "you know, like" and "no problem." They seem to just live in the moment, like our pets do, only less. Our pets show joy, happiness, sadness, anger, and defensiveness. The "disengaged people" seem to have no dreams, no passion, and there are no signs of joy, happiness, anger, or defensiveness there. They seem to be totally indifferent to their circumstances or other people. Some can still smile, but most show no emotion, either good or bad. A "none" could be an unbeliever or a believer. If he is an unbeliever, he would have answered the survey "nothing particular" or "don't know." If he is a Christian, he's like the Prodigal Son, away from his Father, away from his friends, and anything meaningful. What can we do to help him wake-up when we encounter him in one of God's Appointments? Say a quick, silent prayer asking for God's intervention and words, then go straight to the heart of the matter and ask in a kind engaging way, "When you die, will you go to heaven? If he says yes, respond with another question. When you get there and God askes you why should I let you in my heaven, what will your answer be? These are engaging questions that can be used anytime, with anyone, not just the "nones."

The Marine Corps taught me that we learn best through repetition. The instructors repeated their teaching points over and over again. They taught us what to do and what not to do. No matter what – they focused like a laser beam to ensure that we learned. They told us what they were going to teach us, and then they taught us, and then they told us what they had taught us, then we were tested. Next, we reviewed the test. Instructors would test us again and again until we all got it right. The instructors were striving to equip us so that when a situation confronted us, our response would be automatic, swift, and correct. They knew, even if we didn't, that if our response was less than immediate and correct, we or our brothers-in-arms would be dead or wounded, and the mission jeopardized.

The significant difference is that God's mission will never be in jeopardy. The war has already been won, the battle is over, and Jesus has the victory. So, what's our end goal? We are looking for the stragglers, the wounded, and the lost ones. We're on a rescue mission. Some have asked, "Why does God tarry? Why doesn't He come back now?" God doesn't tarry; He's waiting for the late soul who will be saved.

The Marine instructors tested us so they would know what we learned and what we had not learned. Their purpose was to know that we knew the lesson. As Christians, the tests we face are not so God can discover if we have learned a precept, a principle, or a doctrine. He already knows. The purpose of the test is so we will know. If the Bible says something once, it is important. If it says it two or more times, it is very important. Many times, it will say "do something this way," or "don't do it another way." So, as you read through this book, you're going to say to yourself, "I've read this before," or "This seems familiar." That's good. You've found a valuable nugget; just know you may see it again. The fabric of faith is a carefully woven fabric.

His voice will become increasingly profound when we fail to hear Him. Just as He did with David, our Lord will do everything He can to lead us in His ways and keep us on His path. However, in the end, it's our choice to hear and obey. We have volition, (freedom of choice), even in the way we relate to Him. One thing He will not do is violate our volition. We are not robots without a mind or will, and we are not wired to respond this way or that way. God gets no glory when we choose not to obey. "Why does that matter?", you ask. "I'm glad you asked." Some say that when Satan and his angels were thrown out of Heaven, Satan shouted in stunned disbelief, "that's not fair, how can a good God do such a mean thing?" To prove to Satan that His judgment was fair and just, God created man a little lower than the angels. Every time an individual chooses to believe God Satan is proven wrong; at the same time, God and the heavenly host derive much joy.

We, like David and Solomon and any of the Saints, can choose not to relate to Him. When this happens, we imitate the unbeliever by putting ourselves on the throne of our own lives and become consumed in a frantic search for happiness. When we are not in fellowship with God, it becomes increasingly hard to hear His voice because we are listening and flirting with the things of the world. We do not have dual citizenship. We cannot belong to the world and be faithful to Christ. Before we accepted Jesus as our Lord and Savior, we were citizens of the world, enslaved by our nature to sin.

Romans 6:17 (NIV)

17 *But thanks be to God that, though you used to be slaves to sin, you have come to obey from your heart the pattern of teaching that has now claimed your allegiance.*

Ephesians 1:7 (NIV)

7 *In Him, we have redemption through his blood, the forgiveness of sins, in accordance with the riches of God's grace.*

Americans believe that slavery is an ugly blot in our past and that today any baby born in the USA is born free. The Bible teaches that everyone was born an unbeliever, in slavery to sin and that Jesus has redeemed us. Three different Greek words are translated as "redeemed" or "redemption," one means to buy in a marketplace. First-century slave owners could purchase a slave and then sell him again. The second word is stronger and means to buy out of a slave market, never to be resold again. The third word means "to buy and to lose or set free." Jesus Christ paid the ransom price for our sins with His blood. Our sins became His sins, and His righteousness became our righteousness; we were set free. Only one condition is attached to our freedom, and that is we must believe and accept (claim the gift) as our own. Only when we accept Jesus as our Lord and Savior are we truly free.

At that moment in time, when we accept Jesus as our Lord and Savior, we become a child of God and a joint-heir with Jesus. Our citizenship changed. We are now citizens of the Kingdom of God. All we knew was enough to be saved, but at that moment we are appointed Ambassadors for Christ. Much honor has been bestowed on us, and the angels cheered when we accepted Jesus; our lives were forever changed. We can never be the same again. We had been spiritually dead, but now we are spiritually alive. We are privileged as His Ambassadors in this foreign and hostile land, to allow Him to work through us. It is an honor to represent Him, and it is our duty to do it well to accomplish His purpose in our lives.

We can only accomplish this by knowing how He thinks and how He views things. Yes, we can know these things. He is the master communicator. It is fantastic, the length God has gone to ensure His story is known. Yet so many of us know so little. If you believe you don't know enough about being a Christian to share the good news with others or don't even know what I'm talking about, God had you in mind when

He ordered this book be written. It is essential that we know these things, and that we grow in our knowledge of God.

Are our mirrors broken, smudged or filthy? Have they been cleaned recently, if at all? We should be diligent to always reflect a clean, clear and undistorted light of the image of Christ in our lives. In these times, it is entirely possible that you may be the only Jesus those around you may see, and it is your duty to *Light Up The Darkness*.

CHAPTER TWO

God Does Exist

It's essential that we know God and the provisions He has made for humanity. We must get this right. It is imperative that we know God, not just "know about" Him. We need to know Him intimately so we can make Him known to those in our world. We cannot be too embarrassed or too dumbed-down to tell our world what Jesus has done for us. This is our time; we were born to live in and be a part of this time, so let's see if we can make a difference.

Too many voices are demanding that we Christians sit down, shut up, and stop sharing the most significant story of our lives. It's an illusion. Not everyone wants or expects us to be quiet—it's only the loud-mouthed bullies. Your unbelieving friends and acquaintances who know that you are a Christian expect you to be different. When you are not, they are disappointed and may even draw your attention to your lack of fidelity. So, I encourage you, for their sakes and the sake of your witness, always be ready to stand up, speak up, and proclaim the wonders and blessings you have seen. You have seen these marvels and blessings because your eyes have been opened to His glory. In your past, the Holy Spirit used someone to share the Gospel with you. Now it's your turn to share the Gospel with someone else.

Lacking Knowledge, People Will Believe Anything

A survey dated April 12, 2015, by WIN Gallup International (no relation to Gallup Inc.)

reports that 63% of the world's population is religious and 22% are not. Atheists make up 11% of the global population. Global, in this case, refers to the 65 countries from which the pollsters were able to acquire data. An atheist believes there is no God or gods. An agnostic believes that nothing is known nor can be known of the existence or nature of God, or of anything beyond material phenomena. In other words, an agnostic is a person who claims neither faith nor disbelief in God. He is described as a skeptic, a doubter, a rationalist. 63% + 11% +22% = 96% the margin of error was reported to be 2.14 and 4.45 + 3% to 5% and a 95% confidence level.

According to the report, the most "faith-filled" countries in the world have a population of more than 90% who describe themselves as "religious," specifically: Thailand, Armenia, Bangladesh, Georgia, and Morocco. It's worth pointing out that the most "faith-filled" countries are not Christian countries. Seven out of ten (70%) Russians reported they were religious. The USA was lukewarm at 56%. The United Kingdom was reported to be 30% religious. On the other hand, the least "religious" countries were China, Hong Kong, Japan, Czech Republic, Spain, and Sweden the least religious nation reported 10% were religious.

Revelation 3:15-16 (NIV)

15 *I know your deeds that you are neither cold nor hot. I wish you were either one or the other!* 16 *So, because you are lukewarm – neither hot nor cold – I am about to spit you out of my mouth.*

This subject matter brings me to observations from the late John Vernon McGee, Th.D., LL. D, (June 17, 1904 - December 1, 1988). McGee was a great man of God and remains an inspiration to me personally. I include the quote below from this renowned Bible scholar and a graduate of Columbia Theological Seminary and Dallas Theological Seminary to further examine the great "falling away" we see globally, and the status of the churches referenced in Revelation. Notably, McGee served as a Presbyterian pastor in Georgia, Tennessee, and Texas, and moved to Los Angeles in 1949 to become the pastor of the Church of the Open Door, a nondenominational church. He continued as pastor until 1970. In 1967 he began broadcasting the Thru the Bible program, which was a systematic study of each book of the Bible. Thru the Bible has been translated into more than 100 languages and continues to be heard on more than 800 radio stations in North America and is broadcast worldwide via radio, shortwave and the Internet; even today 29 years after his death.

According to Dr. McGee:

"When the Lord Jesus said to the Laodicean Church, "You are neither hot nor cold," they knew exactly what He was saying, and amazingly so do we today. A cold church actually means the church that has denied every cardinal doctrine of the faith. It is given over to formality and is carrying on in active opposition to the word of God and to the Gospel of Christ. You find today in liberalism that they are in active opposition to the Gospel of Jesus Christ. Hot speaks to those with real spiritual fervor and passion like the Christians in Ephesus, although they were even then getting away from their best love. Oh, the Spirit of God, who brought them to a high pitch in their personal relationship with Christ! But the Laodicean church was neither hot nor cold - just lukewarm. Between those positions of hot and cold, you have this lukewarm state. I would say that this is a picture of many churches today in the great denominations that have departed from the faith.

Many churches--both in and out of these denominations -- attempt to maintain a middle-of-the-road position. They do not want to come out flat-footedly for the word of God and for the great doctrines of the Christian faith; and at the same time, they do not want to be known as a liberal church. So, they play footsie with both groups, i.e., a broken fellowship with quite a few men who are extremists in both directions, some extreme fundamentalists and some extreme liberals. And many of these men attempt to play both sides of the street. That is a condition that is impossible. This is the thing that makes the Lord Jesus sick. He is very frankly, saying that he will spew them out of his mouth. In my judgment, this middle-of-the-road position is the worst kind of hypocrisy there is. But the thing that is absolutely startling and frightening and fearful is that he says, I was spitting you out of my mouth. In other words, I will vomit you out of my mouth ... because you are lukewarm. I am of the opinion that if He spoke to a lot of churches today, He would say You make me sick at my stomach. You're professing Christians. You say you love Me. You say it, but you don't mean it."

To expand on the concept of "hot," "lukewarm," and "cold," let's look at statistics regarding United States atheists and agnostics. They make up 6% of the population, while those who describe themselves as "religious" total 56%. Surprisingly 33% consider themselves as "non- religious." There are two surprising things about these United States numbers:

1.) In the U.S.A. where church doors are open, and Christianity is allowed, and Christian radio abounds throughout the nation, 56% claim to be religious. The 56% includes an array of non-Christian organizations. So, according to these numbers, Christianity in America is less than 56%of the population.
2.) A segment of our population, 33%, describes themselves as nonreligious. If these percentages are genuinely representative of our population, we have a huge mission

> field right here in our backyard. My first reaction was that these numbers could not possibly be right. But if Christendom is withdrawing from society, this report may be a warning shot fired across our bow to get our attention. We cannot stay in our boats, in our comfort zones, and succeed in fulfilling our primary command. Christians have always been called to walk in faith, not in our comfort zones. If we think going to church on Sunday is what sets us apart, we are mistaken. Jesus living within us makes the difference in our lives and sets us apart. If we put His light under a basket and refuse to light up the darkness, we have lost our purpose for being.

Another study, The 2014 Religious Landscape Study (RLS) by Pew Research Center gives another view of how Americans see themselves regarding religion.

CHRISTIANS	70.6%	
Evangelical Protestant		25.7% to 21.7%
Mainline Protestant		14.7%
Historically Black Protestant		6.5%
Catholic		20.8%
Mormon		1.6%
Orthodox Christian		0.5%
Jehovah's Witness		0.8%
Other Christian		.0% to 4%
NON CHRISTIANS	6.0%	
Jewish		1.9%
Muslim		0.9%
Buddhist		0.7%
Hindu		0.7%
Other World Religions		0.3%
Other Faiths		1.5%
UNAFFILIATED (religion none)	23.5%	
Atheist		3.1%
Agnostic		4.0%

Nothing Particular	15.8%
Don't Know	0.6%

What do all of these numbers tell us? They tell us a lot if we study them. At the most basic level, four things that jumped off the pages:

1.) Humans are really confused about the most important decision they will ever make.

2.) Christians who know the truth are very ineffective at sharing it. Categories such as unaffiliated, nothing particular, and don't know should simply be unacceptable in the Christians in the U.S.A.

3.) The non-Christian activists shout loudly that the U.S.A. is no longer a Christian nation. Religious organizations even mainstream Christian dominations proclaim that America is in a Post Christian era. This report reveals a different, rather convincing story. It shows that a hugh majority of the population declares their Christianity, making America a Christian nation. There is a falling away from traditional Christianity as defined by the church, and that is what needs to be addressed.

4.) That a tiny minatory group, probably 7% of the population is able to speak so loudly that entire national population is believing and following their lead. The rolls are reversed. Christianity is supposed to be winning the world.

~ CHAPTER THREE ~

Christianity and Religion

The atheist declares, "There is no God." God speaks to humanity and says:

Psalm 14:1 (NIV)

[1] *The fool says in his heart, 'There is no God.' They are corrupt; their deeds are vile; there is no one who does good.*

Everyone else knows that God exists and has a personal idea or image of what He is like. In the United States, of those polled in the 2014 Religious Landscape Survey by Pew Research Center, about twenty percent were clueless, claiming "nothing particular" or they "don't know" whether they are religious or not. Here's a mission field at our doorstep. 76 percent claimed to be religious. They worship some kind of god, but not the same god. Eleven different groups identify themselves as religious people. These eleven groups can be divided into two major categories: Christian and Non-Christian. There is a vast difference between Christianity and religion.

Some believe God is so incomprehensible that we as humans can't thoroughly know and understand Him, and that is partly true—but not completely true.

Isaiah 55:8-9 (NIV)

8 "For my thoughts are not your thoughts, neither are your ways my ways," declares the LORD. 9"As the heavens are higher than the earth, so are my ways higher than your ways and my thoughts than your thoughts."

We can and must know and understand as much about God as He Himself has revealed.

Too many of us know about God, but don't know Him as a friend. We fail to spend any time in fellowship with Him and yet we consider ourselves to be a Christians without a functioning knowledge of God presence in our lives. We can grasp an understanding of God, but not the totality of Him. As humans, our idea of God is finite, but God is infinite. We, therefore, sometimes ascribe to God human traits that He really doesn't have. We use them because they help us better understand His nature and character. The Bible pictures Jesus as sitting at the Father's right hand, etc. These anthropomorphisms are human traits used to describe God. God is Spirit, not human. Jesus doesn't sit, and the Father doesn't have a right hand, but we understand that the Father is the highest authority and Jesus is in the most favored position.

Isaiah 46:9-10 (NIV)

9 Remember the former things, those of long ago; I am God, and there is no other; I am God, and there is none like Me. 10 I make known the end from the beginning, from ancient times, what is still to come. I say, 'My purpose will stand, and I will do all that I please.'

God declares His sovereign reign in all creation, His eternal life having no beginning and no end, and the absolute power to make His will so.

Isaiah 45:5a (NIV)

I am the LORD, and there is no other; apart from me, there is no God…

God has no credible rival. We will see in the end that He rules supreme. Satan has declared, "I will be like God," which is not the same as equal to God. He didn't have the power to accomplish his desire when he was a guardian for God's throne room and he has less power now. To each one of us, God has given "free will," and we can use that to put ourselves on the throne during our lifetime. In the end, though, every knee will bow, and every tongue will confess that Jesus is Lord.

Philippians 2:10-11 (NIV)

11 *That at the name of Jesus every knee should bow, in heaven and on earth and under the earth, and every tongue acknowledges that Jesus Christ is Lord, to the glory of God the Father.*

Romans 14:11 (NIV)

11 *It is written: As surely as I live, says the Lord ever knee shall bow before Me; every tongue will acknowledge God.*

1 Samuel 2:2 (NIV)

2 *No one is holy like the LORD! There is no one besides You; there is no Rock like our God.*

As a side note, where the Bible reads LORD, it is referring to all three members of the God Head. When it reads Lord, it speaks of Jesus the Christ. When it reads lord, it isn't identifying deity at all but is human in nature.

There is only one God, and He has made His desires known to man. So why is there so much confusion concerning who He is, what He requires, and how we should worship Him?

The simple answer is, man doesn't have the capacity to understand spiritual things, and God is Spirit. Man was initially created with a "spirit," and Adam and Eve were able to communicate and understand spiritual things through that "spirit." This was a human spirit, not the Holy Spirit. When Adam and Eve sinned, the human spirit died and can't function in natural man.

Genesis 1:26-27 (NIV)

> 26 *Then God said, "Let us (The Father, the Son, the Holy Spirit) make mankind in our image, in our likeness, so that they may rule over the fish in the sea and the birds in the sky, over the livestock and all the wild animals, and over all the creatures that move along the ground."* 27 *So God created mankind in his own image, in the image of God he created them; male and female He created them.*

What do you suppose the scripture means when it says God created us in His image? In Their image would indicate that humans would be a reflection or a likeness of Him. Well, we certainly don't look like God. We are unique in the way we look; no other person looks or acts exactly like anyone else. We may be similar in appearance, but there are no replications. We may act or react similarly, but each one of us is unique, just as each snowflake is uniquely designed. No two are exactly alike. Therefore, God isn't saying that we look like Him or that we will act like Him. We don't even have the attributes of God. He is God, and we are not. However, He is saying that each person would be a three-part being, with a body, soul, and spirit.

We, like God, are triune beings. The body allows the soul and spirit to live in Earth's atmosphere; it is our space suit, so to speak. The soul is our identity. It houses the real us. It's our memory center, our norms and standards, our emotions, our frame of reference, our viewpoint, vocabulary, self-consciousness, volition, conscience, and everything that makes us uniquely us. The human spirit is that part of us that allows us to understand spiritual phenomena. It's the speaker and amplifier of God's unique communication system.

That's the way Adam and Eve were created and lived until Eve ate of the forbidden fruit. She believed Satan instead of God and ate so she could be like God. She was tempted to have that very same desire that got Satan thrown out of heaven. Adam believed Eve and followed her lead instead of believing God. In doing so, Adam gave up his position of being the head of the household and of having dominion over the Earth. God had given dominion over the Earth to Adam, and Adam surrendered it to Satan by not believing God.

The disbelief on that day still has repercussions to this very day. This is serious business. Do you think not believing God always has serious consequences? You can bet it does! At that moment, they died just as God said they would. They died spiritually, not physically. When they sinned, they lost the ability to understand spiritual things. The human spirit shriveled up and died. Also, because of Adam's choice, the nature to sin has infected all humanity. We all inherited Adam's nature to sin; his "sin nature," and we have an empty spot or (vacuum) where the human spirit was originally located. When we become Christians, that human spirit is rejuvenated or born again, it lives again and is the home of the Holy Spirit, but the "sin nature" remains with us.

The unbelievers have a void where the human spirit should be. This void creates a vacuum, and without the Holy Spirit, it becomes the resting place for any religion that man can create. Man, instinctively knows there is a higher authority. "Christianity" is not "religion!" Let me say that again: "Christianity is not a religion!" I want to shout that out again "Christianity is not a religion!!" Sometimes in our past, Christians allowed people to perceive Christians as religious, and as a result, we are lumped together with those who have fallen for one of Satan's greatest lies. In fact, Satan loves religion because it deceives so many into thinking that man can somehow earn God's favor. The "somehow" is wide open, so if man can imagine it and convince others it's the true way, it might become a major religion someday. Religions refuse to believe God, even though its followers believe there is a god.

Christianity is God reaching down to lift man up. Christianity is all about what God has done to reinstate fellowship with man. Man does nothing but accept it. Any good deed that a Christian does must be in appreciation of God's love for him or her, not an effort to gain God's approval. Religion is man reaching up to God attempting to gain favor. Religion requires man to consistently perform deeds to earn his salvation, and thereby gain God's favor for a time. But that salvation can be lost by displeasing God. Religious activities are a stench in God's nostrils; they are an abomination to Him.

**"Religion is DOING,
Christianity is DONE!"**

~ Dr. James Merritt ~

CHAPTER FOUR

How God Chose To Reveal Himself

Some may be confused when we talk about God the Father, God the Son, and God the Holy Spirit, and then we say that God is One. Which is it? Is God One or is He (they) three? Let me be emphatic with my answer. God is one, not three!

There are not three Gods! We do not worship three Gods! God is three in function or personalities, and one in essence. It's as simple as that. We should not be confused. All of our praise, adoration, and prayers should be directed to the Father. God has revealed Himself as our Heavenly Father, as Jesus, and as the Holy Spirit. That's the way He chose for us to relate to Him. Jesus said, "I and the Father are one. I must go so the Spirit can come."

THE TRINITY

God the Father, God the Son, and God the Holy Spirit is the Trinity – always capitalized, just as we typically capitalize all holy references of His name. As a side note, I capitalize the pronouns he, him, and his when referring to God the Father, God the Son, and God the Holy Spirit. This capitalization may or may not appear in certain translations of the Bible from which I quote, but certainly appear in my own writing in deference and respect.

God is truly indescribable, exceptional perfection. However, He wants us to know Him on the deepest level within our realm of human understanding. Therefore, He manifests in three separate and distinct personalities, but one in essence. He does so to allow us to relate to Him.

Some good examples of worldly trinities exist, but none are perfect examples of God.

1. The egg is a trinity. It has a shell, a yoke and a white. All three parts are different, but it is one egg. The shell by itself is not an egg; neither is the yoke nor the white. Therefore, the simple egg illustration isn't an excellent example because it would indicate there are three parts to God. This is not the case. Again, God is revealed in three separate and distinct personalities each one is complete, and each one is God, but they are one in essence.

2. Light is a better example. It is one in essence and has three properties. You don't have to understand light it to use it.

Actinic: A property (UV) of light that is neither seen nor felt. It illustrates the Father.

Luminosity: This is the light; it is both seen and felt. It illustrates the Son.

Calorific: The production of light generates heat. Heat is felt but not seen and illustrates the Holy Spirit.

3. Water is sometimes used to illustrate the Trinity. Water is one. There can be a lot of it or just a drop of it, but it is still water, and it is one. We can change the form of water, to a solid (ice); to gas (steam); or it can be liquid ...but it is still water. It is composed of two parts of Hydrogen and one part

of Oxygen. This is not the best example; sure, it's available in three forms and consists of three parts, but the two parts of Hydrogen are identical. $H^{2}0$ by any name is still and always will be water.

4. I can use myself as an example. I am a son, I am a father, and I am a husband—but I am one. Ask my parents, my children, and my wife who I am, and you'll get three different answers. I fill a different need and have a different purpose for each of them, but I am still just one.

You get the idea. Many examples of trinities are seldom thought of in that way. Have fun thinking of some.

THE THREE PERSONALITIES and FUNCTIONS of GOD

~ GOD THE FATHER ~

God the Father is the planner, the head. He is the architect of our salvation and our life after being "born again." Western society is obsessed with the idea of becoming a matriarchal or even an asexual society, thus eliminating the father lead and the patriarchal role.

But Jesus taught us to pray to the Father, not to Him nor the Holy Spirit. He addressed God as "Father," followed by "Abba" (or Daddy). The father figure in society has the God assigned responsibilities of protecting, providing for, and planning for his family. God also holds the father responsible for training the children in the way he should go, which includes the spiritual instruction and discipline.

Our earthly fathers are supposed to be living pictures of our Heavenly Father. Many of us have failed, and our children have a distorted or even harmful, mental picture of God the

Father. I, for one, have fallen short of the assume responsibility too often. But remember that God is not a man, and man's failures must not be attributed to God.

Try to think of what a perfect earthly father would be like, and that may give you just an inkling of what God the Father is like. While you're running through this exercise, know that our heavenly Father has none of the shortcomings of our earthly fathers, and He knows exactly what we need. Trust that He is always working to your benefit so that you can be the best you can be.

Today, many families and homes have no father present, he has died, divorced or has abandoned his family. He may be present physically but has refused to accept the spiritual leader of the home responsibility. God has not relieved him of this responsibility, but if anyone is going to see to this most critical responsibility, it will be the Mom who willingly takes on one more care giving role. God bless her.

~ GOD THE SON ~

The Son is the executor of the Father's plan. He is the unique person of the universe, both 100% God and 100% man. The Son is God with flesh. He became man via the virgin birth. Sin had infected the human race through Adam's seed. Jesus, through the virgin birth, escaped that infection and is without the sin nature. Jesus had a step-father, but no natural father. A feat that is just as amazing is Jesus, in His humanness, lived a sinless life without calling on His divine capabilities. These two facts made Him the perfect sacrificial lamb for our sins. The justice and righteousness elements of God's essence were satisfied with His sacrificial death because He had neither committed sins of His own nor inherited a sin nature from Adam! He was the spotless lamb.

Therefore, His death was the perfect payment in full of all of our sins. He became our sacrificial lamb. If we repent (turn from) and confess our sins (agree with God that we have sinned), and ask Jesus to come live in us, He becomes our Lord and Savior. Our salvation is a free gift because Jesus has paid the price for every sin that we will ever commit. He had to because we couldn't.

Some say Jesus cannot be God. They are basing that assumption on their interpretation of Biblical scriptures when Jesus is speaking.

The rebuttal is simple. They are wrong because they fail to recognize the uniqueness of Jesus. They see only the humanity of Jesus, but Jesus is entirely God and fully human at the same time. No one else could qualify to fill this unique position. He was and is the unique person of the universe. He divested Himself of His divine authority and became a man. He was tested far beyond the ways that man could be tested because He was God and could have exercised His divine power at any time. However, doing so would have destroyed the Father's plan for our salvation.

He was tempted to turn stones into bread when He was very hungry, and this was a real temptation for Him. After all, He could easily turn stones into bread and completely satisfy His hunger. That test would not have tempted us because we absolutely can't turn stones to bread. He submitted His will to the Father's will 100% of the time. Furthermore, Jesus did not become God after dying on the cross, as some say. He didn't earn His position in heaven as others surmise. He has always been God and was in Heaven before He came to earth. Jesus did not earn His place in Heaven, and neither can we earn our place in Heaven.

When Jesus is quoted in the Bible, He was speaking to humans in His humanity using terms, words, and examples that the people would understand. He is the master communicator. The world sees only the humanity of Jesus and says that Jesus was a great moral teacher. Some even say he was a prophet. Peter had been with Jesus from the beginning of His ministry, and still didn't fully understand who Jesus was. Even when he responded to the question "Who do you say I am?" he responded with, "You are the Messiah sent by God." Peter didn't observe something that the others hadn't seen. He hadn't pondered the subject. His answer just rolled out of his mouth, as smooth as silk. It was revealed to Peter by the Holy Spirit. Jesus was the one who reveals the source of Peter's wisdom. Peter still didn't understand completely, and neither do we. Today, people recognize who Jesus is the exact same way. The Holy Spirit reveals Jesus to us.

The book of James can be misunderstood. The Holy Spirit inspired the stepbrother of Jesus (James) to write to us saying if we have Jesus, our works will prove that we are Christ followers. James is not saying we must or can work to earn our way into heaven. We were saved to serve and evangelize. We don't serve to be saved. James is saying that without good (divine) works, there will be no rewards or crowns given at the Judgment (Bema) Seat of Christ. These rewards will be presented on a raised platform in heaven, after the Rapture of the Church, to His followers in the presence of all the Saints and God the Father.

In scripture, the picture of the Bema Seat is likened to that of an athlete who has won his event and is receiving the winner's wreath (crown). We humans see the word "judgment" and say, "Uh-oh." We automatically think that bad things are going to happen. That is not the case at the Bema Seat of Christ. Only good things happen there. There will be no sadness, no tears, no grinding of teeth. Even the human goods that we have done during our lifetime will be destroyed as filthy rags during our ascension to Jesus. Only the good deeds we have done in God name will withstand the trip. Please, if you don't get anything else out of this whole book, understand this: the human race will not be judged for any sins it has committed. Jesus has already been judged and found guilty and paid the penalty for every sin that will ever be committed, past, present, and future. The judgment (Berna) Seat of Christ and the Great White Throne judgment are two very different events for two very different groups of people. Still, there will be no judgment for sins at either.

~ GOD THE HOLY SPIRIT ~

The Holy Spirit indwells the believer at the moment of salvation. At that wonderful moment, you have all of the Holy Spirit there is (100%). There is no "second blessing," "return visit," or "additional blessings." In the Old Testament days, the Holy Spirit did indwell the believer for an unspecified amount of time to accomplish a specific deed. That supernatural work complete, He would then depart. The Day of Pentecost changed that scenario.

Jesus said He had to leave so the Comforter (Holy Spirit) could come. At Pentecost, the Holy Spirit came and permanently indwelled the believers. He is the Seal, guaranteeing we are saved. The Holy Spirit is the manifestation of God's presence, (Psalms 51:11, Matthew 20:29-34, Psalms 139:7, and Haggai 2:4:5). The Holy Spirit is God. He is not an "it." He is not a ghost, nor is He a mystical concept. He is God and has the same essence as the Son and the Father. His purpose is to motivate, direct, and train the believer to become "Christ-like."

You alone have the power to "quench" the Holy Spirit—that is, to put out the fire or lamp and extinguish the fire. The Holy Spirit was and still is often pictured as a fire. We Christians have the fire of the Holy Spirit within us, so we should feed the fire, not throw water on it. Don't close Him off. Give Him full access to your life. How much of "you" will you grant access to the Holy Spirit?

The Holy Spirit Came to turn Weaklings into Mighty Witnesses!

Our goal should be to submit our human will to our heavenly Father's will 100% of the time. Unfortunately, because we lack training, strength and because we have a sin nature, we fail too often. We can do much better; it requires only desire, discipline and putting God first in everything we do. When we submit to His will, it is a fantastic journey.

Before Pentecost, the Holy Spirit would be poured out on an individual person to direct, guide, and otherwise help that person accomplish a divine purpose. When the mission was completed, the Holy Spirit left that person. It was a temporary indwelling (Judges 14:6-15:4, Genesis 31:8, Numbers 11:17, Judges 6:34, and Chronicles 28:12). About 59 days after Jesus was crucified and had ascended to heaven, during an event known as "Pentecost," the Holy Spirit descended permanently to indwell anyone who becomes a follower of Christ (John 14:16). This is one of the 38 things that happen to new Christians the moment they accept Christ as Lord and Savior (see Chapter 16: Mission Impossible).

The Holy Spirit came to enable us to know Christ and to teach us the ways of God. He empowers us to fulfill our divinely ordained purpose in life. The Holy Spirit inspired holy men to write the Scriptures. He dictated the Scriptures without violating the scribes' vocabulary, experiences or personality. He has protected the Scriptures throughout history so that today we have the completed Bible, "the mind of Christ" (1 Corinthians 2:16) in writing, without error or contamination from the world. He makes the Scriptures relevant and meaningful. Where there is confusion about what it says, it stems from our own weak minds, or from false teachings that have infiltrated our minds.

When the Holy Spirit Speaks

The Holy Spirit will not violate or be inconsistent with the Word of God. As you read the Bible, the Holy Spirit gives it new life. If what you hear violates the Scriptures, it's not the Holy Spirit talking.

Put the voices to the test. Don't let the impressions go unchecked.

- The Holy Spirit will motivate or compel us to obey God.
- The Holy Spirit speaks to clarify directions.
- The Holy Spirit speaks to help us do and doing right gives us peace.
- The Holy Spirit speaks to give us revelation.
- The Holy Spirit speaks to put us into our ministry.
- The Holy Spirit completes the work of God. He moves us to completion.

We need to do what the Holy Spirit directs us to do.

When we are out of fellowship with God, we need to claim the promise of 1 John 1:9 and confess our sin—name it. Only when we do will we be restored to fellowship.

God chose to reveal himself as a Father, as a Son. and as the Holy Spirit. God is one in essence and three in personality: God the Father (planner), God the Son (executor of the plan), and God the Holy Spirit (revealer, motivator).

As you can see, I have no problem with the Trinity and hope this has helped you defend your faith. So now let's take a closer look at the "One."

When a believer dies the responsibility of the Holy Spirit in that believer's life passes to the Heavenly Father. All three members of the God Head, the Son, the Holy Spirit, and the Father are actively involved with the believer.

CHAPTER FIVE

God is One In Essence

The essence is the fundamental nature of a thing: the quality or qualities that make a thing what it is. It is what it is at its most basic level.

God's essence is identical for all three personalities of the God Head. While there is a difference in function, there is no difference in the essence. To help us understand the nature of God, here are ten fundamental qualities that make up the "Essence of God."

Sovereign

There can only be one. All things are under God's rule and control, and nothing happens without His direction or permission. R.C. Sproul asks in his seminary classes, "Is God in control of every single molecule in the universe?" He adds, "The answer to that question will not determine whether you are a Christian or a Moslem, a Calvinist or an Arminian but it will determine whether you are a theist or an atheist." He concludes that "If there is one maverick molecule in the universe, it would mean that God is not sovereign."

Ephesians 1:11 (KJ21)

[11] *God works not just some things but all things according to the counsel of His own will.*

His purposes are all-inclusive and never thwarted (see Isaiah 46:11). Nothing takes God by surprise. God created the universe and all that is within it. He has the right to govern all things, and He does. God is sovereign in principle and practice.

A few more Biblical references to the Sovereignty of God are: Isaiah 11:2; Psalms 2:6; Psalms 33:6-9; Psalms 83:18; Matthews 6:10; Matthew 28:18; Romans 14:11; Corinthians 12:11; Philippians 2:9-11; and Revelation 19:6.

Omnipotent

God is all-powerful. God's power has no limitations. There is nothing that God cannot do. There are things that He chooses not to do, such as violate our free will. He will not make anyone accept Him.

The number one question—the one that has eternal consequences—is the same question Jesus asked His disciples: "Who do you say I am?" The answer you give is your choice. However, even those who have not acknowledged Him when it was to their advantage to do so, will bow their knee in acknowledgment of who He is at the Great White Throne of judgment. Then it will be too late!

Genesis 1:1 states, *"In the beginning, God created the heavens first and then the earth."* He spoke them into existence! Imagine that! Earth is and has always been, far enough away from the sun so it would not over-heat and explode. Yet it is and has been close enough so it would not freeze.

God spoke the earth into existence, and the command was complete; and its completeness was instantaneously full, far more complicated than this example. It must have been something like, "Earth, orbit around the Sun at a speed of 67,000 miles per hour. Tilt on your axis so that the maximum intensity of sun rays hits the earth 23.4° north of the Equator at the June Solstice and 23.4° south of the Equator at the December Solstice. Rotate from the west to the east and turn counter-clockwise."

This tilt, working with the gravitational forces of the Sun and Moon, provides the stability that has lasted from the earth's creation and will continue until God, Himself, destroys it. The tilt is also the reason for the seasons. Those who study the universe and such things say that the Earth's rotation, tilt, axis, and speed are so stable that it could last for millions of years to come. Imagine the power to speak, and the entire universe obeys. Only man and angels with their free will can say "no" to Him.

When Satan led his great rebellion in heaven and tried to remove the sovereign being of the universe, God had the power to cast Satan's followers— one-third of all the angels in heaven and Satan himself—out of heaven. Satan was the most beautiful creature God had created; he was one of the guardians of the God's throne room. Satan had to be incredibly charismatic to influence a third of the angels to follow him to steal the authority and the throne. As great as God had created him to be, he didn't have the power to overthrow God. What was his problem? It was pride!

Proverbs 6:16-19 (NIV)

16 There are six things the LORD hates, seven that are detestable to him: 17 haughty eyes (pride), a lying tongue, hands that shed innocent blood, 18 a heart that devises wicked schemes, feet that are quick to rush into evil, 19 a false witness who pours out lies and a person who stirs up conflict in the community.

At the top of this list is pride!

A few other Biblical passages that speak to the omnipotence of God: Psalms 139:7-12; Jeremiah 23:23-24; Matthew 28:20; John 1:3-4; John 14:20; and Revelation 1:8.

Omniscient

God has all knowledge of all things at all times. Never has there been a time when God didn't know everything. God does not learn one precept at a time, and then create knowledge by adding precept on top of precept as man does. God always knows the thoughts and intents of every mind and is not fooled by the words on our lips. God knows everything! He knew billions of years ago everything that would happen in the past, present, and future. His knowledge is not limited to time; He is outside of time.

Other verses that speak to God's Omniscience: Deuteronomy 29:29; 1 Samuel 2:3; 1 Samuel 16: 6-7, 1 Chronicles 28:9, Job 21:22; Job 28:24; Job 36:3-5; Job 37:15-16; Psalms 139:1-6; Psalms 147:5; Isaiah 40:28; Jeremiah 1:5; Jeremiah 23:24; Jeremiah 29:11; Isaiah 40:13-14; Isaiah 40:28; Isaiah 42:9; Isaiah 55:8-9; John 21:7; Romans 11:33-36; 1 Corinthians 2:11; and Hebrews 4:13.

Omnipresent

He is present in all places at the same time. God doesn't leave one place to go to another place. He occupies all places at all times. He doesn't sleep or daydream. He isn't distracted by something going on here or there. He is totally attentive to all things at the same time.

Other verses that speak to God's Omnipresence: Genesis 17:1; Job 11:7; Zechariah 3:6; Luke 1:37; Acts 1:8; Romans 1:4; Romans 1:20; Romans 15:19; and Revelation 4:8.

Just

God judges with perfect justice. Because He is also omnipresent and omniscient, His justice is not impaired by the imperfections of a human justice system, no matter how well-intentioned it may be. God hears everything and sees everything and knows the intentions of our hearts. It is impossible for God to be unjust or unfair. His judgments are perfect.

Bible verses confirming the Justice of God: Deuteronomy 10:18; Deuteronomy 32:4; 1 Samuel 24:15; 2 Chronicles 19:7; Psalms 9:7-8; Psalms 99:4; Psalms 140:12; Psalms 146:7-9; Proverbs 11:1; Nehemiah 9:31-33; Job 34:12; Isaiah 30:18; Isaiah 61:8; John 5:27; John 16:8; Acts 10:34-35; Romans 3:20; Romans 12:9; Colossians 3:25; 2 Thessalonians 1:8-9; 2 Timothy 4:8; and Revelation 20:12-13.

Righteous

God's perfect righteousness is free from sin. God's absolute and perfect righteousness cannot be compared to any other righteousness. Man's righteousness is relative righteousness. One person is righteous compared to someone else. Have you ever heard, "I may not be perfect, but I'm better than Joe over there?" We always compare ourselves to someone else, and most of the time (in our mind, at least), the person we compare ourselves to is inferior to ourselves, we seldom compare ourselves to someone we believe is superior to ourselves. We compare ourselves to the wrong standard. Our standard should be Jesus, not another human. We should have our eyes on Jesus. No one throughout all of history is absolutely righteous except one: Jesus. The best of us have some bad in us, and conversely, there is some good in the worst of us.

Romans 3:10: *"As It is written: There is none righteous, no not one."* So, how do you decide who is righteous and who is not? What criterion will you use? How will we measure righteousness? God is the only absolute righteous being in the universe. In the end, every unrighteous person will have to proclaim that God's judgment is perfect righteousness.

Other verses confirming the righteousness of God: Isaiah 51:8; Jeremiah 23:16-20; Luke 18:19; John 17:25; Romans 3:21; 2 Corinthians 5:21; Hebrews 7:26; and 1 John 2:1.

Love

His justice and righteousness protect God's love. God's love is perfect love. God loves with no strings attached. Nothing we can do will make Him love us more, and nothing we can do will make Him love us less. God loves all of humanity. We can't buy His love, and we can't earn it because He gives it freely. But an unimaginable price was paid because of this love. 1 John 3:16 tells us, *"God so loved the entire world so much that He gave His only Son, that whosoever believes in Him shall not perish, but have everlasting life."* Roman 5:8 promises, *"But God commended His love toward us, in that, while we were still sinners, Christ died for us."*

He loved us while we were still His enemies, fighting against Him or ignoring Him as if He was not there.

Here's the sticky part. God's love for all humanity does not include a key to heaven's gates for all humanity. Not everyone will go to Heaven, even though that is God's greatest desire. He has made all the preparations and provided all the provisions for all of humanity. While God's love is sufficient to pay the ransom for every sin that has and will ever be committed, it does not provide salvation for everyone. All preparations have been completed; there is nothing to do but accept the invitation, and that acceptance is solely dependent on the one receiving the invitation.

The only way to Heaven is to acknowledge that you have sinned (agree with God that you are a sinner), ask God for His forgiveness, and acknowledge that your request is granted based exclusively on the work Jesus did on the cross. Confess that He is Lord and Savior of your life, and then believe that you are saved.

Some other verses that speak of God's love: John 3:16; John 14:27; John 15:9; John 16:27; Hebrews 12:1-3; and Hebrews 12:6.

Eternal Life

There is no beginning and no end. Never has there been a time that God did not exist, and there will never be a time when God does not exist. God has an eternal existence and eternal life. Humanity and angels, on the other hand, have a beginning but will have no end. We have everlasting life, not eternal life. While our bodies will die, our soul will live throughout eternity. Our souls will never die; our bodies may die but will be raised again incorruptible and reunited with our soul. How you answer the question "Who do you say Jesus is?" determines where you will spend eternity.

Other verses that refer to God's Eternal Life: Exodus 3:14-15; 1 John:1-2; 1 John 5:11; and Revelation 1:8.

Unchangeable

God is dependable and stable; He is unmovable. He is constant. He is the same as He has always been and will always be. He will not change. He is immutable.

Other verses that refer to God's unchangeable nature: 1 Kings 8:56; John 14:16; 1 Corinthians 2; Hebrews 13:8; and James 1:17.

Truth

God is absolute truthfulness. God cannot, and will not, be untruthful. What He says is absolutely dependable. Man, on the other hand, seems to have a hard time telling the truth. We'll bend and stretch the facts to suit our needs. We will deflect questions or change our voice inflection and facial features to convey a meaning different than what we say. We specialize in telling "little white lies" or "bald face outrageous lies," but telling the unvarnished truth is hard for us. Sometimes it seems that we would rather lie than tell the truth, when telling the truth would actually be easier.

Other verses that speak to God's veracity: Numbers 23:9; Job 34:12; Isaiah 65:6; 1 John 5:6; John 14:6; and Psalms 100:5.

Knowing, understanding, and applying these 10 attributes of God will equip you well to answer any objection, question, or attack on God that you may face as you live your life following Jesus—so learn them well.

CHAPTER SIX

The Situation

It is God's written desire for everyone to be saved, and He has done everything to provide us salvation—but the choice is ours. Once saved, it is His desire—no—His command, that every believer grow spiritually in order to become mature, knowing who we are in Christ. Failure to mature can be catastrophic. We cannot afford to remain immature spiritual babies in our faith. There's a good reason God wants us to grow in the faith. He knows our reason for being. Yes, He has a purpose for our birth. We are not accidents or just globs of tissue, as some would have us believe.

A triple-headed threat—the world, the flesh, and the devil—wants to prevent us from achieving our purpose. This unholy trinity has lost the spiritual war, but it continues to propagate a lot of suffering, pain, and confusion. This can be a discouraging distraction from the grace and comfort of God's love. Worse, it can neutralize our witness.

If we can learn to walk in union with our God continually, we can avoid being sidetracked. When we walk in union with God, we will readily recognize God's appointments. He trusts us to glorify Him, just as the heroes of the faith have done. If we do, it will take the wind right out of Satan's sails. Jesus in the Sermon on the Mount said:

Matthew 5:10-11 (NIV)

[10] *Blessed (inner happiness or peaceful) are those who are persecuted because of righteousness, for theirs is the kingdom of heaven.* [11] *Blessed (inner happiness or peaceful) are you when people insult you, persecute you and falsely say all kinds of evil against you because of Me.*

So that we will not become casualties of the terroristic type warfare Satan is fighting and become neutralized, God has recorded some instructions for us to follow.

The Command

2 Timothy 2:15 (KJV) paraphrased

[15] *Study to show yourself approved unto God. A workman that need not be ashamed. (because) You rightly divide (correctly understand) the word of truth.*

The Reason

1 Peter 5:8 (PARAPHASED)

[8] *Be on your guard and stay awake. Your enemy, the devil, is like a roaring lion, always sneaking around to find someone to devour.*

Ephesians 4 14-15 (NIV)

[14] *Then, we will no longer be infants, tossed back and forth by the waves and blown here and there by every wind of teaching, and by the cunning and craftiness of men in their deceitful scheming.*
[15] *instead speaking the truth in love, we will in all things grow up into Him who is the Head, that is Christ.*

Christians are God's children, and our primary purpose is to grow up in the image of Christ. We are not to remain immature Christians but are to grow in wisdom and knowledge. We are to become mature believers so that we do not become compromised in our faith. We will be able to stay close to our Father God and be able to defend the faith so that others in our areas of influence will be drawn to Jesus. Too many Christians fail to grow in wisdom and knowledge of God. When this happens, they remain immature believers, and at best can only reflect dimly what they think God would have us say or do. We are commanded to light up the situations of life by reflecting His light. We can only fulfill this mission through study and training so we can know what He would have us say and do.

There is a world of difference between walking in the spirit and being carnal. At worst, the immature or carnal believer spends his life imitating the unbeliever. There is no distinguishing difference between the carnal believer and the unbelieving lost person except their final destination.

Not too long ago, before commercial chicken farmers and processors, people raised their own chickens. They did this for the eggs and the meat. I remember those chickens would roam around the chicken pen freely. They had eaten all the grass and would eat small rocks. I was told the rocks helped grind up the corn we fed them. Sunday was fried chicken day. In those days the adults ate first, and the children got whatever was left over.

One thing I remember about chickens is that they nearly always walked around with their heads down looking at the ground. Occasionally they would lift their heads, stretch their necks, and (I suppose) swallow, and then their faces were down again looking at dirt. They seemed oblivious to anything going on around them. But they had learned to run to us when we had a pan of food, and to run away from Mom when she had an ax in her hand. Once she had caught the selected chicken, her skill with that ax was superb; no good meat was wasted. If you've ever heard the term "like a chicken with its head cut off" and wondered what that meant, let me explain. The chicken that hardly ever ran before, after losing its head, would run frantically, first here and then there, darting in every direction for what seemed like a very long time, considering it had no head. It was dead, but the body didn't seem to know it.

The unbelievers do the same thing, for the same reason. The point I want to make is that all unbelievers, as well as all carnal believers, are like the headless chicken. It must have been looking for his head, but the lost and those imitating the lost are frantically searching for happiness, running here and there trying to find happiness.

Searching for Happiness

Words are powerful! Words express thoughts, and thoughts create ideas, and ideas create perceptions. Perceptions are compelling because they govern our actions. We respond to life based on our perceptions; I was taught that perception is everything. That's why we dress the way we do and act the way we do. It's why we say the things we say and say them the way we do. It's why we associate with the people we associate with and why we don't associate with others. The way we present ourselves in society reflects what we think about ourselves, it's our self-image.

There was a time when I was in authority, and one of the concepts I taught was—you guessed it—"perception is everything." It seemed so right. But it wasn't entirely accurate then, and it isn't entirely accurate today. It's never been entirely accurate, but it sounds good. You don't have to think long to realize that our perception can be manipulated and misleading at best, and downright deceptive at worst. First impressions may not be the best reflection of the character of a man. How much effort and intelligence does it take to impress someone if you really want to impress him? Our judgment is often clouded, and senses can profoundly influence our perspective. Remember the magician or illusionist who makes a living fooling the eye and doing what the mind says is impossible. We readily accepted the adage, "What you see is what you get" when it sprang into our vocabulary as if it's a virtue. It may be or may not be, but it shouldn't have to be said. The life lived is the validation. Christians should live a lifestyle that reflects the values of their Lord, and there is no deceit in Him.

For some of us, what we see, what we hear, what we smell, what we touch, and what we taste are reality. What could be more real than seeing it with your own eyes, hearing it with your own ears, or touching it? With others, reality is based on the ability to reason. To them, reality is whatever makes sense to them. The problem for the rationalizers is that the mind is very powerful and can rationalize just about anything. For instance, they might assume that all things have always been as they are now. It's so apparent to them; it's what they have observed over the last few years. Any research that is done is done to prove it so. Then it becomes common knowledge; even if it is later proven to be false, they don't seem to care. Someone observes that the world is warmer than it was a few years ago. Then they make the assumption that man's irresponsibility caused it, and his irresponsibility will destroy the world. They can't let that happen, so they double down to develop a plan to correct the perceived problem. It doesn't matter at all that the creator God has told us exactly how the world will be destroyed, and that He will be the destroyer, not man.

For others, faith is the gateway to reality. For them, nothing is impossible. They are the dreamers who take us places no man has gone before and give us products that never existed before. More importantly, faith is the only gateway to spiritual reality. It is only through the portal of faith that Christianity can be understood.

Without faith, we cannot enter the realm of "God moments," "God's realities," or His Appointments. More important than anything else you may read or hear, know this first, that God's reality is more real than anything you can see, hear, smell, taste or touch, and more real than you can reason in your own mind. God loves you, and every day does impossible and supernatural things to prove it is so.

The objective is always to strengthen your perspective of who God is and who we are in Christ. Bombard your mind with some in-depth information and valuable tools (Operating Assets) that God has provided for all believers to use. As valuable as these tools are, they are useless if they remain in the toolbox when we need them. Worse than that, we don't even know these Operating Assets exist in our toolbox, or we don't know we have a toolbox.

The major problem is that too many genuine believers, who should honor God in everything they do, don't honor God anymore. Too many Christians have been neutralized by worldview thinking, the flesh, and their own sin nature. It seems that too many of us have lost our way and are no longer the salt that heals and preserves. We are no longer the light on the hill showing the way and warning of danger. Instead, we have been caught up in our own endless pursuit of happiness. We run from this thing to that thing, convinced that it would make us happy. Our primary objective in life to be "happy" is the wrong objective of us. If we seek Him first, we will find inner joy and peace, and we will be happy.

Everything we do is done to achieve happiness. I have heard many mothers say, "All I want is for little Johnny to be happy." It's been said, "A mother is only as happy as her saddest child." Even many Christian moms want happiness for their children above anything else. What could be wrong with that? It seems to be a worthy objective, but it's the wrong objective. The goal should be to help their children find love, joy, peace, patience, kindness, goodness, and faithfulness (Galatians 5:22) that only springs from being a child of the living God. This higher objective for their children should be that they grow up to be holy (set apart), that they learn to walk with God, and that they desire to live their lives glorying God. Joy is an inner-happiness that is expressed regardless of our circumstances. You can't imagine the pressure that is released when you can be content with what God has provided, and you live your life as He has planned and directed.

In too many cases, there is not enough evidence that God governs our lives to convict us. We spend our days imitating the unbeliever until there is little or no visible evidence that we have a Godly value system. There is little difference in what we think or how we think. We spend too little or no time in fellowship with our heavenly Father. We want what we want when we want it and throw a fit if we don't or can't get it. The preponderance of evidence of our lifestyle would suggest that we think we are God, and that God is our servant—if, indeed, we believe there is a God.

You will begin to understand how much God loves you as we study some of the ways He has always provided for you. He has always extended a pardon and an olive branch to those who have failed, so far, to accept His love.

There has always been 24 hours in each day, but we seem to have too little time or interest in studying God's Word, meditating on Jesus, or spending time in God's house with God's people. Our parents and grandparents worked 14 to 18 hours a day and still made time to study God's word, so why can't we? We act like the political correctness world viewpoint consumes us. Other than "Oh God no!" or "God help me" and occasionally "Yes Lord," our prayer life is nonexistent until we realize that we are unable to solve our problems ourselves. When we finally resort to prayer, all we want is for the pain to go away. When we do pray, too often it's a selfish prayer asking for what we want. The prayers we offer are routine, rote, and without any thought.

Many professing Christians have dust-covered Bibles. The Word of God is not studied or even read on a regular basis. Bibles are not even taken to church by many Christians. When did it become fashionable to leave "The Bible" at home when going to church? I understand that modern man may have his Bible on one or several electronic devices, and I'm delighted. I hope the software permits the user to gain insight into the text in a way an actual Bible does. It's nice to have those clarifications noted for instant recall. However, when the "Word" is not valued enough to be available, it can be an indicator of the lack of spiritual maturity on the part of the individual and the church. We are so immature in our Christianity that we fail to realize that what God wants is an intimate relationship with us. We must take time to have conversations with Him through prayer. We must study His Word to learn what He thinks and how He sees the world and events. We can give God what He wants most of all—we can spend some time with Him! Isn't that amazing? The God of the universe wants to be friends with you and with me. Let's "like" Him with more than a "thumbs up."

Our priorities are misplaced. So many of us are just getting through the day and miss out on the unique adventure that He has for each of us. Our hearts are covered with callouses and scar tissue, and so we cannot make the spiritual connection with our heavenly Father or with the people and to the events occurring all around us. We are in an all-consuming search for happiness, and it eludes us because we are pursuing the wrong source of happiness.

We haven't learned to spell disappointment with an "H," so we don't recognize it as "His Appointment." Not recognizing "His Appointment," we fail to glorify God even when "good things" happen and we certainly don't glorify Him when "undesirable things" happen. To do that would be utterly absurd to us. We then blame God for our disappointments and tragedies. Isn't it strange that man can spend his whole life denying the power of God, and when something tragic happens, blame God for it?

Deep in our subconscious mind, we know that God had the power to prevent whatever has happened, and we think He let it happen anyway. We fail to accept responsibility and usually will not assign blame to anyone but God. In spite of all that, God applies grace and mercy to us.

Grace is God providing us what we don't deserve—life ever after with Him—because the Lamb of God, Jesus, was obedient to the Father and willingly gave His life as payment in full for all our sins. Mercy is God not giving us what we deserve—life ever after without Him— for precisely the same reason. What Jesus did was complete. When the Father looks at us, He sees the spotless lamb, Jesus.

Too many times we put ourselves on the throne of our lives, not God. When we sit on that throne, God does not, and we find ourselves searching for our own happiness. We Christians should know that Jesus is the only source of happiness, inner peace, and joy genuinely available to us. If you are not a Christian, Jesus is the only hope you have for happiness, inner peace, and joy. When Christians enter the frantic search for happiness, we have failed to REMEMBER all that God has done for us, and we imitate the unbeliever.

The Bible indicates that during his reign, Solomon was the richest and wisest man in the world. He had everything, but at some point, quit fellowshipping with God. Consciously or unconsciously, he stopped communicating with God and became unaware of God's presence. He drifted further and further away from God, building up scar tissue on his soul until God was no longer even a thought in his mind. He was in perpetual carnality imitating the unbeliever. He missed God but didn't recognize the problem. He was in a desperate search for happiness. When a believer forsakes the only real source of happiness, it will elude him. Solomon tried to find joy in education. When education failed to provide the satisfaction he sought, he then explored many other things that for a moment seemed they would bring the pleasure he needed. Solomon tried engineering and built just about anything that could be built. Then he started collecting things, redecorating the place, and acquiring servants, cattle, more gold and silver, jewels, peacocks, apes, male and female singers, instrumentalists, and more ...as he searched for happiness. But happiness continued to elude him.

> Ecclesiastes 2:10-11 (NIV)
> 10 *I denied myself nothing my eyes desired; I refused my heart (mind) no pleasure. My heart (mind) took delight in all my labor, and this was the reward for all my toil.* 11 *Yet when I surveyed all that my hands had done and what I had toiled to achieve, everything was meaningless, a chasing after the wind; nothing was gained under the sun.*

Solomon could surely say, "Been there, done that, got the t-shirt," when he finally realized that there is no substitute for the pleasure of fellowship with the Lord. Solomon was told write the details of his search down—every bit of it—so we will know what it's like to be out of fellowship and then back in fellowship. He did, and it's the Book of Ecclesiastes. He also wrote the book of Proverbs and the Song of Solomon to give us the benefit of his misadventures.

The common belief among Christians is that they are not equipped to answer the questions they may be asked, so they let their witness slide. Before long they are imitators of the lost. My prayer is that these observations will provide ammunition and knowledge that provides believers the boldness we once had. It is meant to help us reload and get back in the battle.

CHAPTER SEVEN

Operation Neutralization

The tragedy is that in succumbing to temptation, we lose our ability to have fellowship with the Father and our opportunity to be a witness for Jesus. These are precisely Satan's goals for the Christian; he wants to neutralize us. The moment Satan loses that most important battle for one's soul, he begins "Operation Neutralize." He comes at the newly saved person with everything in his arsenal, and he is relentless. He never gives up. He cannot leave it alone or say, "No big deal; it's just one."

Satan knows that even "Babes in Christ" now have the power of God in them and that they have the potential to become another Billy Graham, D.L. Moody, Billy Sunday, Peter, or Paul. In Satan's world that would be a nightmare. If this new Christian were to win just one soul to Christ, it would be disastrous. The nightmare of nightmares for him would be if every Christian now on earth was instrumental in just one soul being won to Christ the world as we know it would quickly become a much better place. Satan also knows that he has lost that soul forever. He can never get that soul back, so his best available option is to neutralize the new Christian. His first thought might be to kill the new Christian, but that wouldn't help him. In fact, the new saint would immediately be in God's presence, praising Jesus. What a dreadful thought—can't have that! But an out-of-fellowship believer has distinct possibilities because he or she does very defiantly, although unwittingly, serve Satan. Any Christian who is out of fellowship with God is Satan's trophy because of his love of the world system. An infamous philosopher, Pogo, has said, "I have seen the enemy, and he is me!"

From Satan's standpoint, the Christian who is out of fellowship is a valuable asset and has the capability to immediately discredit himself and his Savior, as well as the body of Christ. Or he can be a "sleeper cell" available at any time to do as much damage as possible to the cause of Christ. Intentionally or unintentionally, the believer out of fellowship has the potential to disrupt and confuse.

The new believer knows only that Jesus loves him, and that's enough for a very short period of time. If the believer doesn't grow to maturity, it will not be enough to withstand Satan's fiery darts. God is not surprised by this. He is prepared and has provided the necessary counteraction for the believer to be restored to full fellowship.

God permanently gives some special "Operational Assets" to every believer very moment we are saved. Each is important, but one of the top three is the "Stall Recovery" technique. It will be covered in detail in chapter 19. Its purpose is to restore the wounded or fallen warrior to the service of his Lord and Savior.

God's goal for us is that we grow into a deeper and more profound relationship with Him. We're able to do this only by communicating, talking with, and listening to Him. He wants to walk in the garden and fellowship with us. He wants to take us to the mountaintop so we can be the shining light of His glory. He wants us to be the lighthouse that protects the mariner from the looming dangers that so easily entrap us. He wants us to be secure in our faith when we feel disappointment, stress, and trials. He is sufficient to meet our needs. His desire is to meet our needs, and He wants us to know it and act accordingly. We cannot be satisfied to remain "babes in Christ."

We have failed to prepare ourselves and are not equipped to prepare our children for the spiritual warfare raging all around us, in which we all are already fully engaged. For the most part, that is because we ourselves have fallen short of His goal and are oblivious to this spiritual war that surrounds us.

We all desperately need some "Christian Basic Training." In the days of tall ships, a phrase was born that is still accurate for today's Navy as well as for of our armed services, and all Christians as well:

"When you need to know, it's too late to learn."

We Christians have failed to learn that simple truth. We go out every day poorly trained and under-equipped for the battle that awaits us in the spiritual realm.

1 Peter 5:8 (NIV)

8 *Be alert and of sober mind. Your enemy, the devil, prowls around like a roaring lion looking for someone to devour.*

The Marine Corps Drill Instructor School has this motto mounted on the front gates:

"Let no Marine's ghost say, 'If my Drill Instructor had only done his job.'"

It's not a bad reminder if we substitute "Drill Instructor" with dad, mom, preacher, small group teacher, or friend.

The Boy Scout motto is "Be Prepared," and the purpose of the organization is to train boys to be prepared to face any adversity that he might encounter. Christians should "Be Prepared" to be the best they can be. This is accomplished the same way through study and training in God's ways.

When I was asked to teach the college and singles group at our church, I was told the way to get them involved was to feed them often. I intended to do that, but I was going to feed them spiritual food. The core of the curriculum would be R.B. Thieme's 1962 Basics course because it would be a great beginning and it would give them a strong foundation in their faith.

That first Sunday morning after introducing myself, I asked, "What has Jesus done in your life this week?" It was a question they were not prepared to answer. There was absolutely no response. Every student looked stunned; their eyes popped wide open their jaws dropped. They were startled, like deer trapped in the headlights of an oncoming car, and no one said a word. It was if they had never been asked that question, maybe they hadn't.

They were uncomfortable. I think that for the first time they realized they didn't have sufficient knowledge or had even thought a whole lot about Jesus. He was not playing even a minor role in their lives, and they didn't even realize that they were incapable of remembering even one interaction with their Lord and Savior. Does this describe most of the Christians in America? Finally, after a minute or two of deafening silence, the associate teacher broke the silence by saying, "That's a question, people. It demands an answer." The question was so fundamental that any of them should have been able to immediately answer it. That's what I thought anyway.

God requires it, and the Bible commands it.

1 Peter 3:15 (NIV)

> 15 *But in your hearts revere Christ as Lord. Always be prepared to give an answer to everyone who asks you to give the reason for the hope that you have. But do this with gentleness and respect.*

For the Christian, this question should not be hard to answer; every hand should have gone up as each one in the class eagerly wanted to share their story. Their response should have been second nature to them. Finally, Jake spoke up. There were twenty something in the class and, six finally struggled to give an answer.

If we don't make Jesus an active part of our lives, we can't see the wonders of His blessings, and there are many every day regardless of the circumstances. Oh, we may see some of them. Like a beautiful sunset, we see it but fail to connect the dots and fail to give Him praise. Or by the narrowest of margins, we are protected from a car wreck that happened just in front or just behind us. We credit that good fortune as "luck," when in reality, we have been blessed. Oh, by the way, those who were involved in that wreck were blessed also. The accident was not God's judgment pouncing on them because of something they did or didn't do, and it wasn't a momentary lack of luck that caused the wreck.

The Bible teaches that God can and does use any circumstance to bring blessings. Here's just one. Joseph's brothers hated him and were going to kill him. They chose to sell him instead and tell their dad that he was dead. Joseph was taken to Egypt and sold to Potiphar. Joseph would not be seduced by his master's wife. In her rage at being rejected, she accused him of attacking her, and he is thrown in jail. In the fullness of God's time, Joseph was freed and became the governor of all Egypt, second only to the Pharaoh. My point is that without all of those trials and tribulations happening to Joseph, he would not have been in the position to bless his family and give us this truth through Scripture. Genesis 50: 20 records Joseph's viewpoint: "What you (his brothers) meant for harm, God meant for good."

As I look back on those days, I think that those students thought I was supposed to teach the material, and they would decide whether to accept or reject it. What I was trying to do was teach students the Biblical concepts and principals needed to survive and prosper spiritually. To their credit, the 20-plus continued to come to class, and on holiday week-ends the class had about 60 in attendance. I know they were exposed to the why's and how's of our Christian doctrines and faith.

CHAPTER EIGHT

Political Correctness

Today, as we sit at home in front of the computer surfing the Internet, so much information is available, and much of the information is not good, or even accurate.

Political correctness has overwhelmed our society. Everyone's views and opinions are considered to be equally true. One of the politically correct tentacles that have entangled so many people today is that being reasonable, proper, and fare minded mandates that one must be inclusive of all things. To be inclusive equates in man's mind today with being tolerant. Therefore, we must tolerate all views and all things. There are no absolutes anymore. There is no right or wrong. What is true and right for me is not necessarily true or right for you, and what is wrong for me is not necessarily wrong for you. How convenient is that?

Believe it or not, that is the mindset of our youth today. Societal changes have flourished in the last decade, and these changes rapidly resort to violence, drugs, riots, and protest-filled social media outlets. With the onset of the availability of instant communication, we can see evidence that society has changed, and it's changed for the worse. Just a few years ago no one would have ever thought that being tolerance toward others and their beliefs could be evil. We have confused tolerance with compassion and redefined tolerance.

Compassion is being empathic—caring, sensitive, and understanding.

Webster defines tolerance as "the ability or willingness to tolerate something, in particular, the existence or behavior that one does not necessarily agree with—open-minded, indulgent, charitable, accepting." The world's definition of tolerance is more like "the total acceptance of whatever someone else says or does combined with the absolute dismissal of one's own norms and standards to readily accept whatever behavior or speech is uttered."

If Christians, who have always been the majority in America, were as intolerant as we are reported to be, no religions would have been allowed. The United States is an experiment. All nations before 1776 were ruled by small elite aristocratic groups who told the majority what they could and could not do. They ruled with iron fists and took whatever they wanted with impunity. The colonists in America said, "No, not anymore. We will govern ourselves." A representative government was established giving the majority the power, but the minority had opinions and were not summarily dismissed. A system of counterbalances was set up to ensure that neither the Executive nor the Legislative nor Judicial branches could set up a kingdom. It is a system that has worked well, since its inception, although not perfectly. It does require that the people respect the law and accept the lawfully elected representatives.

All of that is now cast aside. The minority tolerates only their views. The minority now tries to rule through intimidation. If it doesn't like what it hears, there will be riots on the street. The riots are labeled "lawful," but since when has destroying private and public property been lawful? Rioters ranks are swollen by the curious, who likely will get caught up in the disobedience as their minds give way to the mob mentality. The restraints and training are cast aside as they see the police apparently powerless to stop the lawlessness. Protests turn to riots as they draw power from social media and the news coverage is complicit.

Study the rise of Hitler in the early 1930s and consider this: every dictator that we see in the world today achieved his position and took authority because the people tolerated his actions. That tolerance gave strength to the would-be dictator, and strength became power. When he had enough power, he took anything he wanted.

"Evil Preaches Tolerance Until It Is Dominate, and then It Seeks To Silence Good."

~ Charles Chapur ~

Taken to the extreme, here are five ways tolerance manifests itself today:

1. Our children absolutely believe there are no absolutes.
2. All roads lead to God. The belief that all roads lead to God is all-inclusive, and that belief is being accepted by many. It's an appealing thought because no one is accountable for his or her actions or lack of actions. In effect, we are our own gods. Despite all the noise, it is not accepted as valid by a majority of the world's population. Jesus has anticipated and answered that thought.

John 14:6 (NIV)

> [6] *Jesus answered, "I am the way and the truth and the life. No one comes to the Father except through me.*

Jesus is either telling the truth, or He lied. Any honest person after examining the Bible would have to conclude that Jesus is telling the truth.

3. It's not fair that some people have more stuff than others. Since I have less than you have, it's all right for me to take from you. Since some people subscribe to the idea of corporate ownership, it is logical to believe it. Neither socialism nor communism has worked well for all the people. The elites live well on the backs of the peasant people. There is no incentive for the workers to excel, so they do what they must to live, and that's all.

Jamestown, Virginia was established May 13, 1607, when 144 men arrived and began the rigorous task developing a town out of nothing. No one knew how difficult this would be; this is evident when you look at the registration of settlers. 46 were registered as "gentlemen" and didn't know how to work and were not motivated to do so until they got hungry and cold. 24 gentlemen died before December 1607 ended. Four were registered as soldiers, one minister, five boys, 21 tradesmen including one fisherman, 21 mariners, and seven captains or councilors. It got so bad that John Smith had to quote and enforce II Thessalonians 3-10: *"He who does not work, neither shall he eat."* Each man was given his own plot of land to farm and forced to work for his own welfare. Success ensued, the death rate dropped, food was harvested in abundance, a well was dug, and houses were built. Pitch, tar, and soap were made to be returned to England. When Smith made his decree, only 38 of the 144 men were still alive.

The Government's primary responsibility is to protect its citizens from foreign and domestic threats. Secondarily, it is to promote interstate trade. The government does not have a responsibility to care for those who will not care for themselves. Carl Marx taught what our children now believe; everyone should have the same stuff. No one should be allowed to have more than I have because it's not fair. We only have to look at the freedoms the people of Russia enjoy. Look at the prosperity the Russian, North Koreans, Venezuelan, Chinese, and Cuban enjoy. If it's not Communism, it's a definition of socialism. Some pretty influential Americans have said that everyone in the world should be provided what the USA offers to its citizens, at the America tax payer expense. Therefore, the rights of citizenship should belong to everyone who wants them, even if they refuse the responsibilities of citizenship. It has been said that our government is currently handing out social security benefits and medical care benefits and much more, to illegal and legal immigrants alike on the first day they arrive in the USA. Normally legal citizens have to wait until they are 67 or 70 to receive Social Security benefits, and under the current Affordable Care Act (which is not affordable) must purchase medical care benefits; if they don't, they are fined. Where is the advantage of being a citizen? When we fail to listen to God, we can really mess up.

4. Freedom of speech has been yielded by many because they are afraid of offending someone. The politically correct police are brutal in their perceived right to attack anyone who states an opinion that differs from their own. They absolutely believe there are no absolutes and absolutely think they have the right to attack anyone who suggests that there really are absolutes. We have lost what is so dear to us because we are afraid to speak. The church was once the backbone of our moral character, but in 1954 then Senator L.B. Johnson silenced the pulpit with the Johnson Amendment. It forbade the pastors from speaking on political concerns with the threat of taking away the tax-exempt status of the church.

If our pastors had any backbone, they would have said, "Do your worst, we serve God, not the state!"

5. Man is doing what seems right in his own mind. Consumed with living our lives, we are like those in the days of Noah. Most are not doing bad or evil things in our own eyes, but we are ignoring God and His ways (Proverbs 21:2, Judges 21:25).

It's never right to be wrong.
It's never wrong to be right.
Right is always right.
Wrong is always wrong.

What we are experiencing in our society is that those who once demanded tolerance are no longer tolerant, but instead are violent and civilly disobedient and disrespectful of the rights of others and the laws that protect those rights. Even free speech is not tolerated if the lawless ones disagree. Individuals in a mob lose their set of norms and standards. Mob mentality has no respect for others, the laws that protect society, or personal property. People in mobs do not see themselves as criminals, but they are, and they destroy private and public property. These acts, as well as looting, are criminal acts. Those who commit such actions, as well as those who protect them, are committing criminal acts. If those charged with maintaining law and order fail to impose order on the lawless ones, anarchy will reign until the leaders are removed, and enough force is applied to restore order. Those charged with restoring law and order must maintain a great deal of self-control and at the same time restore order. There is no such thing as civil disobedience. Acting in a civil manor is not disobedience. Acting disobediently is not civil.

The very term civil disobedience is an oxymoron.

Archbishop Charles Chaput stated on August 3, 2012: "We need to remember that tolerance is not a Christian virtue. Charity, justice, mercy, prudence, honesty—these are Christian virtues. And obviously, in a diverse community, tolerance is an important working principle. But it's never an end itself. In fact, tolerating grave evil within a society is itself a form of serious evil. Likewise, democratic pluralism does not mean that Catholics (or Christians of any denomination) should be quiet in public about serious moral issues because of some misguided sense of good manners. A healthy democracy requires vigorous moral debate to survive. Real pluralism demands that people of strong beliefs will advance their convictions in the public square—peacefully, legally and respectfully, but energetically and without embarrassment. Anything less is bad citizenship and a form of theft from the public conversation."

Tolerance is not a Christian virtue. So, what are Christian virtues?

The Bible gives us that answer.

Galatians 5:22 (NIV)

22 *But the fruit of the Spirit is love, joy, peace, forbearance, kindness, goodness, faithfulness, gentleness, and self-control*

We have allowed our forbearance, kindness, goodness, gentleness, and self-control to be beaten down by the intolerant. We have been brainwashed into believing that we must tolerate unruliness, contempt for law and order, and the silencing our rights and beliefs by the bullies in the name of being tolerant.

AN AMAZING COINCIDENCE?

We've been taught that diversity is good and America is one of a few countries where it can be celebrated. All people should be proud of their heritage, and it should be celebrated. We as a people should never forget who we were or where we came from.

Several years ago, I attended a high school baccalaureate service. The demographics of this school were diverse, so much so that the graduating class wanted to celebrate that diversity. Somewhere near the end of the ceremony, a Christian boy and girl stood up, went to the podium, and read a passage from the New Testament of the Bible. They then took their positions off to the side and in front of a large unity candle. When they were settled, they lit and held small candles. Then a Jewish boy and girl repeated the procedure, but the boy read from the Old Testament in Hebrew, and the girl interrupted what he had read. They took their place next to the Christians and lit their candles. Then, in turn, they were followed by four other couples representing Islam, Hinduism, Buddhism, and Shinto. Couple by couple, they finished reading their holy books and took their places beside the others and lit their candles.

When all of them were standing together in a circle around the large unity candle with their individual candles lit, simultaneously they placed their flames on the wick of the unity candle. To their surprise, the unity candle's wick would not light. A dozen candle flames licked at the unity candle wick, but it would not ignite. They held their positions for several minutes; you could see the frustration mounting as their individual flames consumed their candles. This wasn't supposed to happen. It was impossible; their flames were supposed to light the unity candle; by all that is natural, that unity candle wick should have ignited. Finally, one of the teachers said, "Let's assume that the unity candle is lit," and they withdrew their smaller candles and continued the service as if everything was all right. But the unity candle did not light.

I don't know how many of those attending the service saw the miracle of the unlit unity candle. Yes, I do—they all saw it. What I don't know is how many recognized what had happened. I believe that God showed all of us that He will not share His light with the manmade religions of this world. He never has and He never will. Furthermore, God showed those with eyes to see that there is no light unless it is His light. It was a reminder that He alone is God; there is none like Him. Throughout the Bible, there are many examples that teach how God refuses to share His glory with any other deity.

We need to be reminded continually that Christianity is not an alternate religion, but a relationship with God. Anyone who responds to God's love becomes His child. The thing that separates us from the world is not a thing at all; it is a who, and that who is Jesus! Christianity is a relationship. It is not a religion. The number one question of our day is, "Who do you say Jesus is?" The good that we do should not be done to gain favor with God; that's what religion teaches. True Christian good deeds are done in His name because He loved us first and sought us out while we were His enemies. If we are to follow the example of Jesus, we must love those who don't know Him, speak softly, stand firm on His teachings and explain the Gospel, making it relevant to those we engage. We do good for one purpose: to bring glory to God alone.

That event reminded me of another event that happened many years ago in another place. It was a showdown between Elijah's God and the prophets of Baal, and it also involved lighting a fire.

1 Kings 18: 15-17 (ESV)

15 *Elijah said, "As the Lord of hosts lives, before*
whom I stand, I will surely show myself to him
today." 16 *So Obadiah went to meet Ahab and told*

him. And Ahab went to meet Elijah. [17] *When Ahab saw Elijah, Ahab said to him, "Is it you, you troubler of Israel?"*

Isn't it interesting how the worldly blame God for their troubles, without REMEMBERING how it was when God ruled their lives? We're always looking for cause and effect. And even the unbelievers who can't reason that God exists can reason that whatever is wrong in their lives is God's fault, but not in this case. Elijah was being held accountable. 1 Kings 16 tells us that Ahab became king of Israel and that he did more evil in the eyes of the Lord than any other king before him. He not only considered it trivial to commit the sins of those who were kings before him, but he also married Jezebel and began to serve Baal. He set up an altar to Baal in the temple of Baal he had built in Samaria. In addition to all that, Ahab made an Asherah temple explicitly built for worshipping Asherah, who was considered a goddess of fertility. God was provoked enough to tell Elijah to give Ahab God's solemn vow that there would neither be dew nor rain for the next few years and then only at God's word.

1 Kings18:18-20 (ESV)

[18] *And Elijah answered, "I have not troubled Israel, but you have, and your father's house, because you have abandoned the commandments of the LORD and followed the Baal's.* [19] *Now, therefore, send and gather all Israel to me at Mount Carmel, and the 450 prophets of Baal and the 400 prophets of Asherah, who eat at Jezebel's table."* [20] *So Ahab sent to all the people of Israel and gathered the prophets together at Mount Carmel.*

Isn't it interesting that King Ahab thought he was in control and had all the power? He despised Elijah for the "no rain situation" and the suffering it caused his nation. Yet he was so subdued and essentially shrugged his shoulders, and said,

"Okay." Elijah had no fear; he knew that the battle was the Lord's. This is a lesson we need to learn. To have the assurance and have no fear, we must walk close enough to God to hear what He wants to say to us and be able to see the world or situation the way He wants us to see it.

1 Kings 18: 21-37 (ESV)

21 *And Elijah came near to all the people and said,*
"How long will you go limping between two dif-
ferent opinions? If the LORD is God, follow Him;
but if Baal, then follow him." And the people did
not answer him a word. 22 *Then Elijah said to the*
people, "I, even I only, am left a prophet of the
LORD, but Baal's prophets are 450 men. 23 *Let two*
bulls be given to us, and let them choose one bull
for themselves and cut it in pieces and lay it on the
wood, but put no fire to it. And I will prepare the
other bull and lay it on the wood and put no fire to
it. 24 *And you call upon the name of your god, and*
I will call upon the name of the LORD, and the God
who answers by fire, he is God." And all the people
answered, "It is well spoken." 25 *Then Elijah said*
to the prophets of Baal, "Choose for yourselves one
bull and prepare it first, for you are many, and call
upon the name of your god, but put no fire to it."
26 *And they took the bull that was given them, and*
they prepared it and called upon the name of Baal
from morning until noon, saying, "O Baal, answer
us!" But there was no voice, and no one answered.
And they limped around the altar that they had
made. 27 *And at noon Elijah mocked them, saying,*
"Cry aloud, for he is a god. Either he is musing, or he
is relieving himself, or he is on a journey, or perhaps
he is asleep and must be awakened." 28 *And they*
cried aloud and cut themselves after their custom
with sword, [s] *and lances until the blood gushed out*
upon them. 29 *And as midday passed, they raved*

on until the time of the offering of the oblation, but there was no voice. No one answered; no one paid attention. [30] Then Elijah said to all the people, "Come near to me." And all the people came near to him, and he repaired the altar of the LORD that had been thrown down. [31] Elijah took twelve stones, according to the number of the tribes of the sons of Jacob, to whom the word of the LORD came, saying, "Israel shall be your name," [32] and with the stones he built an altar in the name of the LORD; And he made a trench about the altar, as great as would contain two seahs (estimated to be 3.84 gallons) of seed. [33] And he put the wood in order and cut the bull in pieces and laid it on the wood. And he said, "Fill four jars with water and pour it on the burnt offering and on the wood." [34] And he said, "Do it a second time." And they did it a second time. And he said, "Do it a third time." And they did it a third time. [35] And the water ran around the altar and filled the trench also with water. [36] And at the time of the offering of the oblation, Elijah the prophet came near and said, "O LORD, God of Abraham, Isaac, and Israel, let it be known this day that you are God in Israel, and that I am your servant, and that I have done all these things at your word. [37] Answer me, O LORD, answer me, that this people may know that you, O LORD, are God and that you have turned their hearts back."

Notice Elijah is in complete control, he is fearless, and he had created an impossible condition. There was no way the fire would burn. Everything was supersaturated with water. Even today water is the primary element used by fire departments to extinguish fires. Elijah's prayer is to glorify God so the people would know that nothing is impossible for God and that they would return to Him.

1 Kings 38:40 (ESV)

38 *Then the fire of the LORD fell and consumed the*
burnt offering and the wood and the stones and the
dust, and licked up the water that was in the trench.
39 *And when all the people saw it, they fell on their*
faces and said, "The LORD, he is God; the LORD,
he is God." 40 *And Elijah said to them, "Seize the*
prophets of Baal; let not one of them escape." And
they seized them. And Elijah brought them down to
the brook Kishon and slaughtered them there.

The devastation of the prophets of Baal and Asherah was complete and just. There would be no prophets of Baal to mislead the people again. In one story the fire that should light doesn't, and in the other the fire that shouldn't light does. Opposite supernatural results created by the one Supernatural God to prove the exact same point. Oh, did I tell you that both stories happened at two separate locations both called Mount Carmel?

CHAPTER NINE

The Awakening

It was winter in Georgia, and by 5 p.m. the darkness had almost overtaken the daylight. It was wet and cold, somewhere between a heavy mist and a light, steady rain. The prelude to the Wednesday night service was—as it had been for as long as I could remember—a delicious hot meal. As everyone finished the meal, we enjoyed fellowship with close friends until it was time to go to classes. Usually, 10 or so different courses were available to choose from, each consisting of approximately 12 sessions. But that night all classes had been canceled so we could hear a special guest speaker.

I was somewhat surprised when I first saw him. By his reputation and the work God had given him to do, I expected to see a trim 6′ man (perhaps taller), maybe in his late 50s with graying hair. He was more round than slim, and closer to 5′5″ or 5′6″. His appearance was pleasing, and he was closer to 50 with blond thinning hair. So much for expectations! What he had to say, however, was one of the most important messages I've ever heard. He strolled to a stool placed on the main floor, not on the raised platform. He sat down and immediately began to speak.

As a young man, Josh McDowell considered himself to be agnostic. He believed Christianity was worthless. When he was challenged to intellectually examine the claims of Christianity, Josh discovered compelling and overwhelming evidence for the reliability of the Christian faith. After he trusted Jesus Christ as his Savior and Lord, his life changed drastically as he experienced the power of God's love. Josh has written or co-authored 142 books in over 100 languages including "More than a Carpenter" and "New Evidence that Demands a Verdict." I encourage you to read them.

What Josh said was shocking to most of us. The two take-a-ways I got were:

1.) Our children are speaking a different language today. It is English or their native language, but the words have a different meaning. We may think we have an agreement, but what the children are saying is entirely different from what we are hearing. A distressing failure to communicate exists between generations. 2.) To our children, no right or wrong exists. There are no absolutes. Truth for me may not the truth for my children. When we think we are communicating, we in all probability are not.

Even more appalling was the statistical data that he presented: "79% of all the children raised in the church will leave the church at the very first chance they get, and they don't plan on returning."

If his statistics are correct, it seemed to me that instead of teaching young people the deep abiding love our heavenly Father has for all of us and the unique Operating Assets He has provided, we had accomplished very little except to inoculate our children against God. They either don't know or have dismissed, knowledge of His provisions that enable us to live in His presence. So maybe, just maybe, we're teaching them the wrong things. One definition of insanity is to continue to teach the same thing the same way and expect a different outcome. They know how to speak "Christianese," but apparently being a Christian means very little to them. If they are saved, they have been neutralized by the world system. They/we are imitating the unbeliever.

Our youth search for ways to express themselves and do not always make right decisions, but they are not reacting like little demons and always looking for any kind of mischief to get into. I think, for the most part, they are "good" people. They are doing what is generally accepted by society as right. But when tempted, they can quickly fall into the trap. They are doing what seems natural, forgetting, or not knowing that they are supernatural beings. They are not dissimilar from the adults, being too poorly equipped spiritually to glorify God when the occasion occurs.

Romans 3:10-12 (NIV)

> 10 *As it is written: "There is no one righteous, not even one;* 11 *there is no one who understands; there is no one who seeks God.* 12 *All have turned away; they have together become worthless; there is no one who does good, not even one."*

Ecclesiastes 7:20 (NIV)

> 20 *Indeed, there is no one on earth who is righteous, no one who does what is right and never sins.*

In 2011, Josh McDowell spoke at another church and said with that the percentage of children raised in the church that will leave the church for good, and they will do it as soon as soon as possible has climbed to 84%.

Those who leave the church doubt the Bible and reject the Christian life, and say the church and Christianity are not relevant to them. The church is exclusive, not inclusive, they whine. Only one way to heaven isn't fair, they argue. There are many ways to heaven, they claim. Everyone's opinions are equally valid, they opine. These moral relativists live as if they doubt there is even a heaven at all. I have been told, "I don't believe there is a hell." The reason given was that a good God would not send anyone to a place like hell. What's ironic is that they absolutely believe that there are no absolutes. They are wrong, but that is what they think, absolutely. There are some relevant prophesies recorded for us so we might learn.

Isaiah 5:20 (NIV)

20 *Woe to those who call evil good and good evil, who put darkness for light and light for darkness, who put bitter for sweet and sweet for bitter.*

Proverbs 1:22-33 (NIV)

22 *How long will you who are simple, love your*
simple ways? How long will mockers delight in
mockery, and fools hate knowledge? 23 *Repent at*
my rebuke! Then I will pour out my thoughts to
you; I will make known to you my teachings. 24
But since you refuse to listen when I call, and no
one pays attention when I stretch out my hand, 25
since you disregard all my advice and do not accept
my rebuke, 26 *I, in turn, will laugh when disaster*
strikes you; I will mock when calamity overtakes
you – 27 *when calamity overtakes you like a storm,*
when disaster sweeps over you like a whirlwind,
when distress and trouble overwhelm you. 28 *Then*
they will call to me, but I will not answer; they will
look for me but will not find me, 29 *since they hated*
knowledge and did not choose to fear the LORD. 30
Since they would not accept my advice and spurned
my rebuke, 31 *they will eat the fruit of their ways*
and be filled with the fruit of their schemes. 32 *For*
the waywardness of the simple will kill them, and
the complacency of fools will destroy them; 33 *but*

whoever listens to me will live in safety and be at ease, without fear of harm.

The church is inclusive. Any and everyone is welcome. God's call is universal. The doors of the church are wide open, and fellowship is available to everyone. But only those who have accepted Jesus as their Lord and Savior have the capacity to fellowship with God. The church does not limit itself to who you are, where you came from, or what you can do for the church. It is an oasis for those who are searching, seeking guidance, and those who worship God. Jesus spent His time on earth teaching and fellowshipping with the ordinary people, not the religious leaders. A true church teaches the truth as God has revealed it in the Bible. When that is done some toes may be stepped on, but they will be the toes of the Christians and non-Christians alike.

There are absolutes! One plus one will always equal two; two plus two will always equal four, $H^{2}0$ will always be water. There is a God. There is a Hell. There is a heaven. There is only one way to get to Heaven. If you are not a child of God, you are on the road to hell. God speaks only the truth, you don't have to agree with what He says, but your disagreement will not change the reality of His statements.

John 14:6 (NIV)

6 *Jesus answered, "I am the way and the truth and the life. No one comes to the Father except through me."*

Everyone is born spiritually dead and physically alive. God wants everyone to be spiritually alive. So, what do you do? You do exactly what God has called you to do.

CHAPTER TEN

We Have Our Marching Orders

The last thing Jesus said to His disciples as He ascended into heaven was not trivial. It wasn't. "see you later," "good luck," "have a good life," or anything like that. Everyone who is dying or leaving for a long time goes right to the important things Jesus was no exception. His directive is short, direct, understandable, doable and extremely important.

Matt. 28:19-20 NIV

19 *Therefore, as you go (through life) make disciples in all nations, baptizing them in the name of the Father, and the Son and of the Holy Spirit.*
20 *Teaching them to obey everything I have commanded you, and surely, I will be with you always to the very end of the age.*

Our marching orders are quite simple: to know Jesus, to make disciples, and teach His truths.

As we go through life, our motive is love. Love for Jesus and love for the lost. The more you know about your faith, the better equipped you will be to let the Holy Spirit use your smile, your knowledge, and all that you are. Don't be afraid, if Jesus means anything to you share what you know and have experienced with your friends, family, and strangers. 99 percent of the time, what you dread will not happen.

We learn more about Jesus by spending time with our Father in prayer and studying our written SOP (Standard Operating Procedures), the Bible. We are not to forsake assembling together because we need the fellowship and encouragement of each other. The church has the extraordinary power to multiply our joys and divide our sorrows.

As long as Jesus means anything to us, the most natural thing to do is to tell others what Jesus has done for us. That's all we could do in the beginning, but as we mature we should remember how simple it was to rely on Him in the beginning. We mature as we grow in the knowledge of Christ and learn that we can trust Him. We should never think or say, "I could never talk to someone about Jesus or my faith." Why do we think we can't tell others what Jesus means to us? Is it because He really doesn't mean much to us? I think it is something else entirely. People say, "I don't talk about Jesus because I don't know enough to carry on an intelligent conversation, and I would embarrass God and myself." If that is truly the reason, it can be fixed. How would you react if your son or daughter, whom you love dearly, were to say, "I could never tell anyone how much my dad or mom loves me; I would be so embarrassed."

Jesus gave this final command to the disciples, and they followed their marching orders very well. Jesus and His most unlikely twelve changed the world. Jesus is the dividing point of history. He is the exclamation point. Jesus's command to make disciples and teach them as recorded in Matthew 28:19-20 still applies today. It is our marching order as much as it was the original disciples.

God's love and the Gospel are clear. As Ambassadors for Christ, our responsibility is to grow in the knowledge of God's ways and to always be ready to represent Jesus and what He means to us. As an Ambassador for Jesus, we are expected to always represent our Lord with excellence. God's plan is for every unbeliever to be so encouraged and convinced by the Holy Spirit, that he or she will be saved. Our Father has developed the plan, and it requires our wiliness to present the Gospel, it's the Holy Spirit's responsibility to draw the unbeliever close. It's the responsibility of the lost one to hear and accept the invitation.

Why is this so important? Spiritual skirmishes are being waged continually between the forces of God and evil. The results of these battles have everlasting consequences; we are our own worst enemy. If I choose to be without God in this life, He will not insist that I be with Him throughout all of eternity. I can choose to accept what Jesus has done for me, or I can choose to try to earn a heavenly pass. The most important thing I need to know is that God says there is no way to earn a heavenly pass; it is a free gift which costs Him more than any of us could imagine. The natural man, through the deceit of Satan, has been infected with the "auto-destruct bug" (ASN – A Sin Nature). This bug cannot be destroyed, but it can be counteracted.

So how does it all end?

ONE DAY EVERY KNEE WILL BOW, ACKNOWLEDGING JESUS IS KING.

The Bible promises what will happen:

Philippians 2:10-11 (NIV)

10 *That at the name of Jesus every knee should bow, in heaven, and on earth, and under the earth,* 11 *and every tongue should confess that Jesus Christ is Lord, to the glory of God the Father.*

Romans 14:11 (NIV)

[11]It is written, "As surely as I live," says the Lord, "every knee shall bow before Me; every tongue will confess to God."

Isaiah 45:23- 24 (NIV)

[23] By Myself I have sworn, My mouth has uttered in all integrity, a word (promise) that will not be revoked: Before Me, every knee will bow; by Me, every tongue will swear." [24] They will say of Me, In the LORD alone are righteousness and strength. All who have raged against Him will come to Him and be put to shame.

You can bet your life, and that's what you are doing, that every knee will bow in acknowledgment of the Lordship of Jesus. Sooner or later you and I and everyone living, and everyone who has ever lived will acknowledge Jesus as Lord and Savior. It will happen so why not do it now?

If you die without acknowledging Jesus as your Lord and Savior or wait until He returns, you will bow before Him as a defeated enemy, and the consequences will be eternally grave. If you bow before Him now, you will rise up as a faithful servant. How important is it to accept Jesus as your Lord and Savior? Christians have an exceedingly better destiny. Therefore, becoming a Christian not only changes your life it changes your destiny.

Philippians 1:9-11 (NIV)

[9] And this is my prayer: that your love may abound more and more in knowledge and depth of insight, [10] so that you may be able to discern what is best and may be pure and blameless for the day of Christ, [11] filled with the fruit of righteousness that comes through Jesus Christ – to the glory and praise of God.

CHAPTER ELEVEN

The Importance Of Remembering

The solution for the Christian's immaturity and lack of commitment is to REMEMBER. REMEMBER what God has already done for you, ACKNOWLEDGE who God is, and then UTILIZE the Operating Assets He has provided. We Christians often fail to recognize our opportunities to glorify God because we have limited knowledge and understanding of who God is and how He has equipped us to face the battles before us. It seems impossible. We, for the most part, have and claim to study the same Bible, which is His Word. It tells us who God is, who we are, and how we are to act and worship. Yet we, much of the time, are paralyzed by fear as we face our personal "giants."

Personal giants are those thoughts and events that tend to overwhelm, paralyze, and dominate our thought processes with fear and other emotions. We should not be controlled by emotions but knowledge and faith. Anger, sadness, pity parties, and fear will keep us from enjoying God's provisions because the focus is on self not on God. Those who study, tabulate and pay attention to such things note that 365 times the Bible instructs us do not be afraid, or says do not fear, and yet the fear remains. Many stories of events recorded in the Bible are not dissimilar from those we face in our lives; the stories are recorded to instruct us. Let's look 2 Chronicles 20:1-17 (NIV) to see how one man, in a moment of time, faced his "Giant."

2 Chronicles 20:1-3 (NIV)

1 After this, the Moabites and Ammonites with some of the Meunites came to wage war against Jehoshaphat. 2 Some people came and told Jehoshaphat, "A vast army is coming against you from Edom, from the other side of the Dead Sea. It is already in Hazezon Tamar." 3 Alarmed, Jehoshaphat resolved to inquire of the LORD, and he proclaimed a fast for all Judah.

Look at verse 3 again. As alarm mounts in Jehoshaphat, he recognizes the fear and pulls out one of the Operating Assets God has given His people: Prayer. He doesn't go crazy running to and fro or even ponder what to do, but instantly prays a prayer of REMEMBRANCE, and the people wait and also REMEMBER.

This passage tells us of a real threat. The people were afraid. The king was afraid, but he knew what to do. His great and great-great grandfathers, King Solomon and King David, had taught him well. When fear gripped him, he didn't wring his hands and said, "Woe is me," or seek counsel from other people. Without hesitating, he prayed to the LORD. Then he proclaimed a fast for the entire nation.

Biblical fasting abstains from food, drink, or even sleep to focus on a period of spiritual growth. We deny something of the flesh to glorify God, enhance our spirit, and go deeper in our prayer life. Jehoshaphat was calling on the nation to pray instead of eating. He called the people together to meet at the "church" for a prayer meeting. Interestingly, the people didn't succumb to their fears and flee; instead, they came from every town to attend the prayer meeting.

Then Jehoshaphat stood up in front of the people and led the prayer. In his public prayer, he reminded the people who their God was by REMEMBERING many of the great and wonderful things God had done for them. As he did, we can see him growing bolder. "We will cry out to you in our distress, and you will hear us and save us."

He acknowledges they are powerless against the vast army and they don't know what to do, except to look to God for deliverance. That is precisely what we are to do.

2 Chronicles 20:4-9 (NIV)

4 The people of Judah came together to seek help from the LORD; indeed, they came from every town in Judah to seek Him. 5 Then Jehoshaphat stood up in the assembly of Judah and Jerusalem at the temple of the LORD in the front of the new courtyard 6 and said: "LORD, the God of our ancestors, are you not the God who is in heaven? You rule over all the kingdoms of the nations. Power and might are in your hand, and no one can withstand you. 7 Our God, did you not drive out the inhabitants of this land before your people Israel and give it forever to the descendants of Abraham, your friend? 8 They have lived in it and have built in it a sanctuary for your Name, saying, 9 'If calamity comes upon us, whether the sword of judgment, or plague or famine, we will stand in your presence before this temple that bears your Name and will cry out to you in our distress, and you will hear us and save us.'"

Jehoshaphat is now in prayer praising God for all the blessings God has given His people and leading the people to REMEMBER that God is in control. They will utilize another Operating Asset God has given all believers – the Trust Factor. No matter what calamity they were about to face, they would trust God completely in the situation.

2 Chronicles 20:10-13 (NIV)

[10] "But now here are men from Ammon, Moab and Mount Seir, whose territory you would not allow Israel to invade when they came from Egypt; so they turned away from them and did not destroy them.[11] See how they are repaying us by coming to drive us out of the possession you gave us as an inheritance. [12] Our God, will you not judge them? For we have no power to face this vast army that is attacking us. We do not know what to do, but our eyes are on you." [13] All the men of Judah, with their wives and children and little ones, stood there before the LORD.

Remarkably, Jehoshaphat refrains from blaming God for what is apparently about to happen. He REMEMBERS obediently doing as the Lord had instructed and spared those who had previously marched against his people. As they face this overwhelming force, he declares they don't know what to do except to look to God for deliverance. It's interesting that Jehoshaphat remembers the property is God's property, and they were allowed to occupy it. We seem to have forgotten that God owns everything. From the time we are babes, we scream, "Mine!" and "That's mine!" and "I want that!" and "Give it to me!"

God responds to this eloquent prayer through the prophet Jahaziel so everyone could hear.

2 Chronicles 20:14-15 (NIV)

[14] Then the Spirit of the LORD came on Jahaziel, son of Zechariah, the son of Benaiah, the son of Jeiel, the son of Mattaniah, a Levite and descendant of Asaph, as he stood in the assembly. [15] He said: "Listen, King Jehoshaphat and all who live in Judah and Jerusalem! This is what the LORD says to you:

> *'Do not be afraid or discouraged because of this vast army, for the battle is not yours, but God's."*

God answers Jehoshaphat's prayer immediately. Jahaziel, a Levite filled with the Holy Spirit, quotes God Almighty: "Do not be afraid or discouraged by what you see. The battle is not yours; it is Mine." God then gives them very specific instructions on what to do and what not to do. Will they follow His instructions or come up with a plan of their own?

> 2 Chronicles 20:16-17 (NIV)
> 16 *Tomorrow march down against them. They will be climbing up by the Pass of Ziz, and you will find them at the end of the gorge in the Desert of Jeruel.*
> 17 *You will not have to fight this battle. Take up your positions; stand firm and see the deliverance the LORD will give you, Judah and Jerusalem. Do not be afraid; do not be discouraged. Go out to face them tomorrow, and the LORD will be with you.*

All the people could hear the prophet speak as God directs, "Listen up, pay attention, this is important," and then he laid out the LORD's battle plan. It is clear and concise, it could not be misunderstood, and the execution of the plan must be perfect. "Tomorrow put your fear aside and go take up defensive fighting positions against the enemy." Then He tells them where they will find the enemy. Take your positions and stand firm (not to be afraid, break ranks, and run away), you will not have to fight the battle. When you do this, you will witness the deliverance of the LORD. Have no fear, don't be discouraged by their numbers the LORD is with you.

To be entirely understood, God told the people not to fight, and that the fight was the LORD'S.

This is important—pay attention—this victory would not just be given to them. They had to demonstrate their faith by overcoming their fears. They knew the approaching army was massive and they had no chance of survival. They had to conquer their fears, obey His commands, and move into their assigned fighting positions prepared to stand firm.

2 Chronicles 20:20-21 (NIV)

[20] *Early in the morning, they left for the Desert of Tekoa. As they set out, Jehoshaphat stood and said, "Listen to me, Judah and people of Jerusalem! Have faith in the LORD your God, and you will be upheld; have faith in His prophets, and you will be successful."* [21] *After consulting the people, Jehoshaphat appointed men to sing to the LORD and to praise him for the splendor of his holiness as they went out at the head of the army…*

In faith, Jehoshaphat and his men did as they were instructed. As they started moving into position, Jehoshaphat reminded the men to believe God and everything would be okay. As an army goes to war, great fear exists among those in the ranks. Their songs of praise to God displaced their fear and bolstered their courage, and they followed their instructions to move forward. Heroes have fear, but it doesn't overpower them. It is laid aside to complete the task before them. God requires a display of faith and total trust because it is in the arena of faith where He does His best work.

2 Chronicles 20:24-30 (NIV)

[24] *When (Not until) the men of Judah came to the place that overlooks the desert and looked toward the vast army, they saw only dead bodies lying on the ground; no one had escaped.*

Here again, I think it is imperative to note that not until they occupied their assigned positions were they able to see the carnage that God had dealt. The entire enemy army was dead. Not one man was left alive.

> [25]*So Jehoshaphat and his men went to carry off their plunder, and they found among them a great amount of equipment and clothing and also articles of value-more than they could take away. There was so much plunder that it took three days to collect it.* [26] *On the fourth day, they assembled in the Valley of Berakah, where they praised the LORD. This is why it is called the Valley of Berakah to this day.* [27] *Then, led by Jehoshaphat, all the men of Judah and Jerusalem returned joyfully to Jerusalem, for the LORD had given them cause to rejoice over their enemies.* [28] *They entered Jerusalem and went to the temple of the*

It took the Israelite Army three days to gather their plunder, confirming that the invading army was indeed massive. The battle was not theirs to fight, and an excellent reward for obeying God was theirs for the taking. Here's another interesting thought: the Israelite army didn't have to go to war to gain the plunder. God had the invaders bring the plunder to them.

> *LORD with harps and lyres and trumpets.* [29] *The fear of God came on all the surrounding kingdoms when they heard how the LORD had fought against the enemies of Israel.* [30]*And the kingdom of Jehoshaphat was at peace, for his God had given him rest on every side.*

When God is with you, who can stand against you?

There was an unexpected but very real and wonderful additional benefit the people of God gained when they trusted God. It was a long period of peace. The kingdoms of the countries feared God when they heard how the LORD had fought against the enemies of Israel. And the kingdom of Jehoshaphat was at peace, for his God had given him rest on every side.

Several lessons can be learned from this historically accurate account of an event that took place in Jehoshaphat's reign:

- When you are afraid, turn to God in prayer.
- When the odds are overwhelmingly against you, quickly turn to God instead of seeking advice from others.
- REMEMBER the many and great things God has done for you.
- Enlist the prayers of friends, family, and people you trust, and don't stop praying until you have an answer.
- Be specific in your prayers.
- Expect you will be directed to do something that may not be rational, or reasonable. Obedience will be your demonstration of faith.
- REMEMBER the battle is the Lord's and let Him fight it.
- Be faithful and accept the outcome, even if it not what you expected.
- When you leave the battle in God's hands and trust Him, you can be at peace.
- Knowing God is in control, you can rest in your faith regardless of what you see.

As I remember the story, shortly after a couple celebrated their 50th wedding anniversary, the wife's cancer, dormant for more than 20 years, savagely returned. By the time it had manifested itself, she was in stage 4. The couple prayed and did all they knew to do, but the cancer quickly and progressively worsened. After a few months of fighting the cancer, the doctor told them it was time for her to go to a hospice care facility, there was nothing else he or the hospital could do for her.

As they waited for the hospice nurse to come and complete the paperwork so she could be admitted, the children, all adults now, snuggled up in her bed REMEMBERING how many ways God had blessed them. They REMEMBERED the fun times, the hard times, and the funny times. She was happier than she had been since this monster reemerged in their lives. She was at peace, knowing that struggle was nearly over and she would soon be in the presence of her Lord in heaven.

From what the doctor had told him, the husband thought she would live for several more months. After the transfer was complete and the children had gone home, he waited for the hospice doctor to return from making his rounds and prayed something like, "Father, how great you are! Thank you for blessing our marriage, for such loving children, and the joy that can only come from You. At last, we're away from the hospital, the prodding nurses who cared so much and were diligent in doing their jobs, all the doctors who were monitoring her everything, and the medicines that only seemed to make her sicker. Now You can heal her.

Thank You, Lord, for the witness she has been to the many professionals that You have brought into her presence. The oncologist has given up. The medicines that were given in an attempt to cure her have been removed from her 'care plan.' What she is getting is for her comfort only. Now it's just us. There will be no glory in her cure that is not Your glory. I turn her over completely to Your care. It is my wish that You heal her Lord, so everyone can witness Your strength and power and be drawn to You because of what You are about to do, but if it is her time, I will rejoice in your love and provision, Your will be done, Lord."

And he believed with every fiber of his being that God would heal her, and the power of God would be revealed for all to see. She passed into glory the next morning with a smile on her face. When he told their pastor, he had prayed she would be healed and he fully expected she would be healed, the pastor's reply was, "And she was, wasn't she?" The husband had to agree, even though the outcome wasn't what he wanted, the prayer was answered. She was in fact healed. It certainly wasn't the outcome he wanted or expected. He wanted God to get the glory, and he wanted her back with him. She was, in the twinkling of an eye, completely healed.

The point is that peace, joy, and happiness came out of remembering a lifetime of service. She passed with a smile, which gave her family the strength and joy to stand firm in the faith and in that moment glorify God through that most difficult time. Her lifelong testimony of God's love was validated through their many friends and extended family. His wish that God be glorified was also honored by the hundreds of friends who suddenly appeared at the hospice center to pray and visit and console the family. That beautiful smile was a testimony to every one of God's great love.

The story doesn't end. In God's perfect time, that husband was blessed greatly when he met the widowed mother of his youngest daughter's best friend. They are now married, and their two families have been blended into one in a most miraculous and wonderful way. When asked, "How many years have you'll been married?" He responds, "108 years. I was married to my first wife 52 years, and Di was married to her first husband 50 years before we were widowed. That's 102 years, and we've been married to each other 6 years, so that's 108 years."

When Job's testing was completed, Job was blessed with twice as much as he had when the testing began. Likewise, when this couple's trials were over, God blessed each of them exceedingly, abundantly, and above and beyond anything they have imagined or dreamed or asked.

You can't count the grains of sand on the seashore, and you can't count the stars in the sky. You'll never know how many ways or how many times God has blessed you, but never, no never, stop REMEMBERING how God has blessed you. If you chose to REMEMBER God's many blessings in your times of testing, you will stand tall and true. I know this is true because I was that man.

CHAPTER TWELVE

God Does Intervene In History

The Old and New Testaments provide many accounts of God's intervention into history, but many people fail to realize such interventions still happen in our day and time. At least three reasons exist for this lack of awareness.

1. Some people reject the notion that God intervenes anymore because they can see no imperial proof that He intervened.
2. God does intervene, and the natural or secular man doesn't recognize the intervention as such. He can't. He lacks the ability to recognize spiritual events, so the reporting and recording of these phenomena go like this: "As luck would have it," and "Strangely," "Mother Nature did this or that," "No one can say for sure," and "Luckily," and so on. But God does intervene, and as a Christ-follower one needs to be able to recognize and identify those special times when He does step into this world to make corrections and change outcomes.
3. We—children of God—have wandered too far from Him. Instead of being sensitive to the leading of the Holy Spirit, as we should be, we imitate the lost and can't see God moving. We mindlessly just move with the crowd. The phase for this setting aside of one's

norms and standards, as well as what he knows to be right, is called the mob mentality. We Christians can and must change our perspective to recognize when God intervenes, and gain wisdom to realize why. When things need to change we need to ask God to motivate hearts, to change or to step in. We should expect Him to answer our prayers and anticipate that He will; then recognize that He did and thank Him. Here are some examples that may illustrate why changing our perspective is so important.

George Washington, Against All Odds, Escapes

In 2015 The American Hero Channel released a very popular, multi-part series with claims to be the true and factual account of the "American Revolution." The producers proclaimed with great pride the extensive research and elaborate expenses that were invested in the production. Assuring the authenticity of the military uniforms and civilian dress apparel would be correct and ensuring the accuracy of the actual events were their paramount objectives. They introduced forgotten and unknown heroes of the cause. They reconstructed events, small and great, with amazing attention to even the smallest details. In the telling of one major event, however, they completely missed a glaring detail about the well-known character and value system of George Washington so, they dreadfully missed the "how" of the outcome of his great vanishing act.

The following is their account of how George Washington and half of his army (9,000 men) escaped certain death and capture, which would have ended the rebellion almost before it began.

"On August 28, 1776, seven weeks after the Founding Fathers had signed the U.S. Constitution, George Washington and 9,000 of his 18,000-man army were surrounded by 32,000 British soldiers on Long Island. The British army was the finest army in the world at that time, and the American army was a ragtag, untrained rabble. The only escape available was to somehow cross the East River into Brooklyn, NY. It seemed that route was going to be denied, as the British warships began to sail up the East River for the express purpose cutting off any possibility of escape and ending the rebellion then and there.

Washington and his men needed time, but time was about to run out. The trapped army was doomed. Sudden furious southernly winds held back the oncoming warships and prevented them from maneuvering up the river into position to set the trap. The wind and luck were with Washington, creating the delay that was so badly needed.

Now General Washington had one night to affect the escape. It would be an impossible feat to pull off, but Colonel John Glover and his mariners were given the task; they gathered as many boats as they could. Most were small rowboats and thus began the evacuation effort. They knew the tides and currents and were both efficient and effective, but the task before them was daunting.

There was a full moon that night, so the fleet of small boats would be seen as they crossed the river. They would be very vulnerable and would be destroyed by naval gunfire as they crossed. Mother Nature provided the cloak of darkness they needed, by providing clouds to hide the moon and provide the essential darkness to conceal the all-night action. Men, weapons, cannons and horses were quietly moved."

Every soldier knows that sound is amplified at night and even more so on the water. Can you imagine moving all that equipment, cannons, men, and horses without being detected? It was impossible, but it did happen. The rear guard maintained the campfires and made regular camp noises to create the illusion that nothing irregular was happening.

"At dawn 1,000 men and George Washington were still on the Long Island side of the river. If they tried to cross the river in daylight, they would be seen by the navy and blown out of the water. If they stayed, they would be captured or killed by the army; they had no chance of escape. A stroke of luck arrived right on cue provided by Mother Nature. A fog developed to cover the final phase of the withdrawal maneuver. It was a miraculous escape."

"George Washington and his men escaped as a result of bold thinking and blind luck."

That's the way it was recorded in this epic story of the American Revolution.

Like it or not, this account will most likely become the standard account of our war for independence. The American Hero Channel's account, though entertaining and informative, is only partially true. Even though it claims total accuracy, it is riddled with many inaccurate conclusions because it excludes well-known facts about George Washington's spiritual life. Leaving Washington's faith out of the account distorts the outcome and invalidates the accuracy of the story.

Stop and think: furious winds blowing against the British warships at just the right time, preventing them from entering the East River and thus protecting the Colonial army. Clouds appeared at just the right time to darken the full moon that night so that the Colonials would be cloaked in darkness as they rowed to safety. The ears of the posted British sentinels on land and on the warships were deafened, resulting in a host of sounds of the evacuation movement that were not heard. Finally, another stroke of "luck" was provided by Mother Nature to provide fog at precisely the right time and obscure Gen. Washington and the rear guard as they were forced to attempt a daylight crossing.

These events cannot be attributed to good planning; even George Washington could not control the weather and make war plans based on his ability to do so. The "American Hero Channel" would have the viewer believe, as it evidently does, that Mother Nature chose to side with the Colonists.

It would be just as easy to believe all the separate parts of your car could assemble themselves together into a marvelous and perfectly running machine and do so without an assembly line and without a mastermind supervising the work. Otherwise, one must conclude that "Mother Nature" is the mastermind who knows all, and she intervened as she willed to control all the documented events that happened. She did it all in the necessary order and at the correct time to protect the Colonial army.

However, if the directors and producers have read the Book of Job—the oldest book in the Bible—one of the many things they would have learned is that it is God who is in control of nature. At least 47 verses in the Bible declare it to be so. This short list of Scriptures follows so you can read them yourself: Job 37-38; 28:25-26; Matthew 8: 26-27; Mark 4: 39-41; Luke 8: 24-25; Jeremiah 10:13; Proverbs 3:19-20; John 3:8; Genesis 8:22; Matthew 5:45; and Genesis 9a:4-16.

It was God Himself, not Mother Nature, who chose to intervene and help the Colonists escape to fight another day. Just as God had helped the Israelites escape from Egypt by providing the supernatural solutions when they were needed, God has always provided supernatural and natural interventions for America, as well as for His people when they were needed.

What prompted God to intervene in this case?

Abundant evidence reveals that George Washington was a man who prayed. He actively sought God's will and leadership. What a unique concept! When we pray asking God's direction in life, we should expect answers and guidance. When we pray expecting a solution, we should be prepared to act on the instructions we receive. When we do, we will stand in amazement and watch God work.

I believe that General Washington prayed for deliverance for his men and himself, and being a man of faith, he believed that God would deliver them. Therefore he, in an act of faith, began preparing for the escape. I believe that God gave him the wisdom to see the opportunities that God was providing as well as the courage to take the actions that were needed. Because the Bible teaches that it is God who directs nature, I believe God took great joy in directing the winds to blow; the clouds to cover the moon; muffling sounds and deafening the ears of the British forces to any suspicious sounds and laying the fog thick on the water. George Washington was in tune with God, and God had a plan for Washington's life and a free America, just as He has a plan for your life.

Think about the men manning the oars of those boats and how many times they crossed the river loaded to the gunnels on the escape leg, and then returning empty. From dark to dawn oarsmen made that risk-filled round trip. One could only guesstimate how many round trips were made that night. Oarsmen rowed from dusk through the night and into the morning hours. Apparently, they did not grow weary. If they did, weariness did not deter them from their seemingly impossible task. Perhaps they claimed the promise of Isaiah 40:31 (paraphrased):

> *But those who wait (as the servant waits) upon the Lord shall exchange their (strength for His), They*

> *shall mount up on the wings of eagles; they shall run and not be faint, they shall (ROW) and not grow weary.*

The oarsmen accomplished their task just in time. As the last boats left the shore, a British patrol saw them and shot, wounding four men. How miraculous is that? All the ammunition, cannons, horses, and 8,996 men escaped without injury and only four men wounded, but none seriously! That's a God thing. I doubt anyone could duplicate the events of that escape today in the same time frame, even if it were attempted during daylight hours.

Another River, Another War; Same Results

To bring perspective to this incredible God intervention, another river had to be crossed during wartime. During World War II as the Allies were closing in on Germany, Hitler gave the order to destroy all bridges that crossed the Rhine River. This was a defensive tactic to delay the Americans until reinforcements could be organized.

Since the time of the Roman Empire, the river's cold, wide, and swift waters had always been a formidable obstacle to any aggressor intending to cross it and enter into Germany. Crossing the Rhine would be a costly and challenging task.

By March 7, 1945, all bridges crossing the Rhine had been destroyed, except one. The Ludendorff Railroad Bridge at the little resort town of Remagen, a few miles to the southeast of Cologne, was intact. About 1 p.m. an American reconnaissance patrol reached the bridge and reported it was intact. The Americans quickly launched a full-scale assault to cross it. At the same time, the defending Germans scrambled to detonate the explosive charges previously placed to destroy it. American soldiers under heavy fire were struggling to dislodge and throw multiple stores of explosions into the river, and the Germans successfully detonated some of the explosives, but not enough to destroy the bridge. By 4 p.m. the Americans had reached the other side of the river and secured the bridge. Within 24 hours General Omar Bradley, 1st Army Commander, had 8,000 of his men and their equipment across the bridge into Germany, but there still wasn't enough force to fully secure the bridgehead against an all-out counter-attack. God uses whatever resources He chooses to accomplish His purposes; I believe it gives Him great pleasure to use men of faith in doing so.

> ***"Our humanity is trapped by moral adolescence. We have too many men of science, too few men of God. The world has achieved brilliance without wisdom, and power without conscience."***
>
> ~ General Omar Bradley

> ***"We live in a world of nuclear giants and ethical infants, in a world that has achieved brilliance without wisdom, power without conscience. We've solved the mystery of the atom and forgotten the lessons of the Sermon on the Mount. We know more about war than we know about peace and more about dying than we do about living."***
>
> ~ General Omar Bradley

> ***"In war, there is no second place for runner-up."***
>
> ~ General Omar Bradley

No army since Napoleon's had successfully crossed the Rhine River, but in 24 hours General Bradley had enough men and equipment across the bridge to sustain the attack. For days the German Air Force and Artillery, which had been so brilliantly accurate until then, tried to blast, and bomb the bridge to smithereens, but no bomb or shell hit it. German artillery poured fire toward the bridge but uncharacteristically continued to missed the target. The Germans even fired V2 rockets at the bridge. V2 rockets were so powerful they just needed to be close. Like a game of horseshoes or a thrown grenade, close should have done the job. The V2s certainly hit close, but the bridge refused to fall.

Later it was discovered that even the dynamite that the combat engineers had wired to the bridge was a less powerful commercial grade, not the more powerful military grade. How did these mistakes and miscalculations happen? By accident? No way! That bridge was the gateway to the end of the evil Nazi regime that had bewitched an entire nation and systematically murdered millions of God's chosen people, just because they were Jewish. Nazi Germany was not going to reign over the earth for a thousand years, but Jesus will. God could, and would, have stopped Hitler's atrocities, but humanity, which thinks it is naturally good, needed to see its true nature. We now know how deceived and depraved we can become.

Now that generation and the one that followed is passing away. The lessons that were learned must be remembered by the new generation, but will we? Probably not. There are those who say the concentration camps and atrocities never happened.

The bridge at Remagen stood until a sufficient number of men and equipment crossed into Germany to protect the building of a replacement bridge, then and only then did it collapse. German firepower didn't cause the collapse; it just lost the strength to hold itself together and collapsed on its own. Remarkable? Yes! But if you know Jesus, it's not unbelievable. It was as if God Himself had been holding it up, and then, in His time, removed His supporting hand and let it go.

It took 24 hours for a modem army with tanks, trucks, cannons, and 8,000 infantrymen, plus the support elements, to cross the Rhine River using the bridge, compared to Washington's great escape of 9,000 men, horses, wagons, and cannons using row boats of varied sizes. Perhaps no evidence exists that God was intervening in the Rhine River crossing, but there is no other accounting for the stability of the bridge, and its refusal to fall. God was in both of these outstanding displays of His overriding will.

Strawberry 5

Another example from our recent past occurred June 4, 1942, when the battle for Midway Island was about to begin. This was the pivotal battle for control of the Pacific Ocean during WWII. Two giant naval forces, the United States and Japan, were looking for each other. The winner of the coming battle would become the dominant force on and in the sea. Lt. Howard P. Ad Jr., the pilot of Strawberry 5 and his crew, manned one of 22 planes that were searching for the Japanese Task Force. Each aircraft was flying its prescribed course radiating out from the Enterprise and Yorktown aircraft carriers. At 5:10 a.m. the first report— a single word "aircraft" crackled through the aircraft carrier's speakers in the Combat Control Center. That word was followed by a second report: "Many aircraft heading Midway." This report allowed the airfield at Midway Island to clear its runway and get fighter aircraft into the air. The American fighters were woefully outnumbered and offered only token resistance, but not one of the remaining operational planes left on the ground was damaged by the more than 100-plane Japanese strike force 45 minutes later.

At 5:34 a.m. a third report crackled through the CCC speakers "enemy carriers" and at 5:52 a.m. another detailed report gave targets as two carriers, main body including the course and speed. That report was the beacon that led to 10 American air strikes and culminated into the most spectacular six minutes in U.S. Naval aviation history when

the Akagi, the Kang, and the Soryu Japanese aircraft carriers were destroyed. The Japanese Navy could not, and did not, recover from this devastating defeat.

Now, here's the rest of the story. The Japanese admirals had also sent their search planes out, and one of them from the Soryu, near the end of its prescribed route, spotted the American fleet. It tried to radio their sighting, but the radio didn't work. Isn't that strange? A functioning radio was the essential reason for the flight. Therefore, that radio had to have been checked out before takeoff, and it was working properly. A properly functioning radio was so vital to the operation that at least one more radio check after takeoff would have been in order, and evidently, it was operating correctly at that time. Remarkably, the radio of the only Japanese plane to find the American Task Force didn't work.

If the American radio had not worked and the Japanese radio had worked, the American fleet would have been destroyed, and the outcome of the war may have been much different. Did God intervene? I think so.

Free At Last

This is a more recent and more personal example of God reaching down into time and intervening in a young boy's life. Just as He has millions of times before and has millions of times since, an extraordinary gift began to be unveiled for me on an April day in 1948 in the Kirkwood neighborhood of Atlanta, GA. A 12-year-old very good friend, Nolan Lassiter, mustered up the courage to do what God asks all of us to do; he invited me to go to the revival at his church that night.

I really wasn't interested; I didn't know why, but I wasn't interested. I would have rather had fun doing whatever I wanted to do, I suppose. I had always been in church. Nine months before I was born I was in church, every Sunday and Wednesday I was in church, my Mom and Dad saw to that! I was one of the "good boys. "Why did I need to go to a silly revival? Nolan countered my "no" with, "Well, Barbara, Peggy, and Faye, Patricia, Mike, and a lot of our friends will be there." Before I knew it, I heard myself say, "What time does it start?" What began that day as an invisible skirmish between the Holy Spirit and my Sin Nature became a fully engaged battle that night. Like the mighty Joe Frazier, the Holy Spirit was assaulting my Sin Nature, who was ducking, weaving, dancing around every issue, and counter-punching. Undaunted, the Holy Spirit pressed on, coming right at me. I was outmatched, but unlike Muhammad Ali, that night I was able to escape the onslaught. I considered that a victory, but in reality, it was potentially my greatest loss.

The church was packed, and everyone in it was oblivious to the mighty battle that was being waged within me; perhaps many of them were engaged in their own battles. Back then children could and did roam freely throughout their neighborhoods, walking or riding bicycles without fear and with full parental approval. At the age of 12, I was on the throne of my life, and I liked it like that. So, remaining on my throne was, in my eyes, a victory, but I was beaten up pretty good. The Holy Spirit had not pulled any punches, and I was on the ropes when at last the invitation was closed. I drew a breath of relief. I had never felt anything that intense before... well, outside of my dad taking the "belt of correction" to my rear end.

The battle was over, I thought. As I remember, no reason existed for me to return on Thursday night and possibly subject myself to that unpleasantness, except for the fact that the Holy Spirit had already gained a foothold in my life. Without hesitation I did go back Thursday; I remember having a really good time during the worship part of the service, but I don't remember a single word that the preacher said. Before the invitation was given, the battle had begun again. Just as if last night had been round one, now round two began. I was hit right between the eyes, my knees buckled, and I was falling backward. I felt as if the ropes caught me. I did a Muhammad Ali "rope-a-dope" until I could regain some degree of composure and effectively block every knockout punch the Holy Spirit threw at me. My will remained in control of my life, as Thursday's round finally ended. I was too dazed to do a victory dance or shout "I'm the greatest." Strangely, I was a little sad, but that feeling was soon over and forgotten. Everything returned to the way it had been, and we all hung out for a while. None of them knew that I had been in a war. One thing God does not do is violate an individual's volition. The choice to obey and keep obeying Him must be ours.

Friday night I found myself back at the church; the gang met outside the church chatting and having fun before the service. As the singing began, we made our way back to the balcony. Although I didn't know it at the time, this was where the most significant battle of my life was to begin. I know now that Satan's cohorts were there, just as they had been the two nights prior, well-armed and ready for battle. The Holy Spirit was there too, ready to harvest the souls that had been prepared. On this, the last night of the revival, neither side was going to be denied. I looked at the round 4-inch brass railing that my white-knuckled hands had clung to the nights before. Would it work again tonight? Equipped with His divine nature, the Holy Spirit fought the fight that night with one hand tied behind His back. Using only three of His attributes: 1.) omniscience (all knowledge), 2.) omnipotence (all power), and 3.) love, He knew what was going to happen, how the evil one would attack and how to counter those attacks, and He had the power to successfully accomplish

His mission. Without violating my free will in any way, He overwhelmed me with His love, and with His love, He lifted me up. With His love, He showed me Jesus; and by the blood of Jesus, He saved me.

I don't know how many verses of "Just As I Am" was sung while the two fought to determine who would have my soul, but I think I bolted during the first verse. I rushed down the steps and down the aisle to the preacher. At that precise moment, I had reached my "age of accountability." For the first time, I clearly understood what Jesus had done for me. It could have been the last time, or it could have been the first and last time, that I would have the opportunity to accept, as my own, the work that Jesus did on the cross on my behalf. If I had continued to stand as a statue like I had the nights before, I might have been lost forever.

Before I stepped sideways to get to the aisle, and before I was walking the aisle, and before I spoke to the pastor, I was saved. I was changed. I was a brand-new person, not repaired, not made over, not refurbished, but an entirely new person! 38 things happened immediately to create me into a new creation. I didn't see them happen; I didn't feel them, I didn't even realize the change had occurred. When I looked in the mirror, I didn't see any difference: Sadly, neither did anyone else. I had never been a "bad" boy; in fact, my world probably considered me to be a "good" boy, and after I was saved, I continued to be a "good" boy. I had no follow-up training to teach me anything about what had happened. I simply went on with my life as if nothing so spectacular had changed me. For 28 more years, I went on as if nothing had changed.

Remember I was a "good" boy and grew up to be a "good" man, humanly speaking. It was only through the Holy Spirit's oversight and protection that I was protected. I was 40 before I began to learn most of what you'll learn in this book.

Wrong Road Correction

The fifth and most personal example of God's intervention occurs in time to change the projected outcome of our future. This is His continuous universal invitation. If we are lost, we are on the wrong road. It leads to destruction and to a place no one wants to go—Hell. You are a unique person, but not in this; every person has been, or is, on this road. There is absolutely nothing you can do to get off this road. You don't even know what your final destination is going to be and haven't spent much, or anytime, even thinking about it. You are in a frantic search for happiness mode, doing this or that, always going here and there searching for an inner joy the world calls "happiness." The world says, "If it feels good, do it" and some sing with pride "I did it my way." But no matter what you do or try, there is no lasting peace or happiness. Perhaps moments of happiness are experienced from the sense of accomplishment or satisfaction, or maybe just relief and momentary rest. Still, there is a sense of being unfulfilled. So off you go to some other project, person, or endeavor.

"Beware not of the enemy from without but the enemy from within."

~ General Douglas MacArthur ~

"Worry, doubt, fear, and despair are the enemies which slowly bring us down to the ground and turn us to dust before we die."

~ General Douglas MacArthur ~

However, before the foundations of the universe were laid, God the Father developed an escape route for us, and 2,000 years ago Jesus completed all the work to ensure that we would have a chance to change our direction and get on the right road—the one that leads to Heaven. At the perfect time, God the Holy Spirit makes sure that we hear the Gospel and motivates us to accept what Jesus has done on our behalf. The Holy Spirit is relentless in His efforts to bring us that point of God-consciousness, and all the way to the point where we can say "I accept," or decide, "No I won't." If you rejected the call, He may persist for a while, but there will come a time when the welcome door may be closed and locked. Don't be caught on the outside.

2 Peter 3:9b (NIV)

> [9] *God is not willing that anyone would perish but wants everyone to repent.*

Still, He will not violate our volition. The outcome is in our hands, not His. Now He's knocking on the door of your heart again. What will you do? No one can guarantee that you'll get a second chance to make this life-changing decision.

You may be a carnal Christian—one who after receiving God's wonderful gift, has drifted from God and is not experiencing the Spirit-filled life. You are living your life as if God does not exist. You bow down to the gods of self-desire. You are like the unbeliever, controlled by your sin nature. You, too, are on a wrong road and need a course correction. The foolish and unbelieving deceivers say that all roads lead to God. That, my friend, is a lie right out of hell. Check it out! Don't believe me, believe Jesus.

John 14:5-7 (NIV)

> [5] *Thomas said to Him, "Lord, we don't know where You are going, so how can we know the way?"* [6] *Jesus answered, "I am the way and the Truth and the Life. No one comes to the Father except through Me.* [7] *If you really know Me; you will know My Father as well. From now on, you do know Him*

and have seen Him" (you know Jesus; therefore, you know God the Father).

Is it possible that people don't fully understand who God is? Yes, it is, and the purpose of *Light Up The Darkness* is fourfold:

- To help people understand who God is and is not.
- To show that God loves every one of us.
- To respond to his love by loving each other.
- To provide some basic understanding of how we are expected to use the Operating Assets, He has provided.

It is my prayer that this information will help His followers see the world as God sees it and understand His Heart and His ways. WWJD (What Would Jesus Do) is not passé. Knowing what Jesus would do is essential to the Christian because it is precisely what the Christian should do in any and every situation.

CHAPTER THIRTEEN

A Mental Adjustment Is Needed

Knowledge of what we have in Christ is everything, and training is vital to gaining that knowledge. Most Christians don't have much training and have forgotten how to effectively apply what they have learned. It's vital we change and REMEMBER who we are and what we have in Jesus.

The Green Bay Packers under Coach Lombardi had to relearn the game of football and return to the basics. The Packers had gotten sloppy in their game, and once they were on that slippery slope, they seemed powerless to escape. As a strong leader, Lombardi knew that discipline and getting back to the basics were needed to get them back on track. We Christians are more like the kid on the block who knows very little about football yet thinks he's the greatest and under-performs terribly. We, like the kid, don't even know the basics. Much can be learned by getting back to the basics and changing our mental attitudes so our aptitude can change. Once you start learning, never stop.

The 1958 season the Green Bay Packers had five future Hall of Fame players on the team but finished the season with one win, ten losses and one tie—the worst record in Packer history. The players were dispirited, the shareholders were disheartened, and the community was enraged. The anguish in Green Bay extended to the NFL as a whole. The financial viability and the very existence of the Green Bay Packers franchise was in jeopardy. On February 2, 1959, Vince Lombardi accepted the positions of head coach and general manager.

He assumed responsibility and total authority and was determined to make change happen. He correctly identified that the team's primary problem was mental in nature. The players had the ability and were furnished with adequate support elements. What was needed was a mental adjustment. The players' view of themselves as exceptional was based on their past performance, and they failed to see that their execution was poor because they had forgotten the basics. Their execution was sloppy. Perhaps they thought they had advanced beyond the basic stuff. But basic is basic because they are the building blocks of achievement. Most Christians haven't even been taught the basic stuff.

Lombardi created punishing training regiments and expected absolute dedication and effort from his players. His introduction to the players was profound. He walked into the first meeting with the seasoned players, many experienced at the highest levels of competition, holding up a football. "This is a football," he said, "and we're going back to the basics. That's where the game is won." The team that executes the basics best and makes the fewest mistakes will always win. We Christians need to go back to the basics to get our heads in the battle.

In his first year at Green Bay, the Lombardi Packers finished tied for third place in the NFL West. In the nine seasons from 1959 to 1969, his teams won five national championships and six conference titles. His teams finished second in the NFL three times. Vince Lombardi (June 11, 1913, to September 3, 1970) was perhaps the greatest football coach who ever lived. He believed and proved we can't stray from basics. There are many distractions, but the grandiose things are deceiving.

Christians have the greatest man who ever lived as our inspiration and coach. Everything He wants us to know has been written for us by the Holy Spirit using 66 different human authors that, according to Peter, sometimes didn't understand what they were writing, but were carried along by the Holy Spirit (II Peter 1:21). We have the Bible, which is "the mind of Christ" (I Corinthians 2:16). It is our playbook.

1 Corinthians 2:14-16 (Phillips)

14-16 *But the unspiritual man simply can't accept the matters which the Spirit deals with – they just don't make sense to him, for, after all, you must be spiritual to see spiritual things. The spiritual man, on the other hand, has an insight into the meaning of everything, though his insight may baffle the man of the world. This is because the former is sharing in God's wisdom, and 'Who has known the mind of the Lord that he may instruct Him?' Incredible as it may sound, we who are spiritual have the very thoughts of Christ!*

1 Corinthians 2:14-16 (MSG)

14-16 *The unspiritual self, just as it is by nature, can't receive the gifts of God's Spirit. There's no capacity for them. They seem like so much silliness. Spirit can be known only by spirit – God's Spirit and our spirits in open communion. Spiritually alive, we have access to everything God's Spirit is doing, and can't be judged by unspiritual critics. Isaiah's question, "Is there anyone around who knows God's Spirit, anyone who knows what he is doing?" has been answered: Christ knows, and we have Christ's Spirit.*

Are we too much like the 1958 Green Bay Packers? What could we accomplish for God if we were to implement His Word in our lives?

CHAPTER FOURTEEN

A Changed Mindset

The expectation of good training is that each Christian would be able to function in a way that glorifies the Savior. To know Jesus with a deep abiding love and to always be prepares to present Jesus to the lost with grace and understanding.

A brief comparison of the levels of training one receives when the individual becomes a U.S. Marine and when he becomes a Christian (a member of God's army) may be enlightening. The one who has just accepted Jesus as his Lord and Savior and the one who has just walked into the Marine recruiting station are absolutely ignorant as to what has just happened, or what lies ahead, or what will be expected of him. Each starts off excited and unsure.

1. Signing on the dotted line to join the U.S. Marines Corps just got me into the brotherhood. It didn't make me a "real" Marine, but I became a member of the Marine Corps fellowship for life.

Agreeing with God that I was a sinner, accepting the work that Jesus died on the cross on my behalf, and turning to Him not only granted me membership into the family of God for the rest of eternity but also made me a "real" Christian immediately. At that moment in time, I was changed radically and completely into a new creation. I could not see the change; I couldn't feel the change. In fact, from my perception, the change was unnoticeable at the time, but many supernatural things happened. They were necessary to made me an entirely new person, one with which God could work.

2. Basic Training at Parris Island, S.C., trained me to look like, walk like, and even talk like a "real" Marine, but I still wasn't a "real" Marine. I was just a recruit. The first day was a traumatic whirlwind of activity. My hair was buzz cut, my civilian clothing was packaged in brown paper, and I was herded into a one- minute group shower. "Turn on the water, turn off the water, soap down, turn on the water, turn off the water, get out of the shower, dry off" were the commands, and they were barked out about as fast as you just read them. First, we were issued skivvies and immediately told to put on a set. As we moved down the line, we were issued a sea bag; the army calls it a duffle bag and civilians call them travel bags. Next, we were issued boot socks and dress socks. Since we would most likely spend most of our time in the Corps on our feet marching, running and fighting the boot and shoe fit was extremely important. Our boots were carefully measured to our feet. Down the line, we went collecting dress uniforms, and utilities (the Marine work uniform) with lots of labels on the trousers and jackets, and finally two dress covers (hats) and a utility cover. When we finished, the sea bag was full of clothing, and we were all clean and wearing the USMC utilities complete with hundreds of labels. We were carrying that sea bag and the little brown package of civilian clothing. Quickly we were ordered to write a short note to our moms and dads, telling them that we had arrived safely and were being well cared for. "Put the

note in the package, address the package and put it in the mailbox," barked the Senior DI.

Straight from there we marched (sort of) to supply and drew our field gear: a poncho, a tent half, a guy line, four tent pegs, a fire bucket, a web belt, a canteen, a first aid pouch with bandage, an entrenching tool, a bayonet, and a scabbard. Without any delay, we marched to the armory where we were issued "our best friend," the Ml rifle. That was the end of the first morning.

Carrying all of our new stuff, we marched to the chow hall for a 30-minute lunch. Reforming in platoon formation, we shouted in unison so the cooks could hear us: "Sir, the chow was outstanding." Afterward, we marched to the Third Battalion area and to our assigned Quonset huts, about two miles away.

All this time Fred, a thin-as-a-rail and five-foot tall recruit directly in front of me, looked like a moving bundle of equipment. We were carrying so much gear that I couldn't see any part of him; he just wasn't visible. As I struggled to keep going under the load and keep it all together (on my shoulders, in my hands, on my head, and around my waist), I remember thinking, *if he can keep going, so can I.* He did, and I did. When we arrived at our assigned area, we laid all of our newly issued gear aside and out of the way, and began to deep clean the outside, inside, windows, floor, and beds. It's called a field day; to this day I don't know why. When it was dry, we moved in.

The point is, our Drill Instructors were telling us what to do and how to do it, faster than we could listen. The Senior DI and Jr. DI were always present to ensure that we did it right, whatever "it" was.

For me, in those critical first days as a Christian, there was no training or guidance on what to do or what might happen. During my life, I have been relocated many times and have seen many churches that had no special training for the new Christian. The new Christian is vulnerable to the "deceivers," as well as counter-attacks and operation naturalization immediately after accepting Jesus as Savior. The new Christian is a changed creature; he has a new commanding officer who leads from the front. The newbie has more than 7,000 promises and many Operating Assets available for use but doesn't know it. He may go through his entire life without learning just how rich he is. Equipping the new saint should begin quickly. Satan's fiery arrows will be fired at him, and he needs to know he has protective armor and how to use it.

3. The Drill Instructor's primary job was to tear out the individualism that made me a civilian and then to rebuild me into what the Marine Corps wanted me to be. I had to become a "me" that was a lean, mean, green, fighting machine. At the end of 13 weeks, I was at one with 46 other men. We moved as one and thought as one. We even looked alike. I think, and the platoon pictures prove my point, we all had a 29-inch waist and were 6 feet tall and weighed 168 pounds. After we graduated, we still just looked like and acted like Marines, but we weren't "real" Marines.

God has decreed that the father, is the head of the household, and as such, one of his awesome responsibilities is to teach his children and his wife the principles that God has laid down in the Bible. It is the father who will be held accountable should he fail to carry out this responsibility. He has the same responsibility as the Drill Instructor. Their motto is on the gates of the DI School and is indelibly ingrained in their very being. The same should be true of the fathers. **"Let not one of my children's soul scream for hell if my Dad had**

only done his job" (paraphrased). Too many times he can't or fails to accept that responsibility, but the responsibility cannot be delegated away. There is nothing more important or rewarding than being the spiritual leader in your home.

No one in the church carries the primary responsibility of training the new Christian in the challenge of becoming a mature Christian. The "babe in Christ" needs a mature believer— thoroughly equipped to become the newbie's champion— to train him or her to continually reflect the characteristics and values of Jesus. The pastor's primary responsibilities are to preach and teach the biblical principles found in the Bible and to ensure no false doctrines are taught. The small group teachers have the responsibility to teach at the group level those biblical principles and doctrines laid out for us in the Bible. The pastors and small group leaders have about 30 minutes each on Sunday morning, and in some churches, an additional 30 minutes Sunday night, to undo the unacceptable lessons learned in the previous six days. It can't be done. That's one reason the primary instructional responsibility belongs to the father. There should be, but is no curriculum available that is specific enough to impart the basic fundamentals of Christianity in a concentrated, intense way to put an individual on a steady course to maturity in Christ. Not many churches provide special training for the new believer. A well-executed program in every church should teach the indisputable truths, facts, and doctrines of Christianity.

With all of this said, enough evidence exists that Jesus lived and died for our individual salvation and that the individual is ultimately responsible for his acceptance or denial of the work that Jesus did on the cross to save him or her. No one will have an acceptable excuse for not accepting Jesus Christ as Savior.

4. We left Parris Island going to Camp Geiger, a satellite of Camp Lejeune, N.C., to continue our training for eight more weeks. Today it's SOI (School of Infantry). After completing SOI, we were deemed ready to go into combat. We were finally "real Marines." Ready for combat, yes; green, yes; and a long way from being "old salts," which keynotes a mature Marine full of knowledge gained from many varied experiences. We were expected to be ready for combat, to protect our unit and fellow Marines, and to be a credit to the Corps and the nation.

Christians are "real Christians" immediately upon receiving Jesus as their savior. Generally speaking, we are woefully unprepared to go into battle, but off we go anyway. The battle I speak of is for our mind, and the battlefield is where we live, work and play, so it cannot be avoided or delayed. Thankfully, in the beginning, most of us have such a great appreciation for what God has done for us that our enthusiasm can win the day.

We don't have to know any more than what we were before we were saved and the difference Jesus has made in our lives. Satan can and will deny, distort, and attempt to discredit everything we now say and do for Jesus, but he cannot deny what Jesus has done in our lives. We are the expert on that matter. Although you may feel as though you are all alone, you are not. The Holy Spirit is there to stand with you as you face the enemy. When facing adversity do not be timid or shy but stand firm in your faith. It is a moment to shine for Jesus; it's one of His appointments. The Holy Spirit will provide the insight and words that are needed. If you do this, you may reap a soul that others have prepared for this moment, or you may be the sower for the Word that someone will reap. In either case, the Lord wins.

With time, that enthusiasm can wane if the "babe in Christ" isn't taught solid Bible doctrine. As the enthusiasm erodes when it is not supplemented by knowledge of God and instructions concerning the Christian life, without God's special provisions to support this new life, the new believer is in mortal danger of becoming a prisoner of war (POW) and returning to the Slave Market of Sin, doing Satin's bidding—not God's. The longer the believer stays out of fellowship with God, the more miserable he becomes, and the more callouses build up on his soul. This build up numbs the senses until the world's view is seen as normal, reasonable and correct. At that point, the Christian has become completely neutralized.

He has not lost his salvation, but now he is double-minded and miserable. He may be a regular churchgoer or not. He may be a small group teacher, a deacon, or a member of the board of elders, but because he is a carnal Christian, he is an unhappy Christian. So once again he is in that frantic search for happiness, running here and there desperately looking for happiness, but it eludes him.

5. If an individual Marine is not assigned to an Infantry unit, the Marine will be trained in a skill for which he has, through testing, shown a natural attribute or learned skill that the Marine Corps wants to develop. The Marine will be assigned to a specific school. More schooling hones the skills of the servicemen regardless of the branch of service. There is always more to learn.

Christians have been given at least one gift they will need to complete their purpose. They also have talents that are natural abilities to be discovered, developed, and dedicated to God's service. Just as the Marine never stops learning and serving, we Christians never stop learning and servicing God. We will never exhaust the information that is available to us. One of the attributes that God says about Himself is that He is Light.

John 1:4-5 (NIV)
4 *In Him was life, and that life was the light of men.*
5 *The light shines in the darkness, but the darkness could not understand (overcome) it.*

Christians are Christ followers. We are commanded to be like Jesus. We are to emulate Him. We can't emulate Him with only an hour a week of instruction. The more we study, the more we understand, and the more we understand, the more we learn, and the more we learn, the better we are prepared to rely on our Lord's leadership.

6. The average serviceman is well-trained in his or her military occupational skill and is highly motivated.

The average Christian is poorly trained and not motivated. The angels must wonder if we are so desensitized that we see no evil, hear no evil and speak only evil. The church is called to make disciples and to train us. Some churches do a good job of answering that commission, but most fail miserably; other projects hold a higher priority. They, like their members, are focused on the details of life, not Jesus.

The tyranny of the immediate must never rule over the Excellency of His Plan.

~ Author unknown

Our Choices Reveal Our Values

Today, Christians in the Far and Near East, Africa, Central and South America, and even in Europe are being imprisoned, suffering terrible atrocities to the point of being put to death because they stand courageously at the moment of their trial and refuse to deny their faith in Jesus. In America, we are being marginalized. In the United States, persecution has just begun. Christianity and Christian values are under attack. Even so, we live in an exciting time in which Christianity is growing rapidly in the most unexpected places. Perhaps that's because ordinary people have been trodden over until they realize there is no hope for them except Jesus. Roman oppression and atrocities could not slow the "Jesus movement" of its day.

Finally, 280 years after Jesus hung on the cross, Emperor Constantine ended the persecution of Christians in AD 313, declaring that Christianity was the official religion of the Roman Empire. His stated reason for doing this was to unite the Empire. The Empire was fragmented with special groups wanting this thing or that thing. What did most Romans have in common? It was their faith. At this moment in history, there were more Christians in the Roman Empire than any religion. Constantine recognized this and used it to unify the nation. Amazing! The more the Christians were persecuted, the faster their number increased.

On November 20, 1620, the Mayflower Compact was signed while the Mayflower was at anchor in Provincetown Harbor near Cape Cod Massachusetts.

It reads "In the name of God, Amen. We, whose names are underwritten, the Loyal Subjects of our dread Sovereign Lord, King James, by the Grace of God, of England, France, and Ireland, King, Defender of the Faith, etc. Having undertaken for the Glory of God, and Advancement of the Christian Faith, and the Honour of our King and Country, a voyage to plant the first colony in the northern parts of Virginia; do by these presents, solemnly and mutually in the Presence of God and one of another, covenant and combine ourselves together into a civil Body Politick, for our better Ordering and Preservation, and Furtherance of the Ends aforesaid; And by Virtue hereof to enact, constitute, and frame, such just and equal Laws, Ordinances, Acts, Constitutions and Offices, from time to time, as shall be thought most meet and convenient for the General good of the Colony; unto which we promise all due submission and obedience. In Witness whereof, we have hereunto subscribed our names at Cape Cod the eleventh of November, in the Reign of our Sovereign Lord, King James of England, France, and Ireland, the eighteenth, and of Scotland the fifty-fourth. Anno Domini, 1620."

~ All About History.Org ~

Jamestown, Virginia's first settlers arrived May 4, 1607. It was established to be a "for profit" venture, but Christians were there, and they attended church.

"Captain John Smith reported that the first church services were held outdoors "under an awning (which was an old saile)" fastened to three or four trees. Shortly thereafter the settlers built the first church inside the fort. Smith said it was "a homely thing like a barn set on crachetts, covered with rafts, sedge, and earth." This church burned in January 1608 and was replaced by a second church, similar to the first. Made of wood, it needed constant repair. Pocahontas and John Rolfe were married in the second church.

In 1617-1619 when Samuel Argall was governor, he had the inhabitants of Jamestown build a new church "50 foot long and 21 broad." It was a wooden church built on a one-foot-wide foundation of cobblestones capped by a wall one brick thick. You can see these foundations under the glass on the floor of the present building. The First Assembly was held in the third church." (historicjamestown.org)

Regardless of what the rewriters of history are selling, the United States was founded as a Christian nation by Christians who embraced Christian values and had done so for 169 plus years before the Declaration of Independence was written. A decade or so ago, someone declared that the United States was no longer a Christian nation and was in a post-Christian era. That's not entirely correct. The influence that the church once had has dissipated, but the vast majority of citizens of this country still describe themselves as Christians. Perhaps it will not go into the Post-era quietly.

Today's culture seems more attuned to political correctness than upholding the traditional values that made this country great: marriage, family, nationalism, and the exercise of our volition. These four values are sanctioned in the first four chapters of Genesis and are the pillars of society for all nations and all people. God is God, and we are not. God has established these institutions for our protection. We can ignore them if we insist, but we ignore them at our peril. God will not be mocked. He has in the past used heathen nations to bring down His people, so it is reasonable to believe He can and will do it again. We are here now, in this time, to REMEMBER our primary responsibility as God's Ambassadors and to stand courageously for the principles He has established. We are to be involved at all levels of life, acting responsibly and representing Christ in whatever we do.

Every Christian should have enough basic training stored in our memory, so we know what to do when the elephant charges. If we do, we will automatically respond with an appropriate action that reflects our Savior's grace.

You have seen that this is precisely what Jehoshaphat did when he was face-to-face with his elephant charge. When you find yourself in an adversarial situation, expect your opponent to bait you so that you will respond in a way to detract from your Christian walk. So, REMEMBER, the battle is the Lord's, and you are His Ambassador and warrior. Your objective is always to represent your Lord well, stand your ground, and let the Lord speak and act through you.

Colossians 3:23-24 (NIV)
23 *Whatever you do, work at it with all your heart, as working for the Lord, not for men,* 24 *since you know*

that you will receive an inheritance from the Lord as a reward, It is the Lord Christ you are serving.

1Corinthians 10: 31b-33 (NIV)
[31b] *Whatever you do, do all to the glory of God.* [32] *Do not cause anyone to stumble, whether Jews, Greeks or the church of God,* [33] *even (just) as I try to please everyone in every way (everything I do). For I am not seeking my own advantage (good), but the good of many, so that they may be saved.*

We must be able to recognize each and every battlefield situation as it confronts us. To do this, our objective is to maximize our time in the presence of our Lord and to ensure we will be prepared to represent Him well. When we do, we won't feel like we've just stumbled into a situation. We will know we have been strategically placed to represent our Lord for a specific reason. That reason would be to present the specific Biblical truths for that situation. He has taught us, "The battle is the Lord's." Our responsibility is to respond to the situation as He leads and marvel as we see Him work, through us.

We are at all costs, at all times, to be ready to take and occupy the high ground, even when we are required to make that quantum leap into eternity. If we are able to do that, know that we will be in the company of the heroes of the faith and will be greeted with a "Well done my good and faithful servant." Matthew 25:21.

Jesus is well-titled "The Good Shepherd" because we Christians, as a whole, are dumb as sheep. We are ill-trained to carry out our primary calling to spread the Gospel as we go through life and to correctly disciple (train) new believers in God's truths. The Good Shepherd ensures His sheep are protected and led to the green valleys and sweet water. He knows us and calls us by name. He protects us because we like sheep are vulnerable and valuable.

John 3:16 (paraphrased)

16 For God so loved the world's people (you and me) that He gave His one and only Son so that whoever believes in Him (even you and me) would not perish but have everlasting life in His presence.

The most pertinent scripture for the lost souls may be the only scripture some believers know. The Bible is a bottomless well of sweet water that refreshes, nourishes, and cleanses. When one is witnessing to the lost, it's one of the best scriptures to use. Just as importantly—maybe more so—we must be able to clearly state what Jesus means to us and how He has changed our lives. If we can't say that Jesus has made a significant difference in our lives, then He must not have, and we may not really know Him at all. If He makes no difference, is He really our Lord?

During the late 1990s, a movement was developing to take Jesus out of our vocabulary. The name "Jesus" has always been a stumbling block to some, and removing the name of Jesus was the first time my generation had seen evidence of an anti-Christian element. This occurred in Atlanta. Suddenly the war was in our hometown. The name "Jesus" was considered religious, and, therefore, it was offensive to a few and considered not to be a politically correct word. Christians were in shock. Unprepared, Christians sat back and failed to confront the threat with the truth, so it grew like an untreated infection. This attitude carried into the Christmas season, to the point many department store employees and clerks were told not say "Merry Christmas" or "Have a wonderful Christmas." Instead, they were instructed use a generic phrase like "Have a happy holiday."

The Christian community was unprepared for this emerging warfare. It was caught off guard and off- balance, and became disturbed, upset, and angry. Our mental attitudes were so distraught that our response was not always what it should have been. Have you felt like that at times?

RAW EMOTIONAL RESPONSES FAIL TO REPRESENT CHRIST PROPERLY

A wonderful Christian lady—I'll call her Rose since I don't know anyone named Rose—was one of the most caring and loving women I've ever known. She stepped outside her beautiful character and proudly proclaimed to her Sunday school class, "I was shopping, and a beautiful young woman pushing her baby carriage looked at me with a smile and said, "Have a happy holiday." I responded by putting a stern look on my face and with my head stuck forward, I growled back at her, "MERRY CHRISTMAS TO YOU, TOO!!"

We have no way of knowing why God had these ladies' paths cross that day. I understand the frustration Rose was experiencing, but her reply was not a winsome one, and it was entirely out of character for her. It was an awful way to respond and in no way reflected the love of Jesus. This true encounter shows dynamically why Christians need to be trained and prepared to glorify Jesus anytime His appointment occurs. A better response would have been something like, "Thank you; I will have a happy holiday. Do you know what this holiday celebrates?" A good conversation about Christmas, the Christ child, and an excellent salvation may have followed. If the young woman was not yet a Christian, the encounter would have been a wonderful way to witness; if she was a Christian, they likely would have had a short but pleasant revival right there, and both would have been blessed. The blessed time may have been witnessed by others who were passing by.

Do you think chance encounters are really by chance? Are encounters God ordained?

Matthew 28: 18-20 (NIV)

18 *Then Jesus came to them (us) and said, "All authority in heaven and on earth has been given to me.* 19*Therefore, as you go, make disciples of all*

> *nations, baptizing them in the name of the Father, and the Son, and of Holy Spirit, [20]and teaching them to obey everything I have commanded you. And surely I am with you always to the very end of the world."*

THE CHRISTIAN'S PRIMARY PURPOSE is to know God and to make Him known, not aimlessly wandering in an attempt to find happiness. We are in God's family now. *Defend the faith* should be our motto.

Know this: the "babes in Christ" and the seasoned follower will most certainly quickly be subjected to a counter-attack by the dark side and will have to defend the faith or be neutralized. Too many have been scarred deeply and mentally because they didn't mature. This is a very serious business. The term "babes in Christ" is not limited to neophyte Christians, but includes some who have been Christians for many years. It seems the church, in general, puts so little emphasis on Christian training, that few Christians learn much about God or how to represent Him.

Jesus is our Commanding Officer, and unlike any other CO's who have a lot of authority in limited areas, Jesus has all authority in heaven and on earth.

Our marching orders are simple. We are to stand in the gap making disciples and teach new and seasoned Christians to obey Jesus' Words, regardless of what they see with their eyes, hear with their ears or reason in their minds. We are to teach others to know and use the Operating Assets He has provided, and to know and use His promises, and to study the Bible, to learn how and what God thinks. We fail Him too often because we lack courage; we lack courage because we believe we are not equipped to take on the situation. We, too, often cower down because we believe we lack the knowledge, and we are right. REMEMBER the battle is the Lord's.

Ask to be His vessel, and then step forward. Even an unbeliever will fall on a hand grenade to save his friends.

Hosea 4:6 (NIV)
[6] *My people are destroyed from lack of knowledge.*

Daniel 3:1-30 (NLT)
Shadrack, Meshach, and Abednego replied, "O Nebuchadnezzar, we do not need to defend ourselves before you, [17] *If we are thrown into the blazing furnace the God whom we serve is able to save us. He will rescue us from your power, your Majesty.* [18] *But even if He doesn't, we want to make it clear to you, your Majesty, that we will never serve your gods or worship the gold statue you have set up.*

2 Timothy 3:16,17 (NIV)
[16] *All Scripture is God-breathed and is useful for teaching, for rebuking, for correction, for training in righteousness:* [17]*So that the man of God may be mature, thoroughly equipped for every good works.*

2 Timothy 2:15 (NIV)
[15] *Do your best to present yourself to God as one approved, a workman who does not need to be ashamed, and who correctly handles the Word of truth.*

Before we get too down on ourselves, remember four things:

1. We can do nothing; it is the power of Jesus Christ that saves and the Holy Spirit who brings the lost to the point of salvation. We just have to be ready, available, and willing to be used.
2. Remember how ineffective the disciples were for the first three years after He invited them to go with Him. Until He was arrested and His trials began, they were

with Jesus continually. After His resurrection, Jesus visited with them several times to prove He was alive. On the day of Pentecost, they were changed forever; they were permanently filled with the Holy Spirit, and they REMEMBERED. They became fishers of men, showing boldness regardless of the consequences. They were all faithful, even to dying a painful martyr's death. John, the only exception, was exiled from civilization until he died. Through the efforts of these unlikely men and the power of the Holy Spirit, the world was changed forever. It is a better place today because of their faithfulness and those who have followed them in Christ. At the moment of salvation, each one of us is sealed and permanently filled with the Holy Spirit. How bold are we?

3. The way God has equipped believers throughout history stands in sharp contrast to those who have followed false gods and false prophets.
4. The U. S. Continental army was poorly equipped, poorly trained, and with a few exceptions suffered from poor leadership. There was no way they should have defeated the finest trained and equipped army in the world at that time, but they did. Divine intervention made the difference. America was destined to be a shining nation on the hill. Being the beneficiary of God's leadership—our purpose—is to lead the world to Jesus, and that starts at home. England had failed at this calling, choosing to build an empire by colonizing and oppressing the nations they conquered or founded.

God rose up a nation and passed the baton of spreading the Gospel from the United Kingdom to the United States. Soon the baton may be passed from the United States to another nation, for precisely the same reason. However, the United States may still be protected by a remnant of believers who boldly stand up and are willing to be lead. If you have accepted Jesus as you Savior, you are a part of the remnant.

CHAPTER FIFTEEN

God Has A Plan For Us

Does it surprise you that God has a plan for you? God loves you! There's never been a time when He didn't love you, and there will never be a time when He won't love you. Nothing you can do will make Him love you more than He already does, and there's nothing you can do to make Him love you any less than he already does. It's incredible, I know. His love for all mankind is so incredibly awesome, it's almost unbelievable, but it is true. Believe it! No love compares to the love God has for you and me! His love is a universal love. His love is so great that all three members of the Godhead are involved in the plan to remove the separation (barrier) that Adam created with his disbelief. God's plan is available for the entire human race. Without exception, God has a perfect plan for our lives. His plan contains three general sections that apply to everyone, and a special section that is specific and unique for each one of us. Will you marry? Who will you marry? Will you have children? Will they be natural born or adopted, or both? What will be your occupation? It's stunning that God knows us so well that before we were even born, these plans could be made. Don't misunderstand; we are not robots or puppets at the end of the string being played by the Almighty. We have volition and are free to choose our steps as we go through life.

What's amazing is that no matter what steps we take, our God has the capacity and the desire to work it all out for good for those who love Him. I never planned I would be writing to people I don't know and never will know in this life. In my years, I've learned and experienced many things and gone many places. I had no idea I was being prepared for this endeavor. It is work, but I'm having a blast doing it.

Jeremiah 1:5a (NIV)

5 *Before I formed you in the womb I knew (selected) you, before you were born I set you apart;*

I've inserted "selected" beside "knew" because that's what it literally says; however, don't let that disturb you. He knew (has always known) all of us. It's not a predestination thing. God doesn't predetermine who will be saved and who will not. He just knows. He is omniscient and has always known everything. His ways are not our ways. His knowledge isn't built precept-upon-precept like ours. He is the Alpha and Omega. He knows from the beginning to the end. God, the Holy Spirit, will for a time do whatever is right to persuade us, but cannot, will not, violate, our free will, to impose His will over our will.

Psalms 139:13 (NIV)

13 *For You created my innermost being; You (Lord) knit me together in my mother's womb.*

God knew you and me before we were a twinkle in our mother's eye. He had a reason and plan for our lives, and no one has ever been born outside of God's love for him or her. If God is not a part of our lives, if He's not active in our lives, it is solely and completely our choice, not His. If you are not saved, you have chosen not to be saved. Because you have not chosen to be saved, you belong to Satan, not God. You may be the nicest person on this entire planet (by human standards) and still not be saved. It's shocking to some Christians, but you can be a cantankerous, unloving, despicable person and be a Christian. Some of the nicest people I've ever known are unbelievers, and some of the worst people I've known are Christians. If you have rejected Jesus, you're a slave to sin, and you are one of God's enemies. Yet He still loves you and continues to stay on post reaching down to pull you out of the Slave Market. You are the reason for the cross. You may even say, "I have nothing against God." Even so, God has something against you. You have rejected all that He has done to provide your salvation. All roads do not lead to heaven, and you are on the wrong road. If you die without accepting His most precious gift, the righteousness and justice of God cannot allow you to enter heaven, even though God's heart will be broken.

God has always known you and me. We cannot surprise Him with our actions or lack of actions. He knew from the beginning how wretched we would be and how badly we needed to be rescued. The John 3:16 passage is found in the New Testament and is one of 2,000 promises directed to unbelievers. It is God's recorded promise that He gave to all of humanity while we are still His enemy. It states that He has developed a perfect plan to rescue any and all who will claim it. I think it is reasonable for us to surmise that if any other plan could have been devised to spare His Son, it would have been activated. It is much more than an excellent plan; it is the only plan that works!

Why did God develop a rescue plan for humanity? In a moment in time, Adam erected a barrier between himself and God through his unbelief, and that error has been perpetuated throughout history through Adam's seed. I had never thought of it as unbelief, but when Adam believed Eve and took the fruit and ate it, he was rejecting God's directive about that one and only tree, and that was unbelief. Adam consciously chose to believe Eve rather than God, resulting in the erection of a barrier between God and man.

This barrier has been described as a vast chasm separating man from God. The cross of Christ bridges that chasm. The work of Jesus on the cross provides the way for us to cross over to God's side. Others have described the barrier as a great wall separating God from man. In either case, God's plan removes the barrier, and it is Jesus who provides the way to freedom. We would have never been able to remove the barrier ourselves. Our efforts to remove the barrier are all called religion, which is man's effort to gain God's favor, but humans have no capacity to remove the barrier because of his own sin. Humanity has an escape plan that works only because the God of Creation has developed and executed it for us. If God had not developed a rescue plan, mankind would have forever been doomed to serve Satan. That was not an acceptable destiny for man.

To illustrate the barrier, let's say that the barrier consists of giant granite boulders constructed to form a wall. Each bolder extends from the Earth's core to Heaven. It is humanly impossible to climb over it, dig under it, or go around it. It completely separates man from God.

The first boulder is Sin. Romans 3:23 tells us: *"For all have sinned and come short of the glory of God..."* We are separated from God.

The second boulder is the penalty for sin. Romans 6:23 tells us *"...for the wages of sin is death..."* This is spiritual death, the inability to commune with God. It is not physical death, for Adam and Eve lived many years after that fateful day, but all of nature in its pristine beauty began a dying process that day.

The third boulder of the barrier is physical birth. Adam and Eve were created spiritually alive and without a Sin Nature. The curse of Adam is that all of humanity, starting with their first born was and continues to be born spiritually dead, physically alive and with a Sin Nature.

The natural man is not capable of fellowshipping with God. Jesus was born perfect, without a Sin Nature, and spiritually alive. God is Spirit and man must be spiritually alive to commune with God. The only way for a man to be spiritually alive is to become a child of God by accepting the work that Jesus did on the cross. Jesus said, *"I am the truth and the light. No one comes to the Father unless he comes through Me."* He was either telling the truth or a colossal lie; He is Absolute Truth so He's not lying. The Bible teaches that salvation is through Jesus, plus nothing. This presents a dilemma for humanity but not for God. We can question the statement that Jesus is the only way with, "That's not fair, what about those who have never heard the Gospel or of Jesus? What about the children who die before they have a chance to accept Jesus?" The answer seems simple, but maybe that just my view. God is God, and I am not. God is also perfect Justice and absolute Righteousness, and perfect Love; the reconciliation of these attributes to the situation is best left to God. He can't lie, He can't be unjust or unfair so, I am content to leave it in His hands. In my mind at least, any child who dies before reaching the age of accountability gets a pass. Also, an adult that doesn't have the mental capacity to process the question gets a pass. That comes from my value system, but you need to understand I've known adults who are so mentally challenged that they are as if they are still very young children, yet their capacity to love makes ours seem infantile, and it seems that there is no place they would rather be than at church, perhaps that because they feel God's love there in the midst of people who also love Jesus. I heard one of these "special" ones ask," Will there be any dogs in heaven?" The answer was very special also, "if you need dogs to be in heaven to be happy, dogs will be there." All of the aborted children also get a pass. Jesus demonstrated His love for the little children. They have an innocence and trust that we adults should emulate. God knows the answer to the "Big" question and the limits to His provision.

The next boulder is the character of God. Man, just can't measure up to the divine character of a perfect God. He just can't. God is the sovereign being of the universe, and there can only be one. God is omnipotent and incorruptible. God is all knowledge and man is not. God is all present. He's everywhere at the same time. Man doesn't have this capability. God is perfectly just, and even Solomon, who was the wisest man on Earth, could not be as just and fair as God.

Another boulder is man's relative righteousness. God is absolute righteousness. He can do no wrong, and man simply can't be that righteous. Man's righteousness is relative righteousness.

Yet another boulder is God's perfect truth. He cannot tell a lie or mislead anyone. Man has a hard time telling the truth. Chapter 5 detailed the ten characteristics of the essence of God, and man falls short of measuring up to any of them.

The work of the Son of God in His humanity was totally sufficient to remove the barrier once and for all, no matter how high, wide, or deep it was. The barrier separating man from God no longer exists.

Hebrews 10:11-14

11 Day after day every priest stands and performs his religious duties; again and again, he offers the same sacrifices, which can never take away sins. 12 But when this priest (Jesus) had offered for all time one sacrifice for sins, He sat down at the right hand of God, 13and since that time He waits for his enemies to be made his footstool. 14 For by one sacrifice He has made perfect forever those who are being made holy.

Our salvation is complete; Jesus paid the price once and for all time. Not only does this salvation deliver us from a life of no hope, it transcends time and carries us through eternity in His Company. Salvation gives us everlasting life so that we will live with Him from the time we are rescued forever more. That's praiseworthy, wouldn't you agree? It is so much more than the Fountain of Youth for which the Spanish explorer Ponce de Leon searched. If Ponce was a Christian, he had the Fountain of Youth in him all along. It was, is, and will always be Jesus. If he had studied his Bible, he would have known he had life everlasting. He would have known death is restricted to the body and everything else about us lives forever. We, like Ponce, have no idea, because we don't take the time to study His Word. Perhaps Ponce would have been an explorer anyway. Who knows? But he would have searched for something else, perhaps the nuggets of golden promises in the pages of the Bible.

Approximately 7,000 gold nuggets are recorded in the Bible for the believer and 2,000 for the unbeliever. These are the promises of God recorded for us to find, know and use. Here's a thought: Why don't you become a prospector for these golden promises? Dig them out, put them in your pouch (mind) and have them ready to use when you need them. Take a trip through the Book of John and see how many golden nuggets you can find. It will be so much fun you'll want to explore other Books of the Bible to pan for gold. Don't neglect the hills and valleys of the Old Testament; they are rich with promises for believers.

John 3:16 (NIV)

> 16 *For God so loved the world that he gave His one and only Son, that whoever believes in Him shall not perish but have eternal life.*

John 3:16 is God's proclamation and promise He loves the world—that's everyone throughout all of time—so much that He developed a salvation plan that without fail will work. Developed in eternity past, even perhaps before there was an

Earth God's plan for you is a complete plan. In its simplest outline, it entails three phases, salvation, the believer in time, the believer in eternity.

The Gospel is not written to make bad men good, but to make dead men ALIVE!

~ Adrian Rogers ~

PHASE I—SALVATION

Salvation is the first phase of His rescue plan that snatches us out of the Slave Market of Sin, cleanses us from all unrighteousness, and provides adoption for us into the family of God. We immediately become joint heirs with Jesus of everything the Father has. Immediately we are members of the priesthood of believers. This means no one has to intercede for us. There is no priest between us and God. Yes, Jesus sits at the right hand of the Father and defends us when Satan accuses. Jesus simply says, "Yes, he is guilty, but I paid for that." At any time, we are welcome in the presence of our LORD. We are Ambassadors for Christ now and are to represent Him vigorously and proudly.

In days of old and even now exalted positions, not nearly as high as this one, were sold at a high price. The more one could pay, the higher one's rank could be. So how much does it cost to become a son and Ambassador of the God of the universe? It is a price beyond anyone's ability to pay. It was unimaginable. It was so high that no man could ever achieve it. So, God sent His only Son to Earth to pay its total cost for all of us. Now He offers it to us without cost, on our part, but with only one stipulation: that we agree with Him that we are sinners and accept the gift. If we do, we will have a new Lord of our life, one that loves us more than we love ourselves.

Developed in eternity past, His plan for all humanity—salvation—was implemented on Earth when the angel told Mary, and she accepted the will of God. Then Joseph, against all human customs and rights, also accepted his calling. This was not a hit or miss search, for God knew their hearts. Consider how little persuasion or explanation was required by Mary or Joseph. It doesn't take much imagination to consider how many young Israelite girls finding they were pregnant out of wedlock claimed to be the mother of God and were stoned to death. But Mary was not, for Joseph protected her. This one point was the pivotal point for one Jewish co-worker who later accepted Jesus as the Savior.

Mary and Joseph refrained from intercourse until after the birth of Jesus so there could be no question that Joseph was not the physical father. After Jesus, they had other children. Jesus grew up from childhood to adulthood and never committed a sin. He was tempted in His humanity, as we all are, but retained a pure heart. At the end of His life hanging on the cross, He became our perfect sacrificial lamb. Jesus paid the price for every sin we ever have or ever will commit. Jesus was our substitute: He was the spotless lamb of the Old Testament. He had neither inherited nor personal sin of His own. Being spotless Himself, He was qualified to be our perfect substitute. As He hung on the cross, He was judged guilty for our sins: neither God the Father nor the Holy Spirit could be in the presence of sin, so metaphorically they turned their backs on our sins He had taken as His own.

Matthew 27:46 (NIV)

> 46 *About the ninth hour (3 PM) Jesus cried out in a loud voice, "Eloi, Eloi, lama sabachthani?" Which means. "My God (the Father), my God (the Holy Spirit) why have you forsaken me?"*

The righteousness and justice of God were satisfied only when the punishment for every sin that was, or ever will be committed had been exacted. Then and only then, Jesus said, "It is finished.

John 19:30 (NIV)

30 *Jesus said, "It is finished." With that, he bowed his head and gave up (released or dismissed) his spirit (or soul).*

Finally, it was done. Jesus stayed the course until every sin that had or will ever be committed had been paid in full, and the righteousness and justice of God was satisfied. Jesus was our sacrificial lamb.

The Hebrews had no concept of the soul, but they realized that with death, the essence of a person went to Paradise or Hades. It was the Greeks who understood the concept that the soul was the essence of a person. The scholars who gave us the King James Bible were not necessarily Christians, they were language scholars. That's why one team of them called the third person of the trinity the "Holy Ghost" and the other team used the name "Holy Spirit." Jesus was not dismissing the Holy Spirit. He was not dismissing the human spirit. "Dismissed" His soul gives us a better understanding than "gave up" His soul. Jesus was the one in control! He exhaled and did not inhale again. He dismissed His soul to the Holy Spirit. This follows the example that The Father has decreed for us. We are to submit our utmost being, all that we are to the leadership of the Holy Spirit. Today, the moment of physical death is recognized as the moment the soul leaves the body. The Romans didn't kill Him; neither did the Jews, your sins and mine did. At any time, He could have climbed down off the cross, called legions of angels to destroy them all, but that was not the purpose of His intervention into history, and the Father's plan would have failed. He was tempted many times but resisted the temptations and in so doing honored the Father by providing the escape for us all. Our sins are paid for, and our accounting ledger sheet is stamped: Paid in Full.

Psalms 34:22 (NASP)

22 *The LORD redeems the soul of His servants, and none of those who take refuge in Him will be condemned.*

The Merriam-Webster Dictionary defines "redeem" as; to make (something that is bad, unpleasant, etc.) better or more acceptable. That is exactly what Jesus did. He made us who were—bad and unpleasant—acceptable to God. But that's not the complete definition because it doesn't say how that was accomplished.

Dictionary.com defines redeem as wider in its application than ransom and means to buy back, regain possession of, or exchange money, goods, etc. to redeem one's property. To ransom is to redeem a person from captivity by paying a stipulated price, or to redeem from sin by sacrifice.

Redeem comes from the French r'edimer, which means "to deliver," and which in turn comes from the Latin for "buyback."

Redeem means "to buy, to purchase, to pay the ransom." In the case of the slave, as we all once were, it means to purchase his or her freedom. We were slaves in the slave market of sin with no hope of escape, and we could never ransom ourselves free. Jesus gave up His heavenly home to become a man, lived a sinless life, and hung on a cross until the ransom price for all humanity was paid in full. The specific word that is used here means to purchase the slave's freedom and to set him free. So, we are really free and not just slaves to a new owner. We will not be condemned for our sin; however, we have not received a license to sin.

Ezekiel 18:4 (NIV)

[4] For everyone belongs to Me, the parent as well as child-both alike belong to Me the one who sins is the one who will die (spiritually).

Hebrews 10:39 (TLB)

[39] But we have not turned our backs on God and sealed our fate. No, our faith in Him assures our soul's salvation.

Revelation 1:5 (NIV)

[5] and from Jesus Christ who is a faithful witness, the firstborn from the dead, and the ruler of the kings of the earth. To Him who loves us and has freed us from our sins by His blood.

Jesus was unique in life and death. He died as we do when His soul left the body. The body was locked in a sealed tomb for less than three days. The tomb was empty Sunday morning. He was the first-born from the grave so that in all things He would have the preeminence (l Corinthians 1:15-18). It emphasizes His position, the most exalted supremacy in rank. Jesus was not the first to be raised from the dead. Jesus was the first to be resurrected to obtain a glorified body, never to die again—l Corinthians 15: 35-44; 1 Kings17:17-23; 2 Kings 4:32-36; and 2 Kings 13:20-21. Jesus Christ was the first to so rise from the dead, that death was forever left behind Him.

Hebrews 9:11-14 (NIV)

[11] but when Christ came as high priest for the good things that are now already here, He went through the greater and more perfect tabernacle that is not made with human hands, that is to say, it is not a part of this creation. [12] He did not enter by means of the blood of goats and calves, but He entered the most high place once for all by His own blood those

obtaining eternal redemption. [13] *the blood of goats and bulls and the ashes of a heifer sprinkled on those who are ceremonially unclean sanctify them so that they are outwardly clean.* [14] *how much more, then, will the blood of Christ, who through the eternal Spirit offered Himself unblemished to God cleanses our conscience from acts that lead to (spiritual) death, so that we may serve the living God!*

Job 19:25 (NIV)

[25] *I know that my Redeemer lives and that in the end, He will stand on the Earth.*

Galatians 3:13 (NIV)

[13] *Christ redeemed us from the curse of the law by becoming a curse for us, for it is written: curse it is everyone who is hung on a pole (the cross).*

Ephesians 1:7 (NIV)

[7] *In Him, we have redemption through His blood, the forgiveness of sins, in accordance with the riches of God's grace.*

1Peter 1:18 (NIV)

[18] *for you know that it was not with perishable things such as silver or gold that you will regain from the empty way of life handed down to you from your ancestors.*

Sin is not the question; all sins have been redeemed. They have all been paid for in full. The real question is, *What will you do about Jesus?*

He stands at the door of your heart and knocks. All He wants from you is an acknowledgment that you are a sinner. If you agree, you turn to Him and away from your previous life and move toward Him. Simple, isn't it? Too simple? Not really! It had to be simple so the simple could grasp it. No advantage is given for intellectuals; salvation is there for them also. If they have a problem with the simple truth of the reality of what Jesus has done for them, their negative volition has caused them to over-think the facts. Believing that's too simple, we assume there must be something we have to do. There is nothing left undone. Just believe. Remember, Jesus has done everything; there is nothing we can do to improve it.

It was God the Holy Spirit who brought us to the point of God-consciousness, so we can't even take credit for that. All that remains is for us to accept the gift.

PHASE II – THE BELIEVER IN TIME

Phase two begins at the point of salvation and ends at the first of two possible opportunities: when the believer physically dies, or at the rapture of the saints. The Tribulation Saints have a different ending, and this occurs at the return of Jesus to this Earth. If we are Christ-followers, salvation did not happen by accident. God, the Holy Spirit, brought us to a point of God consciousness, and we responded positively to that information. If one responds negatively, one could not be a child of God. God is responsible to bring every human to the point of God consciousness at least once in a lifetime, but it may happen many times. The Holy Spirit may use any method at His disposal to accomplish this awareness. I don't know how Job could have known God, but I suspect it was the same way that Adam, Abraham, Jacob, Noah, and many of the believers from the beginning of time up until Jesus walked on Earth. God spoke directly to them, and their belief was credited to them as His Righteousness.

I've been asked many times how a loving God could condemn to hell those who have never heard about Jesus, "Like those in Africa?" My response has been: knowing the character of God and applying just three components of His essence—1.) His righteousness (He cannot be unfair); 2.) His justice (He cannot be unjust); and 3.) His Love (He loves without condition). I can be at peace about how God would judge those who have truly never heard the good news. Then there's a little fact that God is God and I am not. He makes those decisions; they are not mine to make. With that in mind, the question is not what God will do about the "Africans" that haven't heard, but rather what you, who have heard, will do about God. What will you do about Jesus? The Bible also says that if man had never proclaimed God, even the trees and rocks and all of nature reveals Him.

A missionary to Africa, upon presenting the salvation story to an African tribal king, received this remarkable response: "I knew He existed, I just didn't know His name."

So basically, that's how we became Christ-followers. God saw us spiritually dead in the Slave Market of Sin. He, the Father, developed a rescue mission. God the Son accepted the mission and executed the plan to perfection. As the unblemished lamb, His blood paid the ransom price so we can be set free. Only when the righteousness and justice of God were satisfied was the redemption price paid in full, and Jesus proclaimed, "It is finished" and dismiss His soul.

At that point in time His body died. By the way, a few years ago science didn't even acknowledge that humans had a soul, but now science agrees that death occurs when the soul leaves the body. Satan's best tool, the grave, could not defeat or hold Jesus. Before His body was removed from the cross, before the doorway to the tomb was closed and sealed, His soul was in Paradise. I think He waited for the thief who was on the cross next to Him, the one Jesus promised, "Today you will be with Me in Paradise," to physically die that awful, agonizing death so his soul could join the other believers, those who had preceded Jesus in physical death. They had been waiting for Jesus in their designated assembly area, Paradise.

As the Pathfinder and First Fruit, Jesus then led them to heaven and into the presence of the Father. Looking at Luke 16-31, it is clear the beggar, and Abraham were in Hades, and so was the rich man. They are in the same place, but they aren't in exactly the same place. As you read your Bible, you'll see words like She'ol, Hades, Paradise, Abraham's Bosom, and Tartarus. Are they all the same? How do they differ?

Here's a synopsis of what Wikipedia says: She'ol is a Hebrew word for a place where all dead go. Different locations are for the righteous and unrighteous. About 200 B.C. "Hades" the Greek word for "underground," was substituted for "She'ol," and it is reflected in the New Testament. Therefore, Hades and She'ol are the same place. Paradise is the same as Abraham's Bosom, and it is the abode of the righteous believers who throughout time had preceded Jesus in physical death. It is "Heaven like." God was not there, but it had many of the amenities of Heaven. Paradise/Abraham's Bosom was the holding location in Hades until Jesus could lead believers home. They could not go to heaven before Him because Jesus was the First Fruit and the path-finder.

A second holding location is Torment. It is also in Hades, but it is separated from Paradise by a great chasm. The temporary dwelling place of horrors is designed specifically for the unrighteous, the unbeliever, and lost, from the first unbeliever up to and including those who passed from this life into eternity today. They are physically dead and spiritually dead, but their souls live on. All are gathering and suffering as they await the Great White Throne judgment of Revelation 20:11-15. They will be joined by the physically alive and spiritually dead from the Great Tribulation period to be judged, not for their sins but by their works.

Luke 16:23-26 (NIV)

23 In Hades, where he was in torment, he looked up
and saw Abraham far away, with Lazarus by his
side. 24 So he called to him, "Father Abraham, have
pity on me and send Lazarus to dip the tip of his
finger in water and cool my tongue because I am in
agony in this fire." 25 But Abraham replied, "Son,
remember that in your lifetime you received your
good things, while Lazarus received bad things, but
now he is comforted here, and you are in agony. 26
And besides all this, between us and you a great
chasm has been set in place so that those who want
to go from here to you cannot, nor can anyone cross
over from there to us."

One last holding location is in Hades or She'ol, and that is Tartarus. A deep dark pit is where the wicked angels are chained awaiting the final judgment.

2 Peter 2:4-9 (NIV)

4 For if (and it's true) God did not spare angels
when they sinned, but sent them to hell, [Tartarus]
putting them in chains of darkness to be held for
judgment; 5 if (and it's true) He did not spare the
ancient world when He brought the flood on its
ungodly people, but protected Noah, a preacher of
righteousness, and seven others; 6 if (and it's true)
He condemned the cities of Sodom and Gomorrah by
burning them to ashes, and made them an example
of what is going to happen to the ungodly; 7 and if
(and it's true) He rescued Lot, a righteous man, who
was distressed by the depraved conduct of the law-
less 8 (for that righteous man, living among them
day after day, was tormented in his righteous soul
by the lawless deeds he saw and heard) 9 if this is so
(and it's true), then the Lord knows how to rescue

the godly from trials and to hold the unrighteous for punishment on the day of judgment.

Jude 6 (NIV)

[6] *And the angels who did not keep their positions of authority but abandoned their proper dwelling - these He has kept in darkness, bound with everlasting chains for judgment on the great Day."*

The acts of these particular angels were so heinous that God has imprisoned them in chains in utter darkness. They had no awareness of the activities of Jesus and His saving work on earth. They were not aware that Satan had been defeated. It may be they had conscious thoughts that one day Satan will succeed in his rebellion against the kingdom of God. They may have hoped that when that happened, they would once again be free.

1 Peter 3:18-20a (NIV)

[18] *For Christ also suffered once for sins, the righteous for the unrighteous, to bring you to God. He was put to death in the body but (was) made alive in the Spirit.* [19] *After being made alive, he went and made proclamation to the imprisoned spirits* [20a] *to those who were disobedient long ago*

Dr. R. B. Thieme, Jr. in his book Victorious Proclamation states, "Jesus informed these demons that they had failed in their efforts to destroy true humanity and God's plan had moved right on through every satanic attack. He had gone to the Cross on schedule! Christ's sudden appearance to them in a resurrected body was the visual evidence. The penalty of sin had been paid."

Like we might say today, "I win, you lose."

PHASE III – THE BELIEVER IN ETERNITY

Words have meaning, so I hesitated to use the "The Believer in Eternity." Eternity conveys the concept that there is no beginning and no end. Eternal life is the sole possession of God. He alone has always existed and will always exist. Humans, on the other hand, had a beginning and will have no end. That to me is different; it's an everlasting life. It's forever more. Our bodies will degrade and die, but our soul, which is the true essence of us, will live on throughout eternity. *Where* our souls spend the rest of eternity after the body dies is what has always been the question.

God the Father executes this, the final and last phase of the believer's journey, beginning at the point of bodily death and continuing throughout eternity. My first thoughts about this section were that it will be rather short. God's in control, and I am not. It's in good hands, so no worries. What difference would that make? God's in control! How much do we know about heaven anyway? Not much, but more than we realize. It seems that people think heaven is a good final destination, so we all want to go there. Well nearly everyone – a few don't believe there is a God, so they don't believe there is a heaven.

According to the December 18, 2008, Pew Research Center survey, 80% of the United States population believe they will go to heaven when they die. As wonderful as they believe heaven will be, I have not met many in a hurry to go there. In my eighty years, I've known only a very few eager to be called home to glory. Some books have been written about heaven, and maybe room exists for one more, but that's for another day if God so directs. I can, however, recommend one. If you are interested in more in-depth knowledge, read Randy Alcorn's book titled Heaven. As I studied and thought about it, I recognized some things that need to be said:

"Many Christians have a wrong view of death. We think we're going from the land of the living to the land of the dead. But the opposite is true. If you know Jesus, you are actually going from the land of the dying to the land of the living."

In a section titled Frequently Asked Questions About Christian Life, by Keep Believing Ministries: a Bibleinfo.com article these questions were asked, "How long will that take?" "What is Heaven like and where is Heaven?" In the section "How do I get to Heaven?" I found a false piece of information believed by some, stating: "Contrary to popular belief, the Bible says we do not go to Heaven or Hell when we die. We sleep in the grave until the resurrection, which the Bible says: 'and many of those who sleep in the dust of the earth shall awake, some to everlasting life, some to shame and everlasting condemnation'" (Daniel 12:2).

While the Bible does teach the resurrection of the body, it does not teach that the soul sleeps until that time. That's it. That's the short answer.

The more detailed response follows because of the importance of knowing the truth about death.

1. The Bible does not say we do not go Heaven or Hell when we die. The preponderance of scripture says just the opposite that we do go to Heaven or Hell. To be more precise, it is our souls that make the trip; our bodies do not. Our bodies are buried, cremated, lost at sea, and are bound to Earth for a time.
2. Daniel 12:2, when reading in context with the surrounding scripture Daniel 11 through Daniel 12:9, reveals that Daniel is seeing the timeline for the Jewish Age which will culminate at the end of the Great Tribulation with the Battle of Armageddon in Revelation 19:11- 21.
3. The Bible does refer to dead people as sleeping because dead people for a little while appear to be

sleeping. But before long, usually within three days, the bodies are laid in their final resting place until they are resurrected, and then they are united with their souls which had not died or slept but had gone to Hades. Finally, those that were believers were led to Heaven by Jesus as previously discussed. Those Scriptures apply here as well.

4. At its core, the idea of the soul sleeping until the final judgment, which is after the Tribulation and the 1,000-year reign of Christ on Earth, would delay the suffering of Hell's fire for the unbeliever by thousands of years. Believers would be punished by delaying entrance into Heaven by thousands of years. Soul Sleep seems to be neither a righteous nor just solution to the problem, does it?
5. I cannot reconcile the concept that the soul will sleep in the grave with scripture like 2 Corinthians 5:8. At the moment the believer's soul departs the body (the definition of the death of the body), the believer (the real person) is "face to face with the Lord" forever.
6. The subject of Soul Sleep does not harmonize with any scripture in the Bible. It is a misinterpretation of one scripture at best implying that because the body remains in the grave until Jesus summons it, the Soul also stays in the grave.

2 Corinthians 5:5-9 (NIV)

5 *Now the one who has fashioned us for this very purpose is God, who has given us the (Holy Spirit as a deposit, guaranteeing what is to come.* 6 *Therefore we are always confident and know that as long as we are at home in the body, we are away from the Lord.* 7 *For we live by faith, not by sight.* 8 *We are confident, I say, and would prefer to be away from the body and at home with the Lord.* 9 *So we make it our goal to please Him, whether we are at home in the body or away from it.*

CHAPTER SIXTEEN

Mission Impossible

God has a mission for every believer. It's a "Mission Impossible"—impossible, that is, without God's provisions and involvement. Now nothing is impossible because the impossible has changed; it's possible because everything is possible with God's help.

The very moment that we accepted Jesus as our Savior and Lord we were changed. We didn't feel it happen. We could have seen evidence of it if we could have seen the great big grin on our faces and perhaps an inch gain in height due to the extra weight being lifted off our shoulders. Changes were equipping us to do what we had never been able to do before. We were being equipped to participate in His grand plan for humanity.

We are not who we were before. In less than a millisecond we become an entirely new entity, one who now possesses the full potential to become all we can be in Christ and to fulfill His purposes for which we were created. The following is a list of some of the ways we are made new.

1. We now have a living spirit. The spirit within us lies dormant until we accept Jesus as Lord and Savior. It

is the spirit that is reborn. When it happens, we say we are born-again. The spirit makes it possible to discern spiritual things (Genesis 1:26, Genesis 2:7-9). God created Adam in His image so that they would have the ability to communicate spiritually. Man was just a clump of dust until God breathed into his nostrils the breath of life.

Hebrew 4:12—Announces a difference between the soul and spirit. Medicine didn't even acknowledge that man had a soul until the 1900s.

Gen.3:7—Through disobedience, Adam and Eve lost their innocence. Sin disconnected their (human) spirit from God, and they were separated or cut off from their Creator. They were out of fellowship with God. God himself initiated their return into fellowship by seeking them out. When we are out of fellowship with God, He comes looking for us. He is always faithful to initiate contact, we may or may not recognize His effort to re-establish fellowship.

Romans 5:12—Death is through Adam, and life is through Christ. Not physical death or life but spiritual death and life.

1 Corinthians 2:10-16 (NIV)

[10] *these are the things God has revealed to us by His Spirit. The Spirit searches all things, even the deep things of God.* [11]*For who among men knows the thoughts of a man except the man's own spirit within him? In the same way, no one knows the thoughts of God except the Spirit of God.*[12] *What we have received is not the spirit of the world, but the Spirit who is from God; so that we may understand what God has freely given us.* [13] *This is what we speak, not in words taught us by human wisdom but in words taught by the Spirit, explaining spiritual realities with Spirit-taught words.* [14] *The person without the Spirit does not accept the things*

that come from the Spirit of God but considers them foolishness, and cannot understand them because they are discerned only through the Spirit. [15] *The person with the Spirit makes judgments about all things, but such a person is not subject to merely human judgments,* [16] *for, who has known the mind of the Lord so as to instruct him? But we have the mind of Christ. (The Bible is the mind of Christ).*

Jude 17-19 (NIV)

[17] *But, dear friends, remember what the apostles of our Lord Jesus Christ foretold.* [18] *They said to you, "In the last times there will be scoffers who will follow their own ungodly desires."* [19] *These are the people who divide you, who follow mere natural instincts and do not have the Spirit.*

1 Thessalonians 5:23 (NIV)

[23] *May God himself, the God of peace, sanctify you through and through. May your whole spirit, soul and body be kept blameless at the coming of our Lord Jesus Christ.*

Rom 8:16 (NIV)

[16] *The Spirit himself testifies with our spirit that we are God's children.*

Before we became Christians, we were like zombies, dead men walking, we were dead to spiritual things. We were like tombstones, pretty on the outside but full of dead men's bones on the inside.

2. God gives us His Eternal Plan in Romans 8:29, 1 Peter 1:2, and Matthew 22:14.

All three members of the God-head are omniscient. Never has there been a time when God didn't know everything before it happened. He knows the beginning through to the end. His knowledge was not built concept by concept like ours. It was not progressive; it has always been. Therefore, God has always known who would answer His call, and who would not. Although Jesus paid for every sin that has or will ever be committed by all mankind, man must accept His payment. God will not violate man's volition. Those who choose to be debt free are debt free, Jesus has paid it all.

3. We have been reconciled to God as shown in 2 Corinthians 5:18-19.

Reconciled is an accounting term meaning the books are in balance. The account is correct. Jesus through His birth, life, and work on the cross has reconciled our account. It is in balance and paid in full. The barrier that man erected between himself and God has been removed.

II Corinthians 5:18-19 (NIV)

> [18] *All this is from God, who reconciled us to himself through Christ and gave us the ministry of reconciliation:* [19] *that God was reconciling the world to himself in Christ, not counting people's sins against them. And he has committed to us the message of reconciliation.*

4. We are redeemed as shown in Roman 3:24.

Everyone except Adam and Eve and Jesus was born into the Slave Market of Sin. Adam and Eve were created without a SN (Sin Nature), but when they moved from positive volition toward God to a negative volition, the SN was established because they demonstrated by eating the forbidden fruit they didn't believe God. The SN is passed down from Adam to our forefathers and from our forefathers to all of humanity. It's as much a part of us as our DNA. Jesus is the lone exception. The virgin birth of Jesus eliminates the possibility of Jesus receiving the SN. Joseph was not the father, and neither was any other man. You may be tempted into unbelief because that's not possible. Let me remind you that all things are possible with God and He excels in the impossible. No SN coupled with living a sinless life made Him the perfect sacrificial lamb. Having no sins of His own, He qualified to pay the complete ransom price and purchased us out of the Salve Market. Only a free man can purchase a slave. Redemption means to buy or to purchase. If you are a Christian, Jesus bought your freedom.

5. We have been rescued from the final death and spending eternity in Hell with Satan. Romans 8:1 says there is no condemnation. Condemnation is the act of judicially condemning or adjudicating guilty. Because of the redemptive work of Jesus, we—Christ-followers—are found not guilty.
6. God allowed Jesus to be our substitute, shown in Romans:

Romans 3:23-25 (NIV)

23 *for all have sinned and fall short of the glory of God,* 24 *and all are justified freely by his grace through the redemption that came by Christ Jesus.*
25 *God presented Christ as a sacrifice of atonement, ("at-one-meant," i.e., to be at one) through the shedding of his blood to be received by faith.*

He did this to demonstrate his righteousness because in his forbearance He had left the sins committed beforehand unpunished.

7. All of our sins are removed. According to Romans 4:24-25, sin is not a salvation problem; it is a fellowship problem. No fellowship can flourish if we are not His. Once we are saved, our sin removes us from fellowship until we repent and agree with God that we have sinned. Once we repent, we are back in the place of fellowship again.

Romans 4:23-25 (NIV)

23 *The words "it was credited to him were written*
not for him alone, 24 *but also for us, to whom God*
will credit righteousness for us who believe in him
who raised Jesus our Lord from the dead. 25 *He was*
delivered over to death for our sins and was raised
to life for our justification."

8. We are joint heirs with Christ and now spiritually alive as shown in Romans 4:13, Romans 8:17, and Ephesians 3:6.
9. We have been freed from the old Mosaic Law according to Romans 7:4.
10. We are children of God according to John 3:6-7 and Ephesians 2:1, 4-6.

John 3:6-7 (NIV)

6 *Flesh gives birth to flesh, but the Spirit gives birth*
to spirit. 7 *You should not be surprised at my saying,*
you must be born again.

Ephesians 2:1-6 (NIV)

1 *As for you, you were dead in your transgressions*
and sins, 2 *in which you used to live when you fol-*
lowed the ways of this world and of the ruler of the
kingdom of the air, the spirit who is now at work
in those who are disobedient. 3 *All of us also lived*
among them at one time, gratifying the cravings
of our flesh and following its desires and thoughts
(in opposition to the spirit). Like the rest, we were
by nature deserving of wrath. 4 *But because of his*
great love for us, God, who is rich in mercy, 5 *made*
us alive with Christ even when we were dead in
transgressions. It is by grace you have been saved.
6 *And God raised us up with Christ and seated us*
with him in the heavenly realms in Christ Jesus.

11. We were adopted into God's family, shown in Romans.

Romans 8:15 (NIV)

[15] *The Spirit you received does not make you slaves, so that you live in fear again; rather, the Spirit you received brought about your adoption to sonship (with full legal rights) And by him we cry, "Abba," (a term of endearment like "Daddy" or "Father").*

12. We have attained unlimited access to God according to Ephesians 2:18.
13. Christ makes us acceptable to God according to Romans 3:22 and Colossians 3:11.
14. We are justified according to Romans 5:8-10 and 18-20. Vindicated and acceptable, God sees us just as if we had never sinned.
15. We are forgiven of all our sins according to Colossians 1:13-14; 2:13; and 3:13.

Colossians 1:13-14 (NIV)

[13] *For he has rescued us from the dominion of darkness and brought us into the kingdom of the Son he loves,* [14] *in whom we have redemption, the forgiveness of sins.*

Colossians 2:13 (NIV)

[13] *When you were dead in your sins and in the uncircumcision of your flesh, God made you alive with Christ. He forgave us all our sins.*

Colossians 3:13 (NIV)

[13] *Bear with each other and forgive one another if any of you has a grievance against someone. Forgive as the Lord forgave you.*

16. We are brought very close to Him.

Ephesians 2:12-14 (NIV)

12 remember that at that time you were separate from Christ, excluded from citizenship in Israel and foreigners to the covenants of the promise, without hope and without God in the world. 13 But now in Christ Jesus you who once were far away have been brought near by the blood of Christ. 14 For He, Himself is our peace, who has made the two groups one and has destroyed the barrier, the dividing wall of hostility.

17. We are delivered from darkness and its power.

Colossians 1:13 (NIV)

13 For He has rescued us from the dominion of darkness and brought us into the kingdom of the Son, He loves.

18. We are rescued and now residents of Kingdom of the Jesus the Christ.

Colossians 1:13 (NIV)

13 For he has rescued us from the dominion of darkness and brought us into the kingdom of the Son he loves.

19. We have a new foundation according to John 17:6, 11, and 12-21.
20. We are circumcised in Christ. Col. 2:11; Philippians 3:3
21. We received a holy and royal priesthood according to 1 Peter 2:9.

Holy means being set apart to the worship of God and royal means belonging to the King. The priesthood is a term of office lasting from the moment of consecration until death (Hebrews 7:23). Your personal duties are: live a sober life, marry, and live life according to the laws of God. You are one of a "kingdom of priests." As a priest, you have immediate and free access to God, and you enjoy the liberties and privileges of His Kingdom. No one stands between you and God. No one has to speak for you. When you speak with God, we call it prayer, but God calls it fellowship. Satan stands ready to point out your shortcomings to God as if God needed Satan. BUT Jesus is your advocate and says, "I've paid for that one," and He will say that every time.

22. We are chosen, a peculiar people according to 1 Peter 2:9.
23. We are in "much more" care of God according to Romans 5:9-10.
24. We have gained His glorious inheritance according to Ephesians 1:18.
25. Our inheritance according to 1 Peter 1:4; Colossians. 3:24; and Ephesians 1:14.

1 Peter 1:4 (NIV)

4 *and into an inheritance that can never perish, spoil or fade. This inheritance is kept in heaven for you.*

Colossians 3:24 (NIV)

24 *since you know that you will receive an inheritance from the Lord as a reward. It is the Lord Christ you are serving."*

Ephesians 1:13b-14 (NIV)

13b *When you believed, you were marked in him with a seal, the promised Holy Spirit,* 14 *who is (the) deposit guaranteeing our inheritance until the redemption of those who are God's possession to the praise of his glory.*

26. We have the permanent indwelling of the Holy Spirit according to Ephesians 1:14.

27. We have a heavenly association according to Colossians 3:4, Ephesians 2:6, and 2 Corinthians 3:9.
28. We have a heavenly citizenship according to Philippians 3:20 and Luke 10:20.
29. We were drafted into the angelic conflict according to Hebrews 2:14.

With our conversion to Christianity, we were transferred from the kingdom of Satan into the kingdom of God. Satan was not happy with our decision, but since God's salvation was a permanent transfer, Satan cannot get us back. He can, however, use every means possible to neutralize us. Make no mistake; a war rages between the forces of good and evil, and the war is always active in and around us.

Satan is the great deceiver and is always actively trying to deceive us. If we don't thoroughly know God's viewpoint, and try to wing it, we will be deceived, neutralized and maybe even rendered useless. The question is, will we become more like Jesus or will our witness be neutralized? We cannot be the person God intended us to be if we are not equipped with the weapons of God and if we lack the Bible knowledge to understand what's happening. Even Jesus relied on the sword of Scriptures when Satan tempted Him. Angels defer to God's defense when confronted by Satan. Unless we know God's provisions, how can we stand against Satan's attacks?

Hebrews 2:14 (NIV)

14 *Since the children have flesh and blood, He too shared in their humanity so that by His death He might break the power of him who holds the power of death-that is, the devil.*

Satan must have thought he had at last won the cosmic war as Jesus hung on the cross and died. He had to be jubilant and hardly able to contain himself. That was Friday, but

Sunday was coming. While man thought Jesus was sealed in the tomb, Jesus got up and went to complete a twofold purpose. First, to be the pathfinder for those saints who had died before Him and were waiting for Him in Paradise. He was the first fruit, and no one could go to heaven before Him. As He left, the gates to Paradise were chained and locked, for there was no further need of Paradise. All believers who died after Jesus are face to face with Him in heaven in the twinkling of an eye.

30. We are members of the family and household of God according to Ephesians 2:19.
31. We are the light of the Lord according to 1 Thessalonians 5:4.
32. We are vitally united to the Trinity according to 1 Thessalonians 1:1; Ephesians 4:6; John 14:20; and 1Corinthians 12:13.
33. We are blessed with the Holy Spirit according to John 3:6; 1Corinthians 12:13; and 1 Corinthians 6:19.
34. We are glorified according to Romans 8:30.
35. We are made complete in Him according to Colossians 2:10.
36. We possess every spiritual blessing according to Ephesians 1:3.
37. Our transgressions have been blotted out according to Isaiah 44:22.
38. We are given a gift or gifts to enable us to accomplish God's purposes in our life according to Romans 11:29; Romans12:6-8; 1 Corinthians 12:1-11, 1 Corinthians 12:28; and1Corinthians 14:1.

Romans 11:29 (NIV)

29 *For God's gifts and his call are irrevocable.*

Romans 12:6-8 (NIV)

6 *We have different gifts, according to the grace given to each of us. If your gift is prophesying, then*

prophesy in accordance with your faith; [7] if it is serving, then serve; if it is teaching, then teach; [8] if it is to encourage, then give encouragement; if it is giving, then give generously; if it is to lead, do it diligently; if it is to show mercy, do it cheerfully.

1 Corinthians 12:1-11 (NIV)

[1] Now about the gifts of the Spirit, brothers, and sisters, I do not want you to be uninformed. [2] You know that when you were pagans, somehow or other you were influenced and led astray to mute idols. [3] Therefore I want you to know that no one who is speaking by the Spirit of God says, "Jesus be cursed," and no one can say, "Jesus is Lord," except by the Holy Spirit. [4] There are different kinds of gifts, but the same Spirit distributes them. [5] There are different kinds of service, but the same Lord. [6] There are different kinds of working, but in all of them and in everyone it is the same God at work. [7] Now to each one the manifestation of the Spirit is given for the common good. [8] To one there is given through the Spirit a message of wisdom, to another a message of knowledge by means of the same Spirit, [9] to another faith by the same Spirit, to another gifts of healing by that one Spirit, [10] to another miraculous powers, to another prophecy, to another distinguishing between spirits, to another speaking in different languages, and to still another the interpretation of languages [11] All these are the work of one and the same Spirit, and he distributes them to each one, just as he determines.

1 Corinthians 12:28 (NIV)

[28] And God has placed in the church first of all apostles, second prophets, third teachers, then miracles, then gifts of healing, of helping, of guidance, and of different kinds of language.

1 Corinthians 14:1 (NIV)

[1] Follow the way of love and eagerly desire gifts of the Spirit, especially prophecy.

Immediately we were changed into someone God can work with. Following Him, we will accomplish specific objectives that we never would have done before, and we will recognize His leadership in these impossible and improbable works.

"When the Holy Spirit moves us, we are moved from compliance to radical."

~ Chip Ingram ~ "Living On The Edge,"

We now have a purpose or mission in life far more than the self-serving goals we may have had previously set for ourselves. To live our lives as Jesus would will be a magnificent journey.

Today our soldiers and marines own the night. They have night-vision equipment that enables them to see almost as well as if it were daylight while maintaining the concealment of darkness to hide their movements. Christians while in fellowship have the remarkable ability to see through the darkness to accomplish their missions as well.

Beyond changing us, He has equipped us with the Operating Assets that we will need to accomplish our mission.

OPERATING ASSETS – A Partial List:

1. God unilaterally and completely removed the barrier that separated God from man. Nothing separates God from His children.
2. As a member of the Priesthood of Believers, no one stands between God and you. Before Jesus paid the

ransom for us, only the priest was allowed into the Holy of Holies, and that was only once a year. He wore bells so other priests could hear him walking. He had a rope tied around his waist so they could pull him out if he stopped moving. But now we can run freely into the presence of God, climb up in His lap, and call Him Daddy. This is only possible because Jesus loves us so.

3. Jesus paid the purchase price in full to purchase you out of the Slave Market of Sin; He alone is worthy of your service.
4. You are a NEW YOU! Not modified, changed, made over or refurbished—a COMPLETELY NEW AND DIFFERENT YOU.
5. You have a human spirit that enables you to recognize, commune, and communicate in the spiritual realm.
6. God—the Holy Spirit—has set up permanent residence in your soul. He will never leave you.
7. We have the complete Bible, containing the Old and New Testaments, which communicate the thoughts and viewpoint of God on everything we need to know.
8. More than 7,000 promises are recorded and signed by God for the believer to use in time.
9. More than 2,000 promises for the unbeliever regarding His free gift of salvation.
10. The best communication system ever devised -- prayer.
11. A Stall Recovery promise (1John1:9) that enables us to reestablish fellowship with God.
12. More than abundant blessings and continual communications create a new mental attitude, one of selflessness and service.
13. The gift to be able to trust God when facing challenging circumstances.
14. A new way of life, one based on grace living.
15. A new family, the church, and a brotherhood that transcends national borders and race.

The four Operating Assets that will be discussed in the next four chapters are crucial to the Christians well-being.

A. The Bible is Reliable in all that it says
B. Stall Recovery - To sour with the eagles we must learn to recover from stalls
C. The Trust Factor - God, has earned our trust and demands our trust
D. Our Communication Provision - Prayer

CHAPTER SEVENTEEN

Operating Asset—The Bible

The Bible is the only reliable source of information regarding spiritual matters.

I used to say, "I believe the Bible from cover to cover," or "from the index to maps." I was saying I believed every word of it, even though in the beginning I hadn't read the entire Bible or studied many of the maps. My reasoning was the Bible is the Word of God. God doesn't lie therefore the Bible is true so, I should believe it. I made a conscious decision to believe what it said. If I had been asked to prove it, I would have been unequipped to do so. We do need to be equipped to defend our faith with facts. Not that we need our faith shored up, if we needed facts, we couldn't exercise faith.

Faith is believing even when no evidence exists or is not known. Unbelievers lack faith and will need proof. It's good to know why we believe and what we believe. Providing whatever information may be needed is noble. We must use whatever ammunition is available to back-up and prove our point, for someone's destiny could be changed. This information is intended to give you confidence in what you say, but it is the job of the Holy Spirit to bring the lost to Jesus.

Some people can read a passage of the Bible and have no problem believing it. Others can read the same passage, believe it, and still say, "So what?" Others can read the passage and say they don't believe it. They don't believe it happened, or that it happened that way, or they think it is impossible, and therefore it couldn't be true. They fail to realize that God excels in doing the impossible. They rapidly develop rational reasons why something doesn't make sense to them. Even so, the Bible is also for them.

Rationalization is not the gateway to spiritual understanding. Neither is empiricism. Faith is the only gateway to understanding spiritual phenomena. If you read a verse or hear one from the Bible that seems unacceptable to your values and/or understanding, don't just throw up your hands and say, "I don't believe that." Write it down, remember it, ask God to clarify it for you and give you wisdom. Then do some research.

Each religion on Earth has its own holy books. What's so special about the Bible? How is it different from other books? What's important about its authorship, history, and language? Is the Bible a reliable information source? Can we really believe the Bible is absolutely true? Why should we follow Biblical teachings?

First, realize that Christianity cannot be lumped into a category titled "religion," because Christianity is not a religion. That may be a sobering message to the world. It should be because it is true. Christianity is nothing like the "religions" of the world. The world is confused and doesn't understand Christianity because it applies religious understanding to Christianity and that doesn't work. As a result, the Bible seems like foolishness.

1 Corinthians 2:14 (NIV)

[14] The person without the Spirit (natural man, the unbeliever) does not accept the things that come from the Spirit of God but considers them foolishness, and cannot understand them because they are discerned only through the Spirit.

Religion has to be defined as man trying to gain favor with a deity of some sort: man reaching up to a god and man doing things to please a god and gain favor. Any act, from sacrificing babies or animals, to blowing themselves up with dynamite to kill the infidels, to protecting cows, to equating or elevating plants and animals to human life, or doing good deeds—if man can think it, he can believe it to the point that it is defied. He can whip himself, walk on hot coals of fire, disfigure himself with sticks and stones, charm snakes, or stand on stakes sharp as needles to prove his devotion to his god.

There is a massive rock called the Great White Throne in Zion National Park. The native Indians of Utah threw their virgin daughters off the rock, believing they would gain redemption. Over and over again, archaeology proves that man is prone to worship. Worshiping the wrong god is religion; the true God is not impressed with these acts.

Christianity, on the other hand, is a relationship with God. This relationship is initiated by God, not man, as God himself reaches down to lift man up. Man can do nothing to make God love him more or love him less. His love for us is complete and everlasting, unending and beyond our ability to understand. Absolutely Amazing!! A Christian is a joint heir with Christ; he is adopted into the family of God. All we can do to become a Christian is simply believe the testimony of the Holy Spirit and turn to Christ. God insists man must trust Him. Our trust is what God desires most, and if we do not trust God, we don't believe Him.

Romans 8:14-17 (Phillips)

[14-17] *All who follow the leading of God's Spirit are God's own sons. Nor are you meant to relapse into the old slavish attitude of fear - you have been adopted into the very family circle of God, and you can say with a full heart, "Father, my Daddy." The Spirit Himself endorses our inward conviction that we really are the children of God. Think what that means. If we are His children, we share His treasures, and all that Christ claims as His will belong to all of us as well! Yes, if we share in His suffering, we shall certainly share in His glory.*

AUTHORSHIP OF THE BIBLE

The Bible reveals God's character. The Bible is written without error or omission and consists of 66 books written by 40 different human authors over a period of 1500 years, in four different languages (Arabic, Chaldean, Hebrew, and Greek). The message is cohesive, complete, and contains a consistent narrative. It would be astonishing, no, impossible, if it had been written by men. Men were not the Bible's authors; its author was the Holy Spirit, and the Bible validates its divine authorship. The Holy Spirit is the agent responsible for recording a written record of the mind of Christ.

1 Corinthians 2:16b (NIV)

[16] *But we have the mind of Christ (the thoughts, feelings, will, and understanding).*

Recording this was too important and impossible to be left to human skills of communication. How could man accurately write of things that preceded him by thousands of years, and events that will happen thousands of years after his passing? He cannot! The Holy Spirit was the author of the Bible, and He used men to write it. The Holy Spirit has also protected the written Word throughout the ages. Many ancient manuscripts were rejected and not included in the Scriptures because they disagreed with the books that had been accepted. The rejected books taught contrary doctrine, such as witchcraft, and to believe them one would have to reject the Biblical teachings. The Bible, as we have it, is the complete revelation of God; no book was mistakenly omitted. Other passages say the Bible is the "mind of Christ" are Romans 3:2; Psalms 147:19; Acts 7:38; Deuteronomy 4:8; 1 Corinthians 2:17; and John 17:7. What the Bible says once is important; if it says it more than once, even more important. It is important that we know we have the mind of Christ in written form. We can know what and how He thinks, as well as what God expects from us. Paul amplifies the importance and origin of the Scriptures in 2 Timothy 3:16-17:

> 2 Timothy 3: 16-17 (NIV)
>
> 16 *All* (How much? <u>All</u>) *Scripture is God-breathed* (exhaled -breathed out) *and is useful for teaching, for rebuke, correcting, for training in righteousness.* 17 *So the servant of God* (all believers) *may be mature, thoroughly equipped* (completely equipped) *for every good work* (to do divine good deeds).

When we recognize that our death is imminent, we stop delaying and emphasize the urgent matters and details. We concentrate on what is most important. Peter was no different. He was compelled to write his second Epistle know to us as II Peter. He was near death, and he knew it, so with a sense of urgency, his pen exploded with the things he considered most important for us to remember. After 19 verses of introduction, he writes above all those that this is the most important.

> 2 Peter 1:20-21 (NKJV)
>
> 20 *Knowing this first (this is most important thing Peter wanted us to know) that no prophecy of*

Scriptures is of any private interpretation (a better translation of the Greek is "springs up," or "has its origin," or "originates from one's own explanation") [21] *for prophecy never came by the will of man, but holy men of God spoke as they were moved by the Holy Spirit.*

Peter wrote, "Most importantly, know that the Scriptures include both the Old and New Testaments did not originate in man's mind but rather it was written by man as the Holy Spirit dictated every word without violating the vocabulary, and experiences of the writers."

This passage is saying not just prophecy, but *all* Scriptures are inspired by God. Anyone who spoke for God was called a Prophet and what He wrote was prophecy.

The modern-day definition of prophecy is "the inspired utterance of a prophet viewed as a revelation of divine will; a prediction of the future, made under divine inspiration; a foretelling or prediction of what is to come." Most certainly, the Bible contains prophecies that fall under this definition. Prophecy occupies one-fifth of all Scriptures and one-third of that one third concerns prophecies pertaining to the second coming of Jesus Christ.

There are 660 general prophesies, and 335 are concerning Jesus. 109 were fulfilled in the first coming, and 224 are yet to be fulfilled. The Old Testament contains 1,527 passages refer to the second coming of Jesus. Of the 7,959 verses in the New Testament, 333 refer directly to the second coming of Jesus. That's one in 24. I'm not sure who gets the credit for the research behind these statistics, but think I got them from a tape study by Dr. John MacArthur

Next to the subject of Faith. The subject of the second coming is the most dominant subject in the New Testament. 21 times the Lord refers to His return, and more than 50 times we are exhorted to be ready. I think He's coming back, don't you?

HOW DOES THE BIBLE DESCRIBE ITSELF?

Hebrews 4:12 (NKJV)

12 *The Word of God Is living (always alive) and powerful sharper than any two-edged sword, piercing even to the division (dividing) of the soul and the spirit, and the joints and marrow, and is a discerner of the thoughts and intents of the heart.*

Even though we don't have much use for a sword in battle today, when this was written the sword was the individual soldier's main battle weapon, and it was used extensively by civilians as a self-defense weapon well into the 1800s. It's shortened version when affixed to the end of a rifle or musket (a bayonet), and it is still a terrifying weapon.

Even today the U.S. Marines are trained in the proper use of the bayonet because of its effectiveness in close quarter fighting. With a bayonet attached to the end of a rifle barrel, the rifle's effectiveness is extended threefold. It can fire bullets, be sword-like, or be a lance extending the soldiers' reaches beyond their arms. In combat, when the soldier is out of bullets, and hand-to-hand fighting is the only defense, the bayonet becomes the most significant weapon. What is this verse is saying to us today? Is still pertinent?

"The word of God is alive" — through generation after generation its message remains clear and understandable. The New Testament is mostly pure doctrine; it is the mind of Christ. Unlike any other book that has ever been written, it lives. It's alive. It is as current, up-to-date, understandable, and meaningful today as it was when it was written — "and powerful" as well (the Greek word is "dymidimus," the same word we translate as dynamite.) Today many things are more powerful than dynamite, but nothing is more powerful than the Bible. The word "powerful" still conveys the meaning of what is being said and has staying power that can reach into your mind with the ability to change how you think about anything.

Consider these phrases: 1.) "sharper than any two-edged sword" (Macharia is the word for sword); 2.) "piercing even to the dividing of the soul and the spirit" (not until the 20th century did scientists discover there is a difference between the soul and the spirit, yet the Bible said there was a difference in the book of Hebrews, which dates back to before AD 70); 3.) "and the joints and marrow" (it cuts to the essence of the problem, and it's sharp enough to separate the joints and marrow); and 4.) "and is a discerner of the thoughts and intents of the heart." We don't think with our hearts. Our heart is a pump, and its only function is circulating blood. The function of the mind is to think. But this was written when people believed the heart was where thoughts originated and that the stomach was the seat of their emotions. Today we Know better but consider this; even today we can get so emotionally upset that it affects our stomachs and Valentine's Day is a celebration of letting our hearts rule. When we are in love, we can do some of the dumbest things because we try to think with our hearts. We still understand what the writer is saying.

Our thoughts and intentions stem from the set of norms and standards we have accepted. Our emotions are a part of our soul. For us today, the word "heart" should be "mind," but when this was written, the heart was considered to be the seat of the emotions. This portion of Scripture should read, "and is a discerner of the thoughts and intents of the mind." We are as much what we think as we are what we do. We can never fool the Holy Spirit.

One of our major problems today is our emotions ruling our actions when it should be our mind ruling our actions. Two examples are the increasing reports of "road rage" and protests in the streets that are supposed to focus attention on a problem. Instead, riots destroy public and private property and become detractions from the original intent. The Prodigal Son's brother appeared to be the better of the two brothers, but when he consistently refused to celebrate his brother's return, he showed his calloused heart. As far as we know, he never reconciled with his brother or father.

"When the book of Hebrews was written, five different kinds of swords were in use and well known:

1. The Romphaia was a two-handed Thresian broadsword. Its blade was attached to a short pole that made it as long as the soldier was tall. It had one sharp edge with no point. The soldier swung the Romphaia like we swing a baseball bat. As he walked forward swinging the sword, the idea was to cut off as many heads as possible—terrifying—but the Romphaia had some problems. The soldier was vulnerable and off-balance at the end of his swing, so the Holy Spirit didn't use the word Romphaia to describe the Bible. When you use the Bible, you will never be vulnerable or off-balance.
2. The Akinekes was a Persian ordinate sword. Made of gold and embedded with precious stones, it was elegant and for dress-up affairs only, NOT for fighting. The Holy Spirit didn't use the word Akinekes to describe the Bible because the Word of God is not meant to be carried in formal dress affairs; it's meant to be used in battle.
3. The Xiphos was a thin, narrow sword that had a point but no cutting edges and was made for thrusting only. The Holy Spirit didn't use the Xiphos because the

Word of God was not written to only make a point here and there.

4. The Dolon was a hidden sword usually in a walking cane or whip. Dolan was not used to describe the word of God because the Word of God is not something you hide. There is no Secret Service in God's Army. The Bible is not merely a defense weapon to be used only in emergencies.
5. The Macharia is the sword the Holy Spirit used to give the readers of Hebrews a word picture that perfectly describes the word of God. The Macharia has a point, so you can jab or thrust to make your point. Both sides were very sharp so that you can swing forward and backward and cut to the quick of the problem. It was light, short, and easy to use, so you will never be off-balance when you use it. It was equally useful as an offensive or defensive weapon. It was the nuclear bomb of its day."

~ R.B Thieme, Jr. 1961 Basics ~

The Greeks used a Macharia like weapon to conquer the world. The Romans used it to conquer the Greeks and an even larger known world. Rome ruled the world for more than 500 years. Rome's demise was the result of moral decay, greed, poor leadership, immigration, diversification, the inscription of foreign fighting units into the army, and the high cost of welfare.

THE LANGUAGES OF THE BIBLE

The Old Testament was recorded in Hebrew, Aramaic, and Chaldean. The structure of these languages is relatively simple: translating them in to any language is relatively easy and fast..

The New Testament, particularly the epistles, is almost complete doctrine and is written in Koine Greek (koine is the

Greek word meaning common). It is correctly named because it became the universal world language as the Greek empire expanded, having originated about 350 B.C. It was the language of the world during the first advent and the time when the New Testament was written. It was the language of the street people as well as the people in the exalted places.

Koine Greek was an excellent language for communicating one's ideas, instructions, and conversation because it could not be misunderstood. Changing the meaning of what was said with voice inflection or eye movement or even body language, or deliberate miscommunication through the choice of words, was impossible. Words had a precise meaning and could not be misunderstood. Therefore, ideas and instruction were communicated concisely. One word in Koine Greek could convey a thought that might require a paragraph of the English language to explain. It was the perfect language for God to use to express His teachings and desires. Was it a coincidence that Koine Greek was the language of the people when the New Testament was written? I don't think so. I think it was part of God's grand plan. God has no problem understanding man, and He knows the intent of our heart, so He doesn't need words, voice inflection, rolling of the eyes, or body language to understand us. But man needed the clear, precise words of a language that could not be misunderstood.

However, Koine Greek is not so common anymore. Today there are many dialects and eight of them are derivatives of Attic Koine, a blend of the original language of Plato and Aristotle and the ancient city-state of Athens and Alexander's common no-nonsense Koine language. The supreme purpose for the development of Koine was to convey God's thoughts to man precisely, but don't tell Alexander that. More than 400 years have elapsed since the King James Version of the Bible was published, and some words and expressions have changed since then. They may no longer convey the meanings they once did. For instance:

Matthew 6:6 (KJV)

> [6] *But thou, when thou prayest enter into thy closet, and when thou hast shut thy door, pray to thy Father which is in secret; and thy Father which seeth in secret shall reward thee openly.*

The NIV translation of the same verse reads:

Matthew 6:6 (NIV)

> [6] *But when you pray, go into your room, (or a private place) close the door (so you will not be disturbed) and pray to your Father, who is unseen. Then your Father, who sees what is done in secret, will reward you.*

In 1611 when the King James Version of the Bible was finished, a closet was a private place, not a room to store clothing. It may still be a private place, but it seems strange to us to go into a closet to pray. It simply means to get alone, away from the hustle and bustle, and close the door so you will not be disturbed. Make preparations and expect to hear from God. This is instruction on how to prepare for an intimate conversation between you and your heavenly Father. These intimate conversations are best done privately so you can open up and say what you really need or want to say and are free to hear what you need to hear. This secret conversation is not a clandestine conversation, but a private one. The privacy eliminates the temptation to impress a third party or repeating those same worn-out words, or the possibility of being embarrassed. You can speak openly to your Father about anything without filtering your words.

Yet the original languages of the Bible are never outdated. They communicate to modern man as they did to all previous generations. The word of God is still alive and powerful.

How Koine Greek, the language of the New Testament, came to be is an outstanding example of God's overriding will. This is an excellent starting place to understand some of the wonders of the Bible. Isn't it amazing God looked out over the expanse of time, and as He watched the development of man, He orchestrated the events so that at the precise and perfect time and place the Son of God became the unique person of the universe? Jesus was 100 percent God and at the same time was 100 percent man. He is the perfect mediator between God and man. As a man, Jesus lived some 33 years, was tempted far beyond our capacity to be tempted, and yet remained sin free. God planted a stake in the ground with His Son nailed to it because of His unbelievable and astonishing love of us.

The message of His love for humanity was so important it required a language that was precise and could be clearly understood. There could be no chance that the message could be misunderstood. Some 383 years before the crucifixion, God raised up a brilliant heathen who hated miscommunication and double talk and invented a language that could not be misunderstood. The love letter, our SOP (Standard Operation Procedure) manual that would be written and protected by the Holy Spirit would be absolutely true because it is His nature to be absolute truth. It also had to be understandable without the possibility of being misunderstood. That language became the common language throughout the known world. This intense planning was for our benefit, so we would have His recorded Word; it is to guide us in His ways.

Greece was not a united nation as we think of it today. No central government existed; instead, each city was an independent city-state. Each one was autonomous and fought for supremacy over the others. Athens and Sparta had fought as allies in the Greco Persian Wars (B.C. 499 - 444). With their victory at hand and Persians withdrawing from Greece,

Athens grew more powerful. Tensions grew between the two city-states, and a war erupted that lasted almost 30 years, known as the Peloponnesian Wars lasting from 431- 404 B.C. As the war was winding down, Sparta defeated Athens and then marched against Thebes, a much smaller city-state.

Macedonia, another Greek city-state, would from time to time; dispatch raiders down out of the mountains and raid Thebes. During one of these raids, the Macedonian king's son was captured. He was held hostage because the Thebans didn't need any harassment or raids from Macedonia as they prepared for the coming war with Sparta. As a king's son, Philip II had the freedom to go where he pleased, but he couldn't leave. Philip was observant as he moved about and became very impressed with the organizational skills and other aspects of his captors. He was really shocked and amazed when the smaller Theban army with less training and substandard equipment decisively defeated the Spartan army which was well known to be the prominent warrior nation. When the war was over, Philip was freed. When he left to return to Macedonia, he took with him all the knowledge and items that he would need to reorganize his city-state, Macedon.

Under the leadership of King Philip II, Macedonia emerged as a well-organized and powerful kingdom. In 338 B.C. Philip conquered Greece and laid the foundation of what was to become a mighty empire. His marriage to Olympias resulted in the birth of a son they named Alexander. We know him as Alexander the Great. Schooled by Plato and Aristotle, Alexander was a genius who was the right man at the right time, in the right place; he changed the direction of history.

By the time Alexander was 16 he was already a divisional commander in his father's army. This was not a political appointment, he was a natural leader and earned his commission. Phillip was assassinated, and Alexander ascended to the throne. Alexander maintained his Kingdom and unified the fragmented armies. He positioned himself as a liberator who would defend all Greece by defeating the Persians that had continually conducted raids with such overpowering force that the armies of the city-states were unable to overcome or defeat the invaders.

The merger of such diversified military forces worked in theory, but not in practice. While the combined battle forces presented an impressive sight, they did not, and could not, function as one cohesive fighting force. It has been said that a well-fed army is a happy army and will function properly. That's not entirely true, and Alexander discovered it almost immediately. Good communication is the real key to a successful army. All of Alexander's troops were Greek, and all spoke Greek. The problem was that all the Greeks languages were different. They didn't have a common language. The soldiers from Athens spoke Attic Greek. The soldiers from Sparta knew only enough language to communicate military strategies and tactics, and soldiers from Macedonia spoke a dialect that was completely different, and so on.

In my mind's eye I can see Alexander facing his all-Greek army in brigade formation with the Macedonian division on his left, followed by the Athenian division, followed by the Spartan division, and so on as the other city-states divisions stretched out to his right. The Brigade Adjutant gives the command "Right Face, Forward March," but only the Macedonians understand his commands. They faced right and marched off. The other divisions didn't understand the commands, so there was great confusion.

Alexander realized he had a major problem. So instead of marching to war he dismissed the troops, went to his tent, and developed an entirely new language. Alexander despised double talk and the use of words with multiple meanings, so he developed a language that could not be misunderstood.

When his Koine (common) Greek was spoken or written, it could only have one meaning. Technically and practically there was no way to misunderstand the verbal or written word. Neither gesture nor tone could change the meaning of what was being said. There would be no way to miss the meaning of what was said.

As Alexander conquered the known world, the defeated representatives had to learn his Koine Greek before terms of peace and treaties could be agreed upon. He insisted that Koine Greek language replace the conquered nation's language. As his soldiers retired from his army, they became administrators and politicians in the countries of their new residence. As they did this, they established the organization that Alexander's father had implemented in Macedonia. By 300 B.C. the known world was speaking this new language. Even the Romans realized its merits, and while Latin remained the official language of the Roman Empire, Koine Greek was the language of culture and was spoken by every educated Roman.

Because of its unique quality of communication, the Koine Greek continued to be the preferred language throughout the time the New Testament was written. It is no accident that Koine Greek became the perfect medium for divine revelation. Alexander did not create it for God's purpose, but God orchestrated the need for it and the desire of one man to understand and be understood, therefore God was very much involved in its creation and design. There may be many applications of any given passage in the Bible, but there is only one interpretation. If confusion about a passage is experienced, it may be that the application is confused with the interpretation.

Is There any Evidence That The Biblical Accounts Are Legally Provable?

God began telling the most marvelously exceptional and excellent story ever told in Genesis 1:1a: "In the beginning, God created the heavens and the earth..." Anyone who believes Genesis 1:1 should have no problem believing anything else the Bible says, but it seems that more and more people absolutely refuse to believe the Biblical accounts of history. That behavior puzzled me for a time because the Bible is still the number one bestseller of all times, and no book has ever been so well authenticated as truthful, by non-Biblical sources.

It's incredible that some have committed themselves and their time to the extensive study of the Bible in an effort to find and expose any flaws in it, any contradictions, and any extravagant and unprovable claims in an attempt to prove the Bible is inaccurate and unreliable. If they are intellectually honest, they will eventually prove that they were wrong and God's Word is true. An honest evaluation of the available evidence has converted many unbelievers into Christianity's most ardent apologists (defenders of the faith).

Simon Greenleaf (1783 - 1853) was an agnostic; some even say he was an atheist who believed the resurrection of Jesus Christ was either a hoax or a myth. Greenleaf was a principal founder of Harvard Law School and a world-renowned expert on evidence. He wrote a three-volume legal masterpiece, A Treatise on the Law of Evidence. The U.S. judicial system today operates on the rules of evidence established by Greenleaf. While teaching law at Harvard, professor Greenleaf stated to his class that the resurrection of Jesus Christ was simply a legend; as an atheist, he thought miracles to be impossible. In a rebuttal, three of his law students challenged him to apply his acclaimed rules of evidence to the resurrection account.

In due time, Greenleaf accepted his student's challenge and began to apply the evidentiary rules of evidence of his day to the Gospels of Matthew, Mark, Luke, and John. He concluded that the admissible evidence was sufficient to prove in any fair court of law the resurrection of Jesus Christ was indeed fact—not a hoax, myth or fiction. Greenleaf reasoned that "copies of the original Gospels known to be in existence in his time were at least as authentic as all the works of antiquity, the authenticity of which was acceptable in courts of law, and that the veracity of the testimonies were demonstrable by internal and external examination (i.e.), by examining the consistencies and resolving the paradox is contained between them, and by comparing the Gospel accounts to corroborating of other known writers of the time, such as Tacitus, Josephus, and Seutonius, and that the most plausible, most reasonable, conclusion to be drawn was Jesus Christ not only lived and died but that He rose again from the grave."

In his book "The Testimony of the Evangelists," Greenleaf documents the evidence that caused him to change his mind. In his conclusion, he challenges those who seek the truth about the resurrection to fairly examine the evidence. Greenleaf was so persuaded by the evidence he became a committed Christian. He believed any unbiased person who honestly examines the evidence will conclude what he did, that Jesus Christ had truly risen. My memory recalls being taught that Greenleaf wrote a personal letter to his legal colleagues challenging them to apply the "Laws of Evidence" to Jesus. And he was convinced if they did, they would come to the same conclusion he had discovered.

Robert R. Edwards, at the suggestion of a colleague, decided to apply the more modern 2011 federal rules of evidence to the Gospels and the rest of the New Testament to see if they could still withstand judicial scrutiny and warrant the same conclusion drawn by Greenleaf. In his article "Is Simon

Greenleaf Still Relevant," Edwards states that we not only still have all of the evidence that Greenleaf had, but actually have more evidence today for the authenticity of the Gospels. Edwards points out the starting place is with the fact that copies of lost original documents are admitted into evidence all the time. He points out the data in favor of the authenticity of the New Testament manuscript copies we have today, including the Gospels, are so overwhelming we can only scratch the surface and referred the reader to other works or websites. Minimally, he relies on only two factors. The first is time: how close to the originals were the copies written, and two: how many copies are available. The closer the document is to the time of the event it describes, the more reliable it is, and the more copies we have of those documents, the better we can compare them to each other, and thus gauge their comparison to an "original." As long ago as 1943, having reviewed the information available to him at his time, and drawing from the conclusion reached by Sir Frederick Kenyon, the late Prof. F.F. Bruce in an article entitled, "Is The Bible Authentic?" concluded: "The interval between the dates of original composition and the earliest extinct evidence is so small as to be in fact negligible, especially when compared to the dates of academically excepted historical documents such as those detailing Roman History."

The last foundation of any doubt that the scripts of the old and new Testaments have come down to us substantially as they were written has now been removed. Both the authenticity and general integrity of those works may now be definitely established and proved, probably to be the most authentic historical documents known to man.

But, even more, has been discovered since 1943. In an article published March 5, 2007, Discover Channel contributor Jennifer Viegas reported that the oldest known manuscript copies of the Gospels of Luke and John dated from A.D. 175 to 225 and were found in 1952 at Pabau Egypt. The oldest extant fragments of Mark contained in the "Papyrus 45" along with parts of Matthew, Luke, and John date no later than A.D. 250. Historically speaking, these copies are remarkably close in time the originals of which they purport to be copies. With respect to number, today there are over 5,300 known Greek manuscripts of the New Testament, another 10,000 in the Latin Vulgate, and 9,300 other early versions, giving us more than 24,000 extinct manuscript copies of at least portions of the New Testament. Of those, 230 manuscript portions predate A.D. 600 consisting of 192 Greek New Testament manuscripts, five Greek lectionaries containing Scripture, and others of like consistency. Therefore, even though we do not have the originals, the sheer number of consistent manuscript copies we do have weighs heavily in favor of the authenticity as copies of the originals. The fact, that they have been found throughout the Middle East and the known world as of the dates on which they purport to have been written as consistent with the great commission which, in Matthew 28:16 - 20, Christ tells his disciples to go into all the world preaching the Gospel, or good news, of eternal life through His death and resurrection.

"Compare the above with other works of antiquity, the authenticity of which few, if any, think to question. Aristotle lived from 384 to 322 BC. The earliest manuscript copies of his work, or parts thereof, date from AD 1100 leaving more than 1400 years between the dates on which he penned the originals and the date of the earliest known copies. Moreover, we have only five of those copies. Caesar lived from 100 to 44 BC; the earliest manuscript copies of his original writings date from AD 900 leaving almost 1000 years between the originals and copies. Still, we have just ten. Herodias lived from 482-425 BC; the earliest of his manuscripts date from AD 900 leaving over 1300 years between the originals and their copies. We have eight of those manuscripts.

"Homer lived circa 900 BC. The earliest of his manuscripts extant today dates from 400 BC, leaving some 500 years in between we have a total of 643 copies. Plato lived from 427 to 347 BC. We have seven manuscript copies of his original works, dating around AD 900 that leaves more than 1200 years between his life and the date of the earliest known manuscript copy of his works. Thucydides lived between 460 and 400 BC. We have copies of his manuscripts dating back to around AD 900 leaving 1300 years between his life and the earliest existing copies of his works. Seutonius lived from AD 75 -AD 260 eight manuscripts of work are extant, the earliest of which dates to AD 950, almost 800 years after his death. And, even with the Quran, while the number of extant manuscripts is a matter of debate, the earliest known manuscript dates to AD 750 a young hundred years after the original was written in circa AD 650.

"In light of the above, any objection to Greenleaf's relevance today should and must necessarily be, denied. He is as credible and relevant today, perhaps even more so, as he was in his own day because of the evidence of the authenticity of the documents on which he based his argument are more conclusive today than when it was written."

CHAPTER EIGHTEEN

The Bible and Science

DOES SCIENCE REALLY DISPROVE THE BIBLE?

God is the original scientist. But He did not observe and then try to duplicate in a controlled environment, what He had seen. He didn't postulate and try to make His observation mesh with His opinions. He just spoke everything we see and much more that we cannot see into existence. Being Sovereign and having the power, He did so because it pleased Him and it served His purposes.

Let me narrow that down a bit. He spoke, and the universe was formed. Within the universe, the Earth was formed rotating on an axis from east to west at precisely the correct speed to produce stability. The precise degree (23.5) of tilt of its axis provides seasons and prevents extreme temperatures anywhere on the earth. At the same time, He caused the rotation of the earth around the sun to be precisely at the speed of 67,000 miles per hour. Also, that orbit was exactly far enough away for the sun to prevent destruction by the excess heat, and yet close enough to give the exact amount of heat and light so that vegetation, man, and the animals would have life and flourish.

Our tilted axis points to one star, Polaris (the North Star). Then He said, "Stay there." God is also the author of the Bible which is the recorded mind of Christ (I Corinthians 2:16). No serious thinker would consider that there could or would be any disagreement of the two. Therefore, science does not contradict the Bible; on the contrary, science is continually proving that the Bible is absolutely correct, and it happens every time. Some can't believe that, so they wiggle and squirm like a worm on a hook. But the truth is inescapable. It must be either accepted or rejected. Although the Bible is not a science textbook, it is accurate when it mentions matters of science. The following is by no means an exhaustive list, but rather, a few examples where the Bible statements have been proven by science. It was modern man with his highly tuned intellect who out of unbelief said in effect, "The Bible can't be trusted, look at all the inaccuracies it contains." It is they who are being proved wrong as science unlocks the mysteries of old and validates the Biblical statements.

Man continues to debate the mystery of which came first, the chicken or the egg? This mystery was solved for us in the first chapter of the first book of the Bible.

> Genesis 1:20-22 (ESV)
> 20 *And God said, "Let the waters swarm with swarms of living creatures, and let birds fly above the earth across the expanse of the heavens.* 21 *God created the great sea creatures and every living creature that moves, with which the waters swarm, according to their kinds, and every winged bird according to its kind. And God saw that it was good.*
> 22 *And God blessed them, saying, "Be fruitful and multiply and fill the waters in the seas, and let birds multiply on the earth."*

A cursory reading reveals that the chicken was created first with the ability to make eggs; therefore, the chicken was first.

Neither evolution nor philosophers have any solution to this seemingly unanswerable riddle because they fail to believe or they refuse to believe what is so plainly written.

Astronomy

The Bible is not a book on Astronomy, but when it speaks about astronomical matters, it is absolutely correct and truthful in every detail. The Bible refers to the great number of stars in the heavens many times, and here are three of them.

> Genesis 15:5 Common English Bible (CEB)
> 5 *Then he brought Abram outside and said, "Look up at the sky and count the stars if you think you can count them." He continued, "This is how many children you will have…"*

> Genesis 22:17 Contemporary English Version(CEV)
> 17 *I will bless you and give you such a large family, that someday your descendants will be more numerous than the stars in the sky or the grains of sand along the beach. They will defeat their enemies and take over the cities where their enemies live.*

> Jeremiah 33:22 (CEV)
> 22 *And there will be more descendants of David and of the priests from the Levi tribe than stars in the sky or grains of sand on the beach.*

Once there were thought to be 3,000 stars in the sky because that is about the number one can see with the naked eye, providing that one is looking on a clear night away from the light refraction of the city lights. Galileo using his crude telescope saw a tenfold increase and increased the count to 30,000. Scientists now openly admit that they do not know how many stars there are. They estimate there may be 1021 stars (that's 10 with 21 zeros behind it). The number of grains of sand on earth's seashores is estimated to be 1025. There's no way a man could ever count that many stars. Dr. Werner Gitt states in Stars and their Purpose (Signposts in Space, September 2006): "A computer making 10,000 calculations per second would require 30 million years of non-stop counting to count that many."

The Bible also says that each star is unique.

1 Corinthians 15:41 (CEV)

41 *The sun isn't like the moon, the moon isn't like the stars, and each star is different.*

To the naked eye, all stars seem to be basically alike with only slight differences in brightness and color. Now scientists know from analysis of the star's light spectra that each one is unique and different. Would it be possible for Moses to observe that each of the 3,000 stars he could see would have its own unique characteristics? No, I think not. It was divinely inspired as he wrote; just as Peter tells us in 2 Peter 1:20: "Knowing the first that no prophecy of Scriptures is of any private interpretation." This translates to "springs up" or "originates from one's own explanation."

Science is catching up with and is in agreement with the Bible.

The Bible describes the suspension of the Earth in space.

Job 26:7 (CEV)

7 *Who hung the northern sky and suspended the earth on empty space?*

The Bible describes the earth as a circle or sphere. Many ancient peoples believed that the earth sat on the back of a giant or the backs of animals, like four elephants or a turtle. Others believe the earth was flat.

Isaiah 40:22 (ESV)

[22] *It is He who sits above the circle of the earth, and it's inhabitants are like grasshoppers; who stretches out the heavens like a curtain, and spreads them like a tent to dwell in.*

Believe it or not, there exists today a group of people who call themselves the Flat Earth Society. They believe the earth is a flat disc with a 150-foot high wall of ice around the edge of the disc to keep people from falling off. They also assert that gravity does not exist. If they were serious about their stated belief, there would be no need for the 150-foot ice wall. No one would fall off the disk if there were no gravity. Even if they stepped off the edge of the disc they wouldn't fall, there would be no force to pull them down.

There is much debate over changing the word "circle" to "sphere," and that God was scientifically accurate in His description of the earth. Modern man can view the earth from many vantage points, even outer space, and the earth always appears to be a circle. To me, that is crucial to a description of any spherical object. Viewing the earth from the north, south, east, or west, and from above, beside, or below, it must always appear to be a circle; therefore it is a sphere. If it were a circle in only one dimension, it would be flat on another dimension. Like a basketball without any air in it, it would appear to be round from one dimension, elliptical from another, and from yet another would seem to be a flat line. There was no Hebrew word for sphere, and circle perfectly describes the earth as ancient Israelites would have understood. Christopher Columbus and his peers correctly understood the earth was a sphere, even if he did grossly underestimate its diameter.

Medical

The Bible is not a medical book, but when it speaks of medical matters it is 100% accurate. There are many verses that address medical issues, here are a few. The Bible clearly states that blood is the source of life.

Leviticus 17:11 (ESV)

[11] *For the life of the flesh is in the blood, and I have given it for you on the altar to make atonement for your souls for it is the blood that makes atonement by the life.*

Until 120 years ago, sick people were "bled" to rid the body of disease or infection, and many died as a result of this practice including George Washington, the first President of the United States. The doctors used leeches to suck the blood out of the patient, or a knife to make an incision at the affected site. Today we know that healthy blood is necessary to bring life-giving nutrients to the cells of the body. God declared, "the life of the flesh is in the blood" long before science understood it.

The Bible states that our bodies are made from the dust of the ground.

Genesis 2:7 (ESV)

[7] *Then the LORD God formed the man of dust from the ground and breathed into his nostrils the breath of life, and the man became a living creature.*

Science has confirmed that the human body is comprised of 28 base and trace elements, all of which are found in the earth. God created all mankind from one blood and the dust of the earth.

Genesis 5:1-5 (CEB)

[1] *This is the record of Adam's descendants. On the day God created humanity; He made them to resemble God* [2] *and created them male and female. He blessed them and called them humanity on the day they were created.* [3] *When Adam was 130 years old, he became the father of a son in his image, resembling him, and named him Seth.* [4] *After Seth's birth, Adam lived 800 years; he had other sons and daughters.* [5] *In all, Adam lived 930 years, and he died.*

Acts 17:26 (CEV)

[26] *From one person God made all nations who live on earth, and he decided when and where every nation would be.*

Scientists have now discovered that we are descended from one gene pool. A 1955 study of a section of Y chromosomes from 38 men from different ethnic groups around the world was consistent with the biblical teaching that we all come from one man (Adam). One Blood: The biblical answer to racism (*Christian answers.net*).

Circumcision on the eighth day is the ideal time if it's going to be done. God, the creator of life, knew this, and that's why the instruction He gave specified the 8th day.

Genesis 17:12 (CEB)

[12] *On the eighth day after birth, every male in every generation must be circumcised, including those who are not your own children: those born in your household and those purchased with silver from foreigners.*

Leviticus 12:3 (CEB)

[3] *On the eighth day, the flesh of the boy's foreskin must be circumcised.*

Luke 1:59 (CEB)

[59] *On the eighth day, it came time to circumcise the child. They wanted to name him Zechariah because that was his father's name.*

Medical science has discovered that the blood clotting chemical prothrombin peaks in a newborn on the eighth day. How did Moses know? He didn't, but God knew. God instructed Moses on the how and why the circumcision rite was to be accomplished. There was not a trial and error process to find the best time to execute the rite. It was a process of obedience. Imagine those first parents being pregnant and praying for a son. No one wanted a girl in those days, as life was too hard for women and their perceived value was slightly above worthless. These women were elated that their suffering brought forth a son, and now Moses was telling them that their sons had to be circumcised. Surely some worried that this procedure was too barbaric and too dangerous and that the child could die. Notice that God had already prepared for those concerns by engineering the blood clotting chemical prothrombin.

God has also given us just the right amount of water to sustain life.

Isaiah 40:12 (CEB)

[12] *Who has measured the waters in the palm of a hand or gauged the heavens with a ruler or scooped the earth's dust-up in a measuring cup or weighed the mountains on a scale and the hills in a balance?*

Physics

God established thermodynamics, and around 1850 Rudolf Clausius and William Thomson (Kelvin) observed it and wrote the First Law of Thermodynamics, stating that the total quantity of energy and matter in the universe is a constant.

One form of energy or matter may be converted into another, but the total quantity always remains the same; energy or matter can be neither destroyed nor created. One application of this First Law of Thermodynamics that is seldom acknowledged would be, the creation is and has been finished since the completion of the sixth day:

Genesis 2:1-2 (CEB)
[1] *The heavens and the earth and all who live in them were completed.* [2] *On the sixth day God completed all the work that he had done, and on the seventh day, God rested from all the work that he had done.*

God didn't rest because He was tired, He rested because all of the work had been completed.

The Second Law of Thermodynamics states that everything in the universe is running down and continuously becoming less and less orderly. This law was confirmed before it was written.

Psalm 102:25-26 (CEV)
[25] *In the beginning, LORD, You laid the earth's foundation and created the heavens.* [26] *They will all disappear and wear out like clothes. You change them, as You would a coat, but You last forever.*

Science expresses the universe in five terms: time, space, matter, and energy. God defined the universe in the exact same terms. The Bible is the only source of creation's beginning that is verified by scientific observable evidence.

Genesis 1:1-4 (NIV)
[1] *In the beginning (time) God created the heavens (space) and the earth (matter).* [2] *Now the earth was formless and empty, darkness was over the surface of the deep, and the Spirit of God was hovering over*

the waters. [3] And God said, ''Let there be light" (energy), and there was light. [4] God saw that the light was good, and he separated the light from the darkness.

True science agrees with the Biblical order of creation. Plants require sunlight, water, and minerals in order to survive. God created light first, then water, then soil, and then He created plant life.

Genesis 1:3 (NIV)
[3] *And God said, "Let there be light."*

Genesis 1:6 (NIV)
[6] *Then God said, "Let there be a firmament in the midst of the waters, and let it divide the waters from the waters."*

Genesis 1:6-8 (NIV)
[6] *And God said, "Let there be a vault between the waters to separate water from water." [7] So God made the vault and separated the water under the vault from the water above it. And it was so. [8] God called the vault "sky," And there was evening, and there was morning – the second day.*

Genesis 1:9 (NIV)
[9] *And God said, "Let the water under the sky be gathered to one place, and let dry ground appear." And it was so.*

Genesis 1:11 (NIV)
[11] *Then God said, "Let the land produce vegetation: seed-bearing plants and trees on the land that bear fruit with seed in it, according to their various kinds." And it was so.*

These, I hope, are enough to prove my point. Whenever the Bible speaks of things that are scientific, it speaks with scientific accuracy and authority. To find and record every scientific observation, whether it be in the field of Astrology, Anthropology, Biology, Hydrology, Geology, Medicine, Meteorology, Paleontology, Physics, or any other "ology," would make a fascinating book, but that is not my objective. The objective here is to help you realize that when the Bible speaks, it speaks with absolute truth and authority and that you can rely on its veracity.

When you hear man say, "The world is going to be destroyed," know that his prediction is correct. But if he says or infers anything like, "Man's actions will destroy the world," he is contradicting the Bible, and the Bible contains the recorded Will of God concerning mankind.

Man will not destroy the earth by "excessive" carbon emissions. Man will not destroy the planet by exploding nuclear bombs or with poison gases. Man will not destroy the planet, nor will he cause its destruction. The earth will not be destroyed by melting icebergs or worldwide freezes.

Revelation 20 is a detailed summary of the final events concerning this world and the disposition of its inhabitants.

1. The Battle of Armageddon, which actually will be no battle at all. Jesus will defeat the forces of evil gathered to oppose Him, with one breath. Their defeat will be quick, total, and complete!!!
2. Satan is captured, the Abyss opened, and he is chained for 1,000- years. The earth remains intact.

Jesus the Christ will return just like the Scriptures have promised, and the Jews have always expected Him to come. He will reign on earth for the same 1,000- years, and the earth remains intact. Swords are beaten into plows; sheep lay down with the lions, there will finally be what we have so long prayed for, peace on earth. Satan's influence will not present.

Only the tribulation saints will enter this millennial reign of Christ. Children will be born and they, like everyone else throughout the ages, will have a Sin Nature and must choose to follow Jesus, some will not. There will be tares growing with the wheat. Jesus will rule His Kingdom with one hand covered with silk and the one fist covered with iron. His judgment will be swift and just. The earth still remains!

Satan must be and will be, loosed at the end of the millennial to test the volition of the people. Once again Satan will lead a revolt against God. Amazingly, those who have known only a perfect environmental with no wars or rumors of wars, no pestilence, no sickness, not even death, they will reject the Lord's leadership, proving that the environment one lives in is not the problem and it doesn't lead to happiness. God will call down the fire from heaven will devour the armies of Gog and Magog when they have fully deployed their troops to destroy God's people. These armies are made up of those who witnessed and experienced the marvelous rule of the benevolent King Jesus and rejected the Gospel message to love and be loved by Him. Fire will come down from heaven and devoured that vast army. Satan will be thrown into the lake of fire and brimstone to be tormented day and night for evermore. Yet the earth still remains.

THE DAY OF JUDGMENT OF THE UNBELIEVERS

Revelation 20:11-12 (NIV)

11 *Then I saw a great white throne and Him (Jesus) who was seated on it. The earth and the heavens fled from His presence, and there was no place for them.*
12 *And I saw the (spiritually) dead, great and small, standing before the throne, and books were opened.*

Notice the earth and heavens have fled. They are gone. The judgment will take place somewhere out of this world because it is not here anymore. Some believers think that the world will be destroyed by fire, and maybe it will, but I don't see that in the scriptures.

Isaiah 24:20 (ASV)

> 20 *The earth shall stagger like a drunken man, and shall sway to and fro like a hammock (swinging), and the transgression thereof shall be heavy upon it, and it shall fall, and not rise again.*

There will be no further use for the Earth, it will not be the abode of humanity anymore, the believers will be with Jesus, and the unbelievers will at the Great White Throne waiting for their time to be judged. The Earth's stability will be lost, and it will begin to wobble. The vibrations will worsen and become violent. It would be like being in a 10.0 earthquake that doesn't end until the Earth has shaken itself apart and disintegrates; then it will be no more. However, believing that the earth will one day be destroyed, doesn't release us from our obligation of being good stewardships over it until our master Jesus Christ returns. Knowing that the physical world will end in an apocalyptic way may cause some to avoid caring for creation, but it shouldn't.

The judgment of Revelation 20:12 is for unbelievers only. The books are the Books of Life and the Books of Works. This is explained in more detail in the Section titled His Story. The Book of Life records the names of believers. When it is opened, and the unbeliever's name is not found, the Book of Works is opened; it contains a complete and detailed listing of all the good deeds the unbeliever has done. No matter how long that list is, it will not be long enough for the unbeliever to earn salvation. Salvation cannot be earned. It's a gift that is offered and must be accepted or rejected.

Revelation 21:1 (NIV)

[1] Then I saw "a new heaven and a new earth," for the first heaven and the first earth had passed away, and there was no longer any sea.

Chapter 21:1 confirms that the old earth and heaven will be no longer.

CHAPTER NINETEEN

Operating Asset – Stall Recovery

The most important thing for a student pilot to learn is not take-off procedures, not landing techniques, and not communication procedures. They are all critical, but the most essential principle a pilot must know is Stall Recovery. The student must be able to recognize when the plane has stalled, and even more importantly what to do to regain a proper flight attitude. Stall Recovery is so vital to student pilots that it's the first thing they must learn before flight training can even begin. They will read about stalls in the training manuals, be taught the four principles of airplane flight (weight or gravity, thrust, or speed, drag, which is the force that opposes thrust), and lift, the force provided by the wing surface that allows the plane to fly.

Airplanes will go into a stall when any of these principles of flight are violated.

We who have not earned our wings think of stalls as they relate to automobiles or motorcycles—a stall occurs when the engine stops. But an airplane can stall many ways even when the engine is still running. In aeronautical terms, a stall is a condition that occurs when the lift force has been reduced to the point that the plane cannot sustain flight. It must be instilled in the pilot's head that stalls will occur! So, it is imperative that the pilot is able to recognize the telltale signs of a stall and be able to implement the proper Stall Recovery techniques if he is going to avoid a crash. The pilot will have the head knowledge before he takes off but must demonstrate the ability to translate that head knowledge to the practical application before further training can progress.

Any airplane will stall if it loses lift. There have been enough private and even commercial airlines that crashed because they stalled, and the fatal condition was not recognized or corrected. Telltale signs culminating in airplane crashes and deaths that were missed by flight crews and captains with thousands of hours of flight time, just reinforce how difficult and critical it really is to recognize a stall quickly and apply the Stall Recovery technique.

The Stall Recovery technique is so important that it is taught before the student even learns to take off or land. On the first flight the instructor will take off, and at some point, the student will be given the stick and be told to come to a particular compass reading and a specific altitude, which he or she will likely accomplish very nicely. He or she may become so distracted by this new and exciting view of the horizon, or so intent on watching the gauges, that he or she only notices something is wrong when there's no engine noise (the instructor having turned off the ignition switch). Instinctively, the student reaches for the key to turn the ignition and the engine starts.

Unfortunately, the plane has lost airspeed and its lift and its falling. The nose of the plane wants to dip down. Instinctively the student pilot pulls back on the yoke, forcing the nose up. The aircraft now has a bad flight attitude, nose up with no lift. It cannot maintain its altitude and continues to fall. The only way out of the stall is to do what is unnatural and push the yoke forward, forcing the nose down until there is enough airspeed to level off and regain a proper flight attitude. Once the plane is flying again, the pilot can regain the altitude that has been lost.

Another way an airplane can stall is by flying too slowly. Everything else can be just right, but if the thrust or forward motion is too slow to maintain the lift under the wings, flight cannot be maintained. If lift can't be sustained, the plane will stall. Once again, you have to do the unnatural thing. If there's enough altitude, change the plane's attitude by diving to pick up airspeed, and then level off and regain your flight altitude. If there's not enough altitude, pick out a landing zone that you can get to and land. This is never good; planes are supposed to land on landing strips or at airports for the best possible results. Flying too slow most often occurs during takeoffs and landings, but it can happen while cruising.

We've read about the little engine that could. But sometimes the little engine can't. When you put a plane into a climb, it doesn't matter if it's a steep climb or a shallow climb, at some point, the little engine just will not be able to provide the thrust or energy that's necessary to keep climbing. When that happens, the aircraft will shudder and begin to fall backward. It's in a stalled condition. Again, the pilot's natural tendency is to pull back on the stick or yoke to keep the engine up and keep it flying, but it can't because it's lost its lift and thrust. If the pilot doesn't recognize that the engine has stalled and quickly apply the correcting recovery technique, the plane will fall from the sky maintaining its bad attitude (nose up and no lift) until it crashes. The unnatural thing is to immediately shove the yoke forward, causing the engine to nose down. Now you can begin to build up airspeed, and when there is sufficient speed, ease the yoke back to regain flight.

Now how in the world did flight instructions work its way into this book about spiritual things? It perfectly illustrates what happens to Christians, perhaps many times every day. The Christian goes into a stall every time he slips out of fellowship with his heavenly Father. Stalls occur all the time in the Christian life. We can be walking the walk one minute, and then without warning, we are not. Our stalls are often very subtle. If we as Christians don't understand Stall Recovery, we are just as doomed as the airplane pilot; except his death is physical, and our death is spiritual and happens immediately. Like the airplane that can stall because of a poor flight attitude, the Christian will stall because of a faulty spiritual attitude.

So what is the Stall Recovery? It is a wonderful Operating Asset that God has provided for every believer. It is needed daily to maintain a proper attitude toward God, and yet many of us have never heard anything about stall recovery. Christians stall out when they adopt an improper or dangerous mental attitude. We see and believe the tinsel of the world, and are deceived by the great deceiver. We want what we want, and we want it now. We don't stop and pray, asking God for what is best for us. We just want it. What this really means is we don't trust God to provide for us, even when He promises He will provide in abundance pressed down, shaken together and running over (Luke 6:39). That promise is conditional upon giving and thinking of others' needs before our own desires. God in His omnipotence knew it would be hard—no, impossible—for humans to continually be in fellowship with Him, and He planned for it. He gave us a written promise to rescue us.

1 John 1:9 was written to believers and is for believers only. It is, I believe, the most essential promise God has given to the believer. It tells us how and when to be rescued, and that fellowship will be reestablished as we soar into His waiting arms.

1 John 1:9 (NIV)

9 If (third class condition, maybe we will, maybe we won't) we agree with God that we have sinned and confess our sins (name them), He is faithful and just and will forgive us our sins and purify us from all unrighteousness."

This promise can only be claimed and implemented when Christians recognize that they are on their own path without God. Only the most basic aircraft and stupid aircraft owners don't have stall warnings indicators installed. These warning maybe lights or buzzers and the most sophisticated aircraft have audible alarms. God loves us and will continually alert us when we stall. He will use whatever is necessary to help us recognize our condition so we can regain the proper spiritual attitude.

God promises that the reestablishment of fellowship is available in an instant. God has demonstrated many times that he will attempt to intervene and warn us that we have stalled out, but just as the pilot must recognize that he is in a stall and take immediate corrective actions, we must recognize the warnings and execute the proper recovery technique.

When we recognize that we are in a stall, I John 1:9 is the stall recovery technique. Acknowledge that you are out fellowship by naming it, God will forgive, so believe it. Now live like you are forgiven.

We must agree with God that we have sinned and name the sin or sins, and believe the promise:

1 John 1:9, in essence, says if the believer agrees with God that he or she has sinned, by naming the sin we have judged ourselves and then are immediately back in His fellowship, just as if we had never sinned. There may or may not be

consequences for our actions, but in His arms, we are in a position to take the consequences.

Stall Recovery plays a very significant role in the Christian's life. The Christian will never lose his Salvation even if he becomes neutralized or benched in life. He may be marginalized. He does this when he acts like or thinks he is God. His own views become more important than those of God. This Christian that once was walking arm in arm with God has now become a carnal Christian. Being carnal is being out of fellowship with the Lord. The Christian can't really change sides. Once he accepts Jesus as his Savior and Lord, he becomes an eternal member of God's team, but he can stop playing for God. He may be sidelined, or he may play as if he were on the opposition team.

In either case, REMEMBERING how God has blessed him and recognizing that he has stalled out, and claiming the promise of 1 John 1:9 is in order and is his solution. It is the Christian's primary goal to stay in fellowship with the Lord for a maximum amount of time. When he puts himself on the throne of his life, he is out of fellowship. But God is not surprised. He knew this would happen, and that it happens often. There are some folks who claim and believe strongly that once you are a Christian, you cannot sin. That's simply not true. The Book of 1 John was written to new, immature Christians who were being confused by false doctrines that challenged nearly all, if not all, of the central truths of Christianity.

The logic of the false teachers can seem right and believable, but logic is not the basics of Christianity. Faith is. Secondly, the Book of 1 John was written to believers and is applicable to all Christians. Realize, too, that the Bible is the Mind of Christ. The Bible was not written by man but by the Holy Spirit and is the recorded mind of Christ. 2 Peter 1:21 teaches that truth.

If Christians could not sin, the Apostle John would not have written the following:

1 John 1:8 (TLB)

8 *If we say we have no sin, we are only fooling ourselves and refusing to accept the truth.*

There is nothing in 1 John that gives the slightest inclination it is written to unbelievers. It was written to believers. 1 John 1:9 is one of God's promises to the believer. It is often overlooked but is of paramount importance to the believer. It is God's provision to keep the believer in fellowship. There are no other words or phrases that so readily describe the results of claiming this promise than Stall Recovery. It's the mechanism for changing an improper mental attitude into a proper (right) attitude and regaining a stable attitude by being back in a right relationship with God our heavenly Father.

That's exactly what we do. Believers so easily sin either in thought or through action. When we do, we are immediately out of fellowship with God. The moment we claim the promise of 1 John 1:9, we are immediately back in fellowship with God. It doesn't matter how serious the sin is, humanly speaking. We are immediately in fellowship with God, in His loving arms where we can withstand whatever consequences follow.

The objective is to keep a very short list of sin in our life. Optimally, we should immediately correct our attitude. We should keep the list short, so no callouses can build upon the soul, causing insensitivity. The longer we wait, the longer the list gets, and the harder it becomes to recover from the stall.

Every tool in a carpenter's toolbox is important. None is more important than the other. Each tool has a very specific purpose. A hammer can't be used to cut wood, a saw can't substitute for a pair of pliers, and you can't drive a nail with a plumb line. Some tools will be used more often than others, and so it is with the Operating Assets God has provided for every believer. One of the most important assets is the Stall Recovery.

Technically, implementation of Stall Recovery is a quick, short, and very specific prayer, but it is so important that I have separated it out from the discussion on prayer, our communication asset. They are co-equal in value but different in function.

God has seen this many times before. For our benefit, He has given us detailed accounts of some of them. One thing that makes the Bible so real for me is that the heroes of the faith are not portrayed as perfect men and women. Instead, they are shown with all of their human frailties. King David fell into a familiar trap of doing what he wanted to do without talking to God. He sunk deeper and deeper as he continued to use human viewpoint rather than divine viewpoint and decision making. God tried to get his attention and finally had to send His prophet to open David's eyes. David caused his own disaster, and when he finally realized what he had done, he immediately repented. David's actions had consequences, and if God's judgment seems harsh, but God is Just. He cannot be unfair.

When David repented, he was in a safe place, a place where he could withstand the pain that was a result of his sin. David was able to recover and go on to glorify God. Many of us after many years are unable or unwilling to repent of our sin of dishonoring God.

Remember that David was a man who loved God, and God loved David. As a young man David represented God well, and although David was in mortal danger from a jealous king, he continued to serve the king, always reflecting God's love. God protected David. In God's timing, David became King.

When we think of David and Bathsheba, we think of the sexual immorality story. But that's not the beginning of the story. The Bible is very specific in detailing the specifics of this tragic story so we can know the fullness of it and understand how to prevent it from happening in our lives. This story is a teaching vehicle, so we should be sure to learn all we can.

That God would author, record, and protect the integrity of the Bible through the years should make it even more precious to us. It should have enduring value for us. He also provided the means for it to be printed and produced so you and I can have as many copies of His Story as we want. But even today, there are some who may have only one page of the Bible, and they cherish it. Others don't even have that. Some Christians live in countries that deprive them of openly worshipping God, and they secretly praise God with joyous celebrations after being told about other countries where Christians can openly worship. No one should have to hide when they attend worship services.

I want to retell this well-known story to illustrate how God always gives us an avenue to escape. When we don't take that escape route, callouses or scar tissue will build up on our hearts, as it did on David's heart. Callouses on your heart deaden your sensitivity to God's leadership. It started with just a little thing and moved David further and further from God. If it can happen to David, it can happen and does happen, to us.

2 Samuel 10:17-19 tells us that King David gathered the army of Israel, crossed the Jordan River, and went to Helam where the Arameans had formed their battle lines. The battle began. The Arameans were routed, and David killed 700 charioteers and 40,000 of their foot soldiers. When all the opposing kings saw that they had been defeated by Israel, they made peace with the Israelites and became subject to them. This was a

total victory for David and unconditional surrender of all the kings who had sought to defeat Israel.

We are most vulnerable when we think we are not. David was no exception.

2 Samuel 11:1 (NIV)

> [1] *In the spring at the time when kings go off to war, David sent Joab out with the king's men and the whole Israelite army. They destroyed the Ammonites and besieged Rabbah. But David remained in Jerusalem."*

Notice how specific the Bible is when it tells a story. It was in the spring of the year when kings go out to battle. But David, the king, just back from a glorious victory and confident his army could defeat any opponent, and just as confident of the leadership of his General Joab, David decided he didn't need to go to war. He could just "sleep in," and cool it for a while. He didn't want to go to war; he wanted to stay home, so he did. At that moment David was out of God's will. He should have been leading his army. He wasn't doing what he was chosen to do. He wasn't where he was supposed to be. The moment he decided not to go to work, he was out of fellowship with God and out of God's geographical will for his life. So God, as He is always faithful to do, will reach out to David with a gentle reminder as He tries to get David back in his place of safety.

2 Samuel 11:2 (NIV)

> [2] *One evening David got up from his bed walked around on the roof of the place. From the roof, he saw a woman bathing. The woman was very beautiful.*

David wasn't even running the affairs of state, and there was no urgent state business that needed to be addressed. One evening, the Bible says, he arose from his couch, (what a sleep-in) went upstairs, and saw a beautiful woman. Since the Bible says she was beautiful, she was drop-dead gorgeous. So what? David had at least six wives and ten concubines. These were political marriages. These particular wives may have been beautiful or maybe not. We just don't know, but every woman has her own beauty. The concubines were for pleasure, so they would have been beautiful and trained in the art of sensuality; therefore, this beautiful woman, Bathsheba, should have been a wake-up call for David. A better reaction from David would have been, "Thank you, Lord, for helping me realize that I am out of place." He should have then strapped on his armor and gone as fast as he could to the battlefield.

I know a man who says this really works. As he tells it, in his youth, he was very attracted to looking at beautiful women as they went their way in the downtown area where he worked. He felt drawn to just about all of them, in his mind anyway. He couldn't stop lusting after them, so he asked God to plant a new thought in his mind every time that happened. From that day onward, every time he saw a beautiful woman it triggered this prayer of thanksgiving: *Thank you, Lord, for reminding me that I have a beautiful wife at home who loves me, and children that think I'm a Super dad.* What had been temptations became reminders of God's blessings.

Now back to David. Instead of recognizing God's warning, the temptation grew, and his desire for Bathsheba was very strong. He was used to getting what he wanted and didn't even recognize the temptation; his "wanter" was malfunctioning. His lustful feelings overtook his ability to reason and resist and to do what was right. Layer upon layer of callouses were building over his mind. Now would be the ideal time to recognize that he had stalled out and was going to crash and burn, but he didn't recognize the problem. He was consumed by what he wanted and didn't recognize the warning. His lust should have reminded him this was not in God's plan and didn't glorify Him in any way. But David failed to listen to that still quiet voice. The calluses were too thick now. I wonder how the story would have been recorded if David had acknowledged his problem, said, "Thank you, Lord," grabbed his sword and helmet, and rushed to the battlefield.

2 Samuel 11:3 (NIV)

> 3 *And David sent someone to find out about her. The man said she is Bathsheba, the daughter of Eliam, the wife of Uriah the Hittite.*

To David, at this point, it really didn't matter who she was. It wasn't too late, and God was still trying to get David to snap out of this disobedience. David should have said, "She's married! Thank you, Lord, for your warning me that I'm not where I am supposed to be." Then he should have gotten dressed for battle and headed to the battlefield. His lust should have reminded him, but he was on the throne of his life and failed to listen to that still quiet voice. Now the calluses were thicker.

2 Samuel 11:4 (NIV)

> 4 *Then David sent messengers to get her. She came to him, and he slept with her.*

In those days, she didn't have a choice. When the King summoned, you went. If she had refused him, she probably would have been killed. Once there, if she resisted his advances or acquiesced to save her own life, rape can be added to the sins that are mounting up. But that is not in the story.

Now she had been purifying herself from her monthly uncleanness. Then she went back home.

2 Samuel 11:5 (NIV)

> 5 *And the woman conceived, and sent word to David, saying, "I'm pregnant."*

Oh, this is bad! It's going to be evident to everyone what David has done. But there may be a way out of this mess. Maybe he can escape this embarrassment if he can just get Uriah back home. Hmmm! David was probably thinking he'd be making lemonade out of this sour situation. He may have even thought he'd be a hero. He was scheming. No one will know that I have sinned, and Bathsheba will have cover. Everyone, including Uriah, will think Uriah is the father. Nobody but God, that is, and David was not consulting God. Uriah got a short leave from the battle. He and his wife had several nights together. She would never tell him what David had done, and so Uriah would assume the child is his. What a perfect plan. Everybody wins! There's nothing better than a win-win solution. Isn't it strange how we still worry about how people will see what we have done, and worry about what they will think, without stopping for one second to consider what our Lord will think?

2 Samuel 11:6 (NIV)

> 6 *So David sent word to Joab, "Send me Uriah the Hittite." And Joab sent him to David* 7 *When Uriah came to him, David asked how Joab was doing, how the soldiers were and how the war was going.*

Now David is a hypocrite! He doesn't care how Joab is doing or even how the war is going, but this is his cover for the real reason Uriah is there.

2 Samuel 11:8 (NIV)

> 8 *Then David said to Uriah, "Go down to your house and wash your feet (go inside and relax)." So Uriah went out of the palace, and a gift from the king was sent after him.*

David doesn't make any small talk, but cuts straight to the heart of the matter: go home and enjoy yourself. He even sends a present.

2 Samuel 11:9-11 (NIV)

[9] But Uriah slept at the entrance to the palace with all his master's servants (guards) and did not go down to his house. [10] David was told, "Uriah did not go home." So he asked Uriah, "Haven't you just come from a military campaign? Why didn't you go home?" [11] Uriah said to David, "The ark and Israel and Judah are staying in tents, and my commander Joab and my lord's men are camped in the open country. How could I go to my house to eat and drink and make love to my wife? As surely as you live, I will not do such a thing!"

Is David miserable or what? He should have been shocked back into the reality by such an honorable response and said, "You're right. What am I doing here while the Ark and Israel are on the battlefield? Come on Uriah, let's go." But instead, he is so consumed with deceit, trying to wiggle out of the disaster he created, that now the calluses are continuing to thicken around his mind. Wait, he has yet another trick up his sleeve. He's the king, and nobody can refuse the king, so he decided to invite Uriah to stay for dinner and make him drink until he is so drunk he wouldn't know what he did or didn't do.

2 Samuel 11:12 (NIV)

[12] Then David said to him, "Stay here one more day, and tomorrow I will send you back." So Uriah remained in Jerusalem that day and the next. [13] At David's invitation, he ate and drank with him, and David made him drunk. But in the evening Uriah went out to sleep on his mat among his master's servants; he did not go home.

The cunning craftiness of David trying to deceive Uriah is ineffective again. Still, in a state of near unconsciousness, Uriah spends the night with the guards. He might not know what he did that night, but the guards will know and remember. David was a brilliant man. Doesn't it seem strange that he has no clue that God is still trying to get David to REMEMBER and be honorable again?

The situation is spiraling downward and getting worse the further it goes. It would have been nice if David had the same sense that the rich man's youngest son had when he was reduced to eating the hog slop. Even the prodigal son REMEMBERED that his father's slaves were better off than he was, so he went home to ask his father for forgiveness. But David doesn't. David is so consumed with his situation and trying to solve the problem himself that God is not even in his thoughts.

I've seen situations that were spiraling downward, and no matter what I did it just wouldn't correct the problem. It seemed as though it had a life of its own, and it just had to play itself out. But this is not one of those times. It was always within David's control to recover from this stall, but it's not recorded that he even once thought of God or asked for God's help. Don't we act the same way too? God is just not in our thoughts. We are consumed in our own little world. David thought he was in control, but he would tell us today, "I did it my way, and that was the wrong way, and I should have done it God's way, but the things of God were not on my mind." In David's defense, you may say, "But David didn't have the promise of 1 John 1:9 to rely on." My counter would be, "David wrote Psalm 32:3-4 which tells us how weak he felt when he didn't confess his sin. So the promise was there, and David knew what to do, but wouldn't."

Uriah is a highly valued soldier, but David doesn't hesitate. The calluses are so thick now that David can't think straight. He doesn't realize what's happening and hasn't asked for God's help. All alone in his misery, and knowing that none of his plans have worked, he makes the decision that Uriah must die to protect David's reputation. Knowing that Uriah is an honorable soldier and will not read a dispatch, David will have him deliver his own death warrant.

2 Samuel 11:14 (NIV)

[14] *In the morning David wrote a letter to Joab and sent it with Uriah.*[15] *In it, he wrote, "Put Uriah out in front where the fighting is fiercest. Then withdraw from him so he will be struck down and die."* [16] *So while Joab had the city under siege, he put Uriah at a place where he knew the strongest defenders were.* [17] *When the men of the city came out and fought against Joab, some of the men in David's army fell; moreover, Uriah the Hittite died.*

One might think that when faced with ordering the murder of one of his valiant men, David would snap out of his downward spiral. This should've been yet another wake-up call for David. Remember, David is a man after God's own heart. He's out of fellowship with God now; his heart is hardened from the calluses that he alone has put there. David had a choice to stop this madness, but he just sinks deeper into the pit of sin. Now he's a murderer, and Joab is furious. He has just lost one of his most valiant men, on the orders of the king.

2 Samuel 11:18 (NIV)

[18] *Joab sent David a full account of the battle.* [19] *He instructed the messenger: "When you have finished giving the king this account of the battle,* [20] *the king's anger may flare up, and he may ask you, 'Why did you go so close to the city to fight? Don't you know they would shoot arrows from the wall?* [21] *Who killed Abimelech, son of Jerub Besheth? Didn't a woman drop an upper millstone on him from the wall, so that he died in Thebez? Why did you go so close to the wall?" If he asks you this*

then say to him "Moreover your servant Uriah the Hittite is dead."

Joab knew that David was a brilliant military strategist and that he would, in his right mind, be furious that such a foolish error had been made. So, to protect the messenger and his own reputation, he wanted the king to know this was done to facilitate the instructions to kill Uriah.

2 Samuel 11:22 (NIV)

22 The messenger set out, and when he arrived, he told David everything Joab had sent him to say. 23 The messenger said to David, "The men overpowered us and came out against us in the open, but we drove them back to the entrance of the city gate. 24 Then the archers shot arrows at your servants from the wall and some of the king's men died, moreover, your servant Uriah the Hittite is dead."

The importance of telling the king that Uriah was dead did not escape the messenger. He saw the anger and disgust of his commander. He heard it in his voice. Or, he read the message concealed between the lines of Situation Report. Regardless, he gave a brief account of the battle and went straight to the heart of the message. David's big secret isn't so secret after all.

2 Samuel 11:25 (NIV)

25 David said to the messenger, "Say to Joab: 'Don't let this upset you; the sword devours one as well as another now. Press the attack against the city and destroy it. Say this to encourage Joab.'"

How hypocritical! But at last David has, at a high cost, resolved the problem that he alone had created. He will do the noble thing. He's in the clear now. So, he thinks, but God has seen it all and has tried to get David's attention and warn him, but David hasn't thought one thought about what God wanted. David only thought about what David wanted. David was vulnerable at the beginning of this story and wasn't seeing the events surrounding him with God's eyes nor hearing with God's ears. Wasn't he acting just like we do? Why haven't we learned that we cannot hide from God?

2 Samuel 11:26 (NIV)

> 26 *When Uriah's wife heard that her husband was dead, she mourned for him.* 27 *After the time of mourning was over, David had her brought to his house, and she became his wife and bore him a son. But the thing David had done displeased the LORD.*

And David continued living life normally, just as if nothing had happened. But none of this was normal for David. It was very abnormal. In reality, he was out of fellowship with God, and nothing was going well. Rather than seek the wisdom of God, David continued to react to events as they came up, just as he had gotten into the habit of doing. He had forgotten God. Through this whole story is told in great detail, and there is no mention that David even thought of God, not even once. David's witness was totally neutralized, and he was living a life that imitated the unbeliever. Humanly speaking, he probably did some good things. He married Bathsheba. Maybe that was a noble gesture; however, she was beautiful, so it might not have been as noble as it appears. It was not until Nathan came to David and told him the parable of the poor man with one lamb and the rich man who had many lambs, that David was made to recognize that he had sinned. Immediately he repented in 2 Samuel 12:13.

Notice it was God who initiated the contact, not David, and God initiates the contact with us.

Although David repented and was forgiven, there would be severe consequences for his sin. From God's view, what was David's greatest sin? It wasn't rape, it wasn't adultery, it wasn't scheming to his advantage, or lying, or being a hypocrite, and it wasn't even murder. Those were the result of his greater sin.

2 Samuel 12:10b (NIV)

10b *because you have despised Me.*

2 Samuel 12:14[a] (NIV)

14 *But because by doing this you have made the enemies of the LORD show utter contempt (for My ways) ...*

Strong words, yes, but that was exactly how God saw it. David had not respected God, and that caused his enemies to show utter contempt for God and His ways. Aren't we guilty of the same sin today when we fail to seek God's counsel? As we go through life, aren't we guilty when we fail to stand up for God's principles that are recorded in His Word? Ignorance of His principles are not an excuse, just as ignorance of the law is no excuse for us today. He wrote and protected the integrity of the Bible so that we would learn what and how He thinks, and so we would know and honor His ways.

If someone we know is in a room with us and we ignore him, haven't we disrespected him? It's the same if he ignores you. Hasn't he disrespected you? If you haven't spoken to a friend in months, isn't that disrespectful? Sure, it is.

So, if we go for a day without thinking of God and His ways and what He does, or if we fail to thank the Lord for this or that blessing, haven't we disrespected God? That day stretches to two days and then three, and then four, and God is gone from our consciousness, and we don't even miss Him. Without His presence, what will become of us?

Based on the fact that David and Bathsheba's son was alive when Nathan came to David and died nine days later, David had been out of fellowship for more than nine months. God gave him all that time, enough to come to his senses and repent. When he didn't, God took the initiative.

Remember that when Adam and Eve sinned, God immediately went to them and gave them the opportunity to repent and return to a state of fellowship with Him, but they played the blame game.

Adam's excuse: God, it's your fault. You brought me this woman, and she made me do it.

Eve's excuse: It's the snake's fault, he lied to me.

It's not recorded that they ever asked for forgiveness. The important difference was that when confronted, David immediately recognized his situation. He admitted he had sinned against God by confessing his sin, and as a result was back in fellowship with God. Interestingly, he confessed to sinning against God, not the host of people he had failed and betrayed. Back in fellowship with God, David is in his safe place. Just as it is our safe place. He was in the only place where he would be able to survive the consequences of his sins. He would endure.

David had quit REMEMBERING the many ways God had blessed him, so God reminded him of who was in charge and some of what He had done for David.

2 Samuel 12:7-9 (NIV)

7 Then Nathan said to David, "You are the man! This is what the LORD, the God of Israel, says: I anointed you king over Israel, and I delivered you from the hand of Saul. 8 I gave your master's house to you, and your master's wives into your arms. I

> *gave you all Israel and Judah. And if all this had been too little, I would have given you even more.*
> *9 Why did you despise the word of the LORD by doing what is evil in his eyes? You struck down Uriah the Hittite with the sword and took his wife to be your own. You killed him with the sword of the Ammonites."*

Wouldn't it have saved a lot of grief to be able to see what was happening through the eyes of God? You can! You can see as much as He will allow you to see. When you are in fellowship with God, you will be able to see things as they really are. God desires to have an intimate relationship with you. He wants to fellowship with you continuously. The more you want that same fellowship, the greater that fellowship will be. The better you will be able to see events as God sees them and hear as God hears.

Here's a reality check. What has God done in your life lately?

I can't answer for you. Try as hard as you can, write everything down that you can remember. What has God has done in your life? I guarantee you that your list will be incomplete.

When Solomon, the son of David, ascended to the throne, he was overwhelmed by the task before him. So he went to the Lord with burnt offerings. That's an excellent example for us to follow when we accept the burden of leadership and responsibility. Of course, we don't offer burnt offerings anymore, but we can go to the Lord with a humble spirit asking for guidance with the sure expectation that He will answer our prayers.

2 Chronicles 1:7-12 (NIV)

> *7 That night God appeared to Solomon and said to him, "Ask for whatever you want me to give you."*
> *8 Solomon answered God, "You have shown great*

> *kindness to David, my father and have made me king in his place.* [9] *Now, LORD God, let your promise to my father David be confirmed, for you have made me king over a people who are as numerous as the dust of the earth.* [10] *Give me wisdom and knowledge, that I may lead this people, for who is able to govern this great people of yours?"* [11] *God said to Solomon, "Since this is your heart's desire and you have not asked for wealth, possessions or honor, nor for the death of your enemies, and since you have not asked for a long life but for wisdom and knowledge to govern my people over whom I have made you king,* [12]*, therefore, wisdom and knowledge will be given you. And I will also give you wealth, possessions and honor, such as no king who was before you ever had and none after you will have."*

The Bible indicates that during his reign, Solomon was the richest and wisest man in the world. He had everything, but at some point was out of fellowship with God. Consciously or unconsciously he stopped communicating with God and became unaware of God's presence. He drifted further and further from God, building up calluses on his soul until God was no longer even a thought in his mind. He was in perpetual carnality, imitating the unbeliever. He missed God but didn't know what the problem was. He was in a desperate search for happiness. When a believer forsakes the only true source of happiness, happiness eludes him. Solomon tried to substitute education, then sought self-pleasure of all sorts, then he tried engineering and building. He built just about anything that could be built, even an irrigation system to bring water to Jerusalem. Then he started collecting things. He redecorated the palace, acquired servants, cattle, more gold and silver, jewels, peacocks and apes, men singers women singers, and instrumentalists, trying to find happiness. But it eluded him, and he records this for us.

Ecclesiastes 2:10-14 (NIV)

10 I denied myself nothing my eyes desired; I refused
my heart no pleasure. My heart took delight in all
my labor, and this was the reward for all my toil.
11 Yet when I surveyed all that my hands had done
and what I had toiled to achieve, everything was
meaningless, a chasing after the wind; nothing
was gained under the sun. 12 Then I turned my
thoughts to consider wisdom, and also madness and
folly. What more can the king's successor do than
what has already been done? 13 I saw that wisdom
is better than folly, just as light is better than dark-
ness. 14 The wise have eyes in their heads, while the
fool walks in the darkness.

Solomon could surely say, "Been there, done that, got the t-shirt." When he finally realized there is no substitute for the pleasure of fellowship with the Lord, Solomon was told to write it down—every bit of it—so others will know what it's like to be out of fellowship and to be back in fellowship. He did, and it's the book of Ecclesiastes. He also wrote the book of Proverbs and the Song of Solomon all to give us the benefit of his misadventures and the advice of the wisest man who ever lived.

The common belief among Christians is that we don't know enough to answer questions that we may be asked, and we may embarrass ourselves and God. So we let our witness slide and before long are imitators of the lost. What God wants is our willingness to tell others how we have been changed by Him. Let this book provide the ammunition and knowledge that gives believers the boldness we once had, so we can reload and get back in the battle.

CHAPTER TWENTY

The Trust Factor

Psalms 91:4 (NIV)

4He will cover you with His feathers, and under His wings, you will find refuge: His faithfulness will be your shield and rampart.

Every Christian has trusted Jesus for the most significant thing - salvation. That's the beginning of an amazing life, and we were not supposed to stop there, that is only the beginning. We should trust Him in the everyday difficulties. Do we believe that the Lord has the answer for every adverse situation in life, no matter what it is or how great it is? Yes, He does, and many are found in His Word, the Bible. That's a good reason to study the Bible regularly.

It's certainly not in our nature to want any problems! We would prefer to live a problem free life, but evidently, that's not going to happen. The mistake that so many of us make is that we want an immediate fix for our particular problem. We don't want our boat rocked! If we are in our comfort zone, that's where we want to stay. Don't do anything that takes me out of my comfort zone. If we are out of our comfort zone, we want to get back into it, and we want to really quickly.

It must be in our DNA. We always want a quick, easy solution, but sometimes it seems we will go to any extreme in an attempt to solve our problem before we think to ask our heavenly Father for help. If we had asked Him at the beginning, He may have said: "stand still and watch or wait." The concept of expanding our comfort zone is foreign to us.

You've heard it said before, and maybe you've said to someone who needed to hear it: "God never allows you to be tempted (tested) beyond what you can bear." It's hard to believe when you're the one being tested, but it's true. It's a promise from 1 Corinthians 10:13.

Proverbs 3:5-7 (NIV)
5 *Trust in the LORD with all your heart and lean*
not on your own understanding; 6 *in all your ways*
submit to Him, and He will guide your path.

Psalm 37:3-6 (NIV)
3 *Trust in the LORD and do good; dwell in the*
land and enjoy safe pasture. 4 *Take delight in the*
LORD, and He will give you the desires of your
heart. 5 *Commit your way to the LORD; trust in*
Him, and He will do this: 6 *He will make your righteous reward shine like the dawn, your vindication*
like the noonday sun.

Psalm 55:22 (NIV)
22 *Cast your cares on the LORD, and He will sustain you; He will never let the righteous be shaken.*

Psalm 37:23-24 (NIV)
23 *The LORD makes firm the steps of the one who*
delights in Him; 24 *though he may stumble, he will*
not fall, for the LORD upholds him with His hand.

Matthew 11:27-30 (NIV)

[27] *All things have been committed to Me by my*
Father. No one knows the Son except the Father,
and no one knows the Father except the Son and
those to whom the Son chooses to reveal Him. [28]
Come to Me, all you who are weary and burdened,
and I will give you rest. [29] *Take My yoke upon you*
and learn from Me, for I am gentle and humble in
heart, and you will find rest for your souls. [30] *For*
My yoke is easy, and my burden is light.

1 Peter 5:6-7 (NIV)

[6] *Humble yourselves, therefore, under God's mighty*
hand, that He may lift you up in due time. [7] *Cast*
all your anxiety on Him because He cares for you.

Psalm 68:19 (NIV)

[19] *Praise be to the Lord, to God our Savior, who daily bears our burdens.*

These promises and this lifestyle are available exclusively to believers. When believers find themselves facing a situation that is so hopeless; one where there appears to be no solution, hopefully, they will REMEMBER God's faithfulness during their lives as well as God's written promises. Then they simply go to their place of safety, mentally. They climb up in their heavenly Father's lap, sit back, and turn the battle over to their God and let God resolve the situation.

It makes no difference what or where the battle is: sickness, the death of a loved one, economic loss, attacks on reputation, betrayal by a friend, natural disaster, discouragement, you name it; God wants you to trust Him. Letting go of your struggle and giving it to God like a "hot potato" will demonstrate the believer's faith and trust in Him. Failing to do this, the believer becomes anxious and depressed and acts just like an unbeliever. God is not glorified with this type of response because it appears to the world that God cannot provide for His children, so the world sees no reason to trust God. Failing to trust God deprives God of the joy of providing for us in our time of need.

When a catastrophic crisis occurs, the natural tendency is to do something. The first thing a believer should do is recognize there's a problem, then pray for the wisdom and knowledge to know the appropriate action that should be taken. If the action is to give the problem to God, do it and don't take the problem back. Leave it to Him. It took longer to write that than it will to do. The whole process takes only milliseconds because the believer is trained and prepared to respond. More often, believers are neither trained nor skilled to take action. In this case, believers neither pray nor know what to do. Therefore, they react just like the unbeliever. Or worse, they blame God for allowing the unpleasantness to befall them.

If the situation is beyond your control, don't try to control it. There is no work, no movement involved at all. Turn it over to God and keep on believing and trusting the Lord. Keep on waiting and trusting Him. If nothing seems to be happening, keep waiting and trusting Him until something does happen. If you take back the responsibility for correcting the problem, He can't correct it. The hardest thing for us to do is let it go and let God have it and then to wait for His solution. He has the best solution to solve the problem in a way that will accomplish His purposes.

Sometimes this seems to take too much time; more time than we think it should take so, we are tempted to jump in again. Don't take it back, just keep on trusting God.

Trusting God is merely recognizing that God is God and we are not! It requires that we give the problem/ situation over to God and that we keep on trusting Him for the solution.

This will be, I believe, the hardest concept to explain, but that's okay because it is the hardest to learn and even harder to implement. Believing God and trusting Him in our daily life decisions is living our lives being aware that God wants to, and does, direct us to places of decision for the purpose of blessing us. We please God when we wait on Him. That place may not feel like a place of blessing, but no matter how bad it gets, it will end in a blessing.

Consider Job from the Book of Job. God was pleased with the fellowship He had with Job, but Satan accused Job of loving God only because God had blessed him so abundantly. Job had everything; every day God's blessings were poured out on him and his family. Life could not have been better. Satan was given permission to test Job but was not allowed to kill him. Then in just one day, everything was taken from Job—his crops, his livestock, all of his children, and finally his health. He was so miserable that even his wife advised him to curse God and die.

To their credit, his friends came to minister to him and sat for three days without saying a word. When they spoke, they gave him poor advice which he rightly refused to follow. In those days, just as today, they associated God's blessings with their goodness and their trials as punishment for their evil deeds. But that's not true at all, and Job knew it, so he refused to confess to something that he had not done. The Bible says in Ecclesiastes 1:4-11, "There is nothing new under the sun." The advice of Job's friends stems from a false belief that refuses to die—that God is punishing Job for something that Job has done, even if he didn't know he did it. It wasn't true then, and it isn't true now! When the trials were over, Job's righteousness was validated, and he was rewarded greatly because of his faithfulness.

Our natural response is to respond to what our senses are telling us, and we respond without thinking. Trusting God requires a supernatural response because it involves our supernatural God. We like to live in our comfort zone and getting out of it is hard. Remember, only Peter got out of the boat, and it was only Peter who walked on water. As long as his eyes were on Jesus, Peter did the impossible.

REMEMBER we are called to "live by faith, not my sight." The Biblical foundation is sound, and it has been in plain sight in both the Old and New Testaments. If you'll stick with it, you will see some amazing changes in your life. As you REMEMBER to trust God and keep on trusting Him, you will be amazed as you watch God do the work. God delights in amazing us.

Ephesians 3:20 (NIV)

20 *Now to Him who is able to do immeasurably more than all we ask or imagine, according to His power that is at work within us.*

Faith and fear are always battling to control the Christian's mind. It's all right when we experience fear. In the physical realm a good dose of fear, or respect, or using common sense, is a natural response. However, Christians are more than natural and have the capacity to overcome. Our firemen, policemen, soldiers, and other first responders are trained to ignore the danger and run to the source of danger. Ordinary citizens have been known to put aside their fear and rush to save those who are in danger. They are called heroes. They put love and responsibility first, and in doing so imitated the action of Jesus. Christians are expected to use their discernment to make good decisions. Christians can experience fear, but our faith must overcome the spiritual warfare that produces fear. Our overriding marching orders are to be witnesses for Jesus and to know His ways. Too many times we shrink from those responsibilities because of fear. Jesus does not have a Secret Service Branch of service, but to our discredit, we do try very hard to be invisible Christians.

Faith is doing what God wants us to do whether we want to or not. Faith is doing what God leads us to do even when it doesn't make sense to us. Trusting God when we can't see beyond what we can see equals belief in God. You can count on it—at some point in our Christian walk, we will all be led to a point where we know what God wants us to do even if we can't see or reason how we know it. I think it's one of God's operating principles. We will be brought to a point where we must take that leap of faith and believe God's promises. The sea didn't part before Moses stretched out his hand in faith.

There are many examples in the Bible depicting the results of what happened when God's people were defeated by fear. There are just as many examples when they believed God and overcame their fear as they responded in faith. There are things to see everywhere, but if you're blind, you don't see them. Sound waves are out there to hear, but if you are deaf, you don't hear them. Wonderful smells penetrate the air in flower shops, bakeries, and in your kitchen, but if you 're not in the flower shop, bakery or kitchen, you don't smell them. There are many wonderful tastes to experience, but if your taster is broken (the condition is known as Ageusia) you can't taste them.

Faith is the same way. It's available to everyone, but it has to be activated to be accessed. Everyone accesses faith more than they realize. We reach for the light switch and flip it on, knowing (believing and trusting) that the lights will come on. We do that without having the slightest idea of the physics that are involved to make it happen. We get in our cars, insert the key, and turn the ignition or push the starter button, knowing (believing and trusting) that the engine will spring to life. We move the gear lever from park to drive or reverse knowing (believing and trusting) and even expecting the car to move.

Yet very few of us have an understanding of what makes the car move and can only make feeble attempts to explain every aspect of the actions involved. We don't even know the nomenclature of the many moving parts that engage to achieve the motion that provides the independence we all enjoy so much, but we don't need to know that to use the car. When we do things believing a certain action will occur and it doesn't, we then start diagnosing the problem. Sometimes it's a simple fix, sometimes it's not so simple, but always God is Sovereign and on His throne. He is in control.

The "Trust Factor" is much the same. You don't have to thoroughly and completely understand how it works in order to use it. When it comes to God things, our trust switch should always be turned on, and that should be our default selection. God encourages us with His promises and expects that we let go of the problem or circumstance and relinquish control of it to Him. We are to relax in Jesus, knowing that when He controls our lives, He is completely trustworthy.

Philippians 4:19 (NIV)

19 *And my God will meet all your needs according to the riches of his glory in Christ Jesus.*

When we continually demonstrate that we trust God with the details of our lives, we will be at peace and in a place of rest because we know that God is God and that we are not. We know that His solution is vastly superior to our solution, so we remain in His place of rest, waiting on the Lord to deliver. REMEMBERING His promises and obeying in spite of the consequences—that's the acid proof of our faith. The only part we obey is the part we believe. The failure to REMEMBER the blessings He has already so bountifully given us ensures the failure to enter His rest.

Romans 8:28 (NIV)

[28] *And we know that in all things God works for the good of those who love him, who have been called according to his purpose.*

All things are not good; God never promised that they would experience only the good. In fact, He promised that if we followed Him, there would be hard times. God also promised that we would not face more that we could bare. He also promised that we would always have a comforter living within us. We should always do what 1Thessalonians 5:18 directs us to do.

1 Thessalonians 5:18 (NIV)

[18]*give thanks in all circumstances; for this is God's will for you in Christ Jesus.*

Nothing comes to us that has not been sifted through the fingers of God. When we find ourselves in a storm or if the mountain in front of us seems too high, or too hard to climb, REMEMBER it has been preapproved by God. There can be only one of three possible outcomes:

1. We can seize the opportunity to trust Him.
2. We can forget who we are, and who we belong to. Then we will imitate the unbeliever by reacting to what our senses are telling us. In rough times we gripe, complain, and maybe even blame God for what has happened. In good times, when everything seems to be good, we can just drift away, as we get entangled in the detail of life.
3. If at first, we fail to trust God and begin to act like the unbeliever, we can execute the Stall Recovery technique by claiming the promise of 1 John1:9 and be in the place of complete rest regardless of that's happening all around us.

I went into a stall this morning. I had an early morning dental appointment and got wrapped up in the morning routines. As I pulled into the parking lot I remembered that I had not had a moment of fellowship with God, I sat in the car, and we talked for a while before I went in. The danger was that I could have put that special time aside and forgotten all about God and His plans, for I don't know how long. When we forget to make God a part of our day, we lose the joy of the day and become more vulnerable to Satan's attacks. But this day I was available and quickly recognized two very special appointments that He had arranged. What a great day.

Years ago, when I was transferred back to Atlanta, a much younger couple looked at our home in Birmingham. They really liked everything about the house. There were no negatives in their eyes, and they wanted to make an offer. We were really excited, so much so that we were at rest when they said, "We like your home, and we want to buy it, but we're going home and pray for God's leadership. We're sure God will bless us, but we don't want to be outside His will on this." That was the first time I had seen this principle played out and was pleasantly shocked and at peace with their decision. They called the next morning and said our home was not the one for them. They loved it and wanted it, but God had not given them the peace they needed to proceed. Within two weeks the house was sold for the asking price. It was clear that our home had been reserved for someone else. That lady that bought it has lived there for 42 years. We never heard from the young couple again, but I am confident that they too found the house that God had for them. When you decide to relinquish lordship of your life to your Lord, you will glorify and honor Him and be blessed by Him.

THE TRUST FACTOR ILLUSTRATED

The Israelites had been slaves for hundreds of years (some scholars say over 400 years, and some say just over 200 years). They had for a long time known only hard work. They also knew that no matter what, they could not complain. Complaining always led to more suffering and sometimes death. So why did they complain so much once they were free and on the way to their land of plenty? Every day they experienced God's faithfulness and His provisions for them, yet they had no faith that God would provide. The more they complained, the longer the trip became. It was only because they lacked faith (trust) in God that they could not know peace even as they experienced the Lord's deliverance. That's us today, isn't it? Christians who have a deep faith and are able to remain at rest while they wait upon the Lord have a great peace that most do not understand. However, after this chapter, you should understand and be able to rest in whatever circumstance you find yourself.

We are subject to many barriers in our lives: time, the environment, the economic, social, conversational, political, employer/employee, husbands and wives, parents and child, child and child. How do we overcome them? Can we ignore the barriers, act as if they don't exist, and still be successful transitioning through them? Do we even have to? Can't we just stay in our own little box? Well, yes, we can, but not without consequences. Look at the shape our world is in today. It's apparent that we Christians who have stayed in our boxes, in our very own "comfort zones" are failing to be the salt that preserves or the light that illuminates God's way. Light can shine on the problem, illuminating it. It can also be a warning. It can tell us when to go and when to stop. We have failed to do what we have known to do by not getting out of our boat.

When we fail to trust God, we cannot be at peace with our decision. Joey Hancock once preached a series of sermons entitled "Get Out of the Boat." It is a challenge for us to keep our eyes on Jesus and get out of our places of comfort and step forward in faith when He calls us. As long as we keep our eyes on Him, ignoring the circumstances around us, we are safe. But if we take our eyes off of Him and consider our circumstances, we sink. That's the application we find illustrated below:

> Matthew 14:28-33 (NIV)
> [28] *"Lord, if it's you," Peter replied, "tell me to come to you on the water."* [29] *"Come," He said. Then Peter got down out of the boat, walked on the water and came toward Jesus.*

If you read that quickly, you may miss the miracle. Peter did what no man has ever been able to do: he WALKED ON WATER for as long as he was focused on Jesus. But when he was distracted and took his eyes off Jesus, he saw the storm raging all around him, became afraid, and began to sink. May we learn from this and not be distracted from our Lord's appointments for us. May we keep our eyes steadfastly on Jesus.

> [30] *But when he saw the wind, he was afraid and, beginning to sink, cried out, "Lord, save me"* [31] *Immediately Jesus reached out His hand and caught him. "You of little faith," He said, "Why did you doubt?"* [32] *And when they climbed into the boat, the wind died down.* [33] *Then those who were in the boat worshiped Him, saying, "Truly you are the Son of God."*

Peter "stalled out" and began to sink. Quickly he executed the Stall Recovery technique, cried out, "Lord save me," and immediately, without hesitation, Jesus reached down and grabbed him and brought him to a safe place. Do you think God was surprised or disappointed when Peter took his eyes off of Jesus, became distracted by the waves and wind, and displayed fear? Not at all. God has all knowledge; He is Omniscient. How about Peter? Do you think he was surprised or disappointed?

Jesus said, "You of little faith," which is to say little trust. The wind and waves and storm were very real, but they were under the authority of Jesus and stopped at His command. It is really neat when we are able to dismiss the storms around us and only concentrate on communion with Jesus.

The trust barrier poses a huge problem for every believer because to break the trust barrier we must stop doing and let God take care of the problem. There is no work or planning or effort involved at all – we just believe and keep on trusting the Lord, until something happens. This is an outstanding provision that is available to those who trust Him.

When we are in the grove of fully trusting the Lord, leaning on His everlasting arms and fully believing His promises, we are in a place of joy (inner happiness)! It's a position of strength, and of stability! No matter how difficult the circumstances appear to be, no matter how much pressure is brought to bear, and regardless of how many or what adversities we face, we can have the promise below:

Philippians 4:7 (NIV)

> 7 *the peace of God, which transcends all understanding, will guard your hearts and your minds in Christ Jesus.*

Know that there is a marvelous place or position for everyone who is "in Christ."

Romans 8:1 (NIV)

[1] *Therefore, there is now no condemnation (punishment or even strong disappointment) for those who are in Christ Jesus.*

We can be like Jesus. We have a divine nature. We share life with Christ; it's an everlasting life. His righteousness which is a perfect righteousness has been assigned to us and our sins to Him. His destiny is our destiny. We have been adopted into the family of God we are sons or daughters like He is the Son. We are joint heirs with Jesus. We share His election. We are priests, and Jesus is our High Priest. Our position to God the Father is perfect in Jesus Christ.

According to the Gospel Herald article "Two Parallel Religious Movements" by Taylor G. Bunch, the trip from slavery in Egypt to freedom in the Promised Land should not have taken 40 years. From Egypt to Canaan by the most direct route was only about 250 miles or about a month's journey by foot on an excellent existing road. A few years ago, two men traveled by airplane from the land of Goshen in Egypt to the banks of the Jordon near Jericho in less than two hours.

There were at least four other routes the Israelites could have traveled that were longer and more dangerous, but none should have taken 40 years. The route they endured wasn't a real route but was a way forged by God as the Israelites failed time and time again to see the Lords protection, provision, and love. They failed at every opportunity to appreciate and trust their Lord.

The singing and joy over being freed from the torment of being a slave left them somewhere during the first day's march, probably as they ran out of water. What can we learn from the Bible about what God wants to teach His people? It is pertinent because God is still teaching the same lessons today to His people. Will we learn those lessons any better than the Israelites did?

Genesis 50:24-25 (ESV)

24 And Joseph said to his brothers, "I am about to die, but God will visit you and bring you up out of this land to the land that he swore to Abraham, to Isaac, and to Jacob." 25 Then Joseph made the sons of Israel swear, saying, "God will surely visit you, and you shall carry up my bones from here."

Geneses 50:24-25 Tells us that while Joseph was studying the Scriptures, he learned that God would deliver His people out of Egypt into the Promised Land and he wanted to go with them. Joseph did not want to be left behind so he made the people swear they would not leave him, then he made all the preparations for his death that would insure he would not be forgotten. No one knew when the liberation would come, but he would be ready to go. He would be embalmed as was the custom of the Egyptians and laid to rest in a sarcophagus which is a casket. Extra care was taken so it could easily be extracted from the tomb.

How long does it take to forget a leader of Joseph's status, I don't know? It's been 240 plus years, and we still know who George Washington was and what he did. But a king came to power who didn't know of Joseph, and he was afraid of the Israelites and their great numbers, so he enslaved them. Some scholars say it was perhaps 200 to 300 years later that Moses led the Israelites out of Egypt.

By any count, the children of Israel had been slaves in Egypt for hundreds of years before they were delivered from bondage. Imagine the teaching moments that presented themselves as parents took their children to see Joseph's sarcophagus and would say something like, "Joseph was a super hero for our people. He was a Jew, and he was a ruler of Egypt. While Joseph lived and for many years after his death his people were free and prospered. He believed God's promises and knew that one day they would leave Egypt and go to the land God has promised us. When we do leave Egypt, we must take his sarcophagus with us. I promised my parents that I would not forget, now it's your turn to promise me that you will not forget." Countless times the scene was played out over a period of hundreds of years. Now it was actually happening. As they were leaving Egypt, they gathered an incredible amount of wealth (Exodus 12:36). In their rush, they did not forget Joseph. (Exodus 13:19) Joseph's sarcophagus went with them. Joseph was with them for the entire journey; his final resting place is in a tomb located at the eastern entrance of the valley that separated Mt. Gerzion and Mt. Ebal 300 meters north of Jacob's well. It's on the outskirts of the West Banks city of Nablus, near Tell Balata. That's on the site of Shakmu in the late Bronze Age and later biblical Schechem.

The visual reminder and opportunity to REMEMBER God's faithfulness were in full view of all the people, at all times, as they journeyed to the Promised Land. They had been eyewitnesses to God's mighty deliverance and grace, having passed through the Red Sea. They had seen the destruction of Pharaoh's army as the sea enveloped it. Now Israel has the opportunity to demonstrate for all ages how to respond to adversity. They had followed Moses and Moses had followed the Lord. They had gotten hungry and asked for food, and God delivered. They grew tired of the perfect manna and asked for something else, and God provided in abundance, now there is no water, and it appears they will die from thirst.

What God wanted, was for His people to trust Him. To believe Him and have faith in Him regardless of what they could see, hear, feel or taste. He wanted them to believe the promises He had made and to trust that He would provide. He wanted them to turn to Him in their troubles. The Bible records these events so we can learn God has not changed, what He desires from us is exactly the same thing He has always wanted from His people. He wants us to know His presence, and His promises are more real than anything, and that we can trust and rely on Him regardless of what we could see, hear, feel, or taste. He wants us to believe the promises He has provided for us.

Just as the problem of "no water" touched each and every one of the children of Israel so long ago, we face the same fundamental question today. Will we trust Him? The Holy Spirit used Moses to record their overwhelming problem as well as their reactions.

WE'RE THRUSTY, AND THERE IS NO WATER -- IT'S A TEST Exodus 17:1-45

Exodus 17:1-3 (NIV)

[1] *The whole Israelite community set out from the Desert of Sin, traveling from place to place as the LORD commanded. The Lord was in control. He was in command of the situation and He led them to this specific place where there was no water. They were in God's geographical will when they arrived there.*

They camped at Rephidim, but there was no water
for the people to drink. [2] *So they quarreled with*
Moses and said, "Give us water to drink." Moses
replied, "Why do you quarrel with me? Why do you
put the LORD to the test?" [3] *But the people were*
thirsty for water there, and they grumbled against
Moses. They said, "Why did you bring us up out
of Egypt to make us and our children and livestock
die of thirst?"

Too many of us have heard the evangelists say, "Accept Jesus today, and you will never have problems again." In God's economy, this is entirely true. Our salvation is secure forever and ever. But experimentally, nothing could be further from the truth. In fact, the opposite is more likely the case. As God teaches us, He allows us to be tested for the purpose of validating to us that we have learned what He has taught. He already knows whether or not we will learn the lesson, so it's not for Him. It's for our benefit. His precepts are built one on top of the other. They don't move from the basics to the complex. They are all basic and easy to learn, but sometimes hard to execute especially if we don't REMEMBER who we really are and what God has continually done for us. Then there's Satan, who will attempt anything that God will permit to neutralize our testimony. And he will do his very best to see that it's accomplished.

John 16:33 (NIV)

33 *I have told you these things, so that in Me you may have peace. In this world, you will have trouble. But take heart! I have overcome the world.*

This is the point. When we accept the gift of Jesus Christ, we possess everlasting life. One day we will leave this body which enables us to live on planet earth; exchanging it for a new resurrected body that will permit us to live in the presence of God forever.

We will have troubles in time, but we also have a means of stabilizing, and the means of meeting and facing every problem and every difficulty with peace. Just because we're Christians doesn't mean we are exempt from troubles. In fact, just because we're Christians, we will have more problems than the natural man, and just because we're Christians, we have a supernatural way to deal with them.

When you come to your "trial," will you trust Him? Will you let it go, turn loose, and let God handle it?

God will, in His time, bring every believer to a "trial or test" like He did the children of Israel. God brought two million adults plus children and animals to the wilderness (a desert—dry sand, "testing" location) and their suffering began quickly. God had provided their freedom from Egypt, the destruction of the pursuing Egyptian army, tier leadership, food and everything else, but He didn't make it easy because they needed to learn that they could depend on Him. Now they didn't have any water. He was saying to them, "Will you trust me?" He says the same thing to us today. "Will you trust me?"

Knowing what you now know, do you think your response to your "no water" situation might be something like, "Thank you Lord for giving me this fantastic opportunity to trust You? There's nothing I can do to change the apparent outcome. I'm choosing to look only to You, and I'll wait for Your provision. I'm trusting You for the best solution. I'm simply waiting to see You work, because I remember Your faithfulness in the past, how You have continually blessed me, and I know that You have not abandoned me. REMEMBERING how you have continually blessed me, I'm giving this problem to You and will wait patiently and watch You work."

The chances are that you have never tried this method of problem-solving when you've faced your own "elephant charge" situations. That's why the section on TRUST GOD is so essential. When God brings us to a place of testing, and we fail to REMEMBER all that He has done for us and fail to rest faithfully, believing that He can and will deliver us, we become a carnal believer. Our salvation is secure, but our fellowship with our Creator is broken.

Exodus 17:4-7 (NIV)

4 Then Moses cried out to the LORD, "What am I to do with these people? They are almost ready to stone me." 5The LORD answered Moses, "Go out in front of the people. Take with you some of the elders of Israel and take in your hand the staff with which you struck the Nile, and go. 6 I will stand there before you by the rock at Horeb. Strike the rock, and water will come out of it for the people to drink." So, Moses did this in the sight of the elders of Israel. 7 And he called the place Massah [testing] and Meribah [quarreling] because the Israelites quarreled and because they tested the LORD saying, "Is the LORD among us or not?"

Moses wasn't disheartened by the lack of water and did precisely what he should have done. He when to the Lord. Interesting isn't it that God told him and the leadership team to get in front of the people; in front of the people is the leadership position. If they are in front they can lead; the peoples can see them, they can see unity and dedication, there is no place for back biting, and back room deals, or disagreements, or fear; it also makes them perfect targets for the emotionally angry stone throwers.

Fear had bogged down the 24th Infantry Divisions amphibious assault to take back Leyte Island in the Philippine Islands on Oct. 24, 1944. The defensive fire was so heavy that the 24th was face down on the sandy beach when Colonel Aubrey S. Newman the leading regimental commander, stood up exposing himself to enemy fire and shouted: "Follow Me." Those words became the motto of the 24th Division. That moment of exception leadership is immortalized by the bronze statue named Iron Mike. It stands at the entrance of the Infantry School which includes the premiere airborne and ranger schools at Ft. Benning GA.

When everyone was assembled together, Moses struck the rock once as God had instructed. His obedience demonstrated his trust and faith. Enough water came out of the rock to quench the thirst of two million men, their wives and children, and all of the animals. Can you imagine how much water that was? That's about as much water as Atlanta, Georgia or Seattle Washington needs every day, or one and a half times Charlotte, North Caroline, three times what Columbus, Ohio needs daily, and four times the amount El Paso, Texas needs every day. That's a lot of water! But the children of Israel had failed their test to trust God. Over and over again they had seen the faithfulness of God. He had always supplied their every need, and yet they failed to REMEMBER what He had done and to trust Him. Because of their lack of faith, they would not be able to complete the purposes for their lives of entering and occupying the Promised Land. Instead, they were relegated to wander in the wilderness until that entire generation had passed away. They were the original Dead Men Walking.

THE TRUST FACTOR POSITIVE RESPONSE OF JOSUAH & CALEB

A little over two years after the Israelites triumphantly left Egypt, they were ready to enter the Promised Land. Moses sent 12 spies into Canaan to gather intelligence about the people, land, and buildings so a good plan of attack could be developed. But God had a different plan. It didn't make any difference to God; this was going to be another faith test. God already knew what they would face, and He had promised this land to His people. Therefore, He would deliver it into their hands, if they would trust Him. The question was, would they trust God for what He had promised regardless of what they saw and heard? Ten spies saw too many problems and failed to believe God, so they came back saying, "We can't do it, the people are giants the walls were too well fortified, it will be impossible to take," and they falsified their reports with lies. Joshua and Caleb saw the same things that the ten saw but gave positive reports saying if the Lord delights in us, their fortifications and size will fall before us. Let's go take our land.

Numbers 13:27-33 (NIV)

27 *They gave Moses this account: "We went into*
the land to which you sent us, and it does flow with
milk and honey! Here is its fruit. 28 *But the people*
who live there are powerful, and the cities are for-
tified and very large. We even saw descendants of
Anak there. 29 *The Amalekites live in the Negev;*
the Hittites, Jebusites, and Amorites live in the hill
country; and the Canaanites live near the sea and
along the Jordan." 30 *Then Caleb silenced the people*
before Moses and said, "We should go up and take
possession of the land, for we can certainly do it. 31
But the men who had gone up with him said, "We
can't attack those people; they are stronger than we
are." 32 *And they spread among the Israelites a bad*
report about the land they had explored. They said,
"The land we explored devours those living in it. All
the people we saw there are of great size. 33 *We saw*
the Nephilim there (the descendants of Anak come
from the Nephilim). We seemed like grasshoppers
in our own eyes, and we looked the same to them."

The ten spies did not consider God had led them to this Promised Land. They failed to consider all that God had done to satisfy their needs all the way from Egypt to that location. They failed to acknowledge God's omnipotence or any element of God's essence that had been on display every inch of the way. When they left God out of their evaluation, they were left with their own abilities. Without God, they were probably correct in their assessment of the situation, but they were dead wrong because God was the reason they were there and would have given them the victory. Their human viewpoint made them afraid, and their fear spread through the whole community like wildfire.

FEAR GRIPPED THE PEOPLE, AND THEY FAILED TO TRUST GOD

Numbers 14:1-4 (NIV)

[1] That night all the members of the community raised their voices and wept aloud. [2]All the Israelites grumbled against Moses and Aaron, and the whole assembly said to them, "If only we had died in Egypt! Or in this wilderness! [3] Why is the LORD bringing us to this land only to let us fall by the sword? Our wives and children will be taken as plunder. Wouldn't it be better for us to go back to Egypt?" [4] And they said to each other, "We should choose a leader and go back to Egypt."

The whole congregation experienced a complete breakdown of trust in their leadership and their Deliverer. They were in a mob mentality as their negative volition toward God took control of their emotions. Emotional people out of control become hysterical. As a mob, they lose the restraints of their individual traits of norms and standards. Their character and the essence of themselves are given over to raw emotions. In this case, the people are letting their emotions revolt unchecked and showing the anger that has been stuffed down and held in check for some time. They certainly are not REMEMBERING the faithfulness of God to supply their every need. Now we see the true nature of the people.

Numbers 14:5-9 (NIV)

[5] Then Moses and Aaron fell face down in front of the whole Israelite assembly gathered there. [6] Joshua son of Nun and Caleb son of Jephunneh, who were among those who had explored the land, tore their clothes [7]and said to the entire Israelite assembly,

"The land we passed through and explored is exceedingly good. [8] If the LORD is pleased with us, he will lead us into that land, a land flowing with milk and honey, and will give it to us. [9] Only do not rebel against the LORD. And do not be afraid of the people of the land, because we will devour them. Their protection is gone, but the LORD is with us. Do not be afraid of them."

Joshua and Caleb reminded the people that they are God's people and that their God is able to deliver to them what He had promised He would do. They speak to us down through time and remind us of the same things. God is able and will do what He has promised. Don't be afraid of what you see. Step out in faith to take what He has promised you. It is yours. When they were reminded who they were and what God is capable of, what did they do?

Numbers 14:10 (NIV)

[10] But the whole assembly talked about stoning them. Then the glory of the LORD appeared at the tent of meeting to all the Israelites.

The people revolted against Moses, Joshua, and Caleb, rejecting their leadership, and would have stoned them to death if the Lord had not intervened in a supernatural way. God saw their actions as a rejection of Him and of disbelief. That's precisely what it was, and that is what it is when we fail to trust Him.

Numbers 14:11-33 (NIV)

[11] The LORD said to Moses, "How long will these people treat Me with contempt? How long will they refuse to believe in Me, in spite of all the signs I have performed among them? [12] I will strike them down with a plague and destroy them, but I will make you into a nation greater and stronger than they." [13]

Moses said to the LORD, "Then the Egyptians will hear about it! By your power, you brought these people up from among them. [14] And they will tell the inhabitants of this land about it. They have already heard that you, LORD, are with these people and that you, LORD, have been seen face to face, that your cloud stays over them, and that you go before them in a pillar of cloud by day and a pillar of fire by night. [15] If you put all these people to death, leaving none alive, the nations who have heard this report about you will say, [16] 'The LORD was not able to bring these people into the land He promised them on oath, so he slaughtered them in the wilderness. [17] "Now may the Lord's strength be displayed, just as you have declared: [18] 'The LORD is slow to anger, abounding in love and forgiving sin and rebellion. Yet He does not leave the guilty unpunished; He punishes the children for the sin of the parents to the third and fourth generation.' [19] In accordance with your great love, forgive the sin of these people, just as You have pardoned them from the time they left Egypt until now." [20] The LORD replied, "I have forgiven them, as you asked. [21] Nevertheless, as surely as I live and as surely as the glory of the LORD fills the whole earth (the Lord is making a promise that He will not break), [22] not one of those who saw My glory and the signs I performed in Egypt and in the wilderness but who disobeyed Me and tested Me ten times- [23] not one of them will ever see the land I promised on oath to their ancestors. No one who has treated Me with contempt will ever see it. [24] But because My servant Caleb has a different spirit and follows Me wholeheartedly, I will bring him into the land he went to, and his descendants will inherit it.[25] Since the Amalekites and the Canaanites are living in the valleys, turn back tomorrow and set out toward the desert along the route to the Red Sea." [26] *The LORD said to Moses and Aaron:* [27] *"How long will this wicked community grumble against Me? I have heard the complaints of these grumbling Israelites.* [28] *so tell them, As surely as I live, declares the LORD, I will do to you the very thing I heard you say:* [29] *In this wilderness your bodies will fall- every one of you twenty years old or more who was counted in the census and who has grumbled against Me.* [30] *Not one of you will enter the land I swore with uplifted hand to make your home, except Caleb son of Jephunneh and Joshua son of Nun.* [31] *As for your children that you said would be taken as plunder; I will bring them in to enjoy the land you have rejected.* [32] *But as for you, your bodies will fall in this wilderness.* [33] *Your children will be shepherds here for forty years, suffering for your unfaithfulness, until the last of your bodies lies in the wilderness."*

They spied out the land for 40 days. Now they will wander in the wilderness one year for each day. Forty years! It had taken them just over two years to get to the entrance of the Promised Land because of their unbelief, even as God repeatedly proved Himself. None of them thought they had rejected God through unbelief, but all are sentenced to 40 more years of physical and mental exhaustion.

Numbers 14:34-40 (NIV)

[34] *For forty years - one year for each of the forty days you explored the land - you will suffer for your sins and know what it is like to have Me against you.* [35] *I, the LORD, have spoken, and I will surely do these things to this whole wicked community, which has banded together against Me. They will meet their end in this wilderness; here they will die.* [36] *So the men Moses had sent to explore the land, who returned and made the whole community grumble*

> *against Him by spreading a bad report about it.* [37] *these men who were responsible for spreading the bad report about the land were struck down and died of a plague before the LORD.* [38] *Of the men who went to explore the land, only Joshua son of Nun and Caleb son of Jephunneh survived.* [39] *When Moses reported this to all the Israelites, they mourned bitterly.* [40] *Early the next morning they set out for the highest point in the hill country, saying, "Now we are ready to go up to the land the LORD promised. Surely we have sinned!"*

Interesting, isn't it, that the twelve have given their reports and ten of them failed their trust test and died, apparently immediately because of God's dissatisfaction. The people who also failed their trust test saw the consequences of unbelief—God's displeasure and discipline—quickly changed their minds, but it was too late, the test was over for them.

Numbers 14:41-43 (NIV)

> [41] *But Moses said, "Why are you disobeying the LORD's command? This will not succeed!* [42] *Do not go up, because the LORD is not with you. You will be defeated by your enemies,* [43] *for the Amalelcites and the Canaanites will face you there. Because you have turned away from the LORD, he will not be with you and you will fall by the sword."*

Moses instinctively knows the people will fail because he believes God. He tries to warn them, but they are stubborn, prideful people and are still showing their rebellious ways by refusing to listen to their God's appointed leader. Evidently, they now think they are supposed to take their land but without God. God did promise it to them, didn't He? They were going to take what was rightfully theirs, they thought. Or maybe they thought they could earn God's favor once again. They didn't understand that they had never earned God's favor.

They couldn't and neither can we. In their pride, they determined to do their will and call it God's will.

TAKE AWAY # 1. We can never earn God's favor. Whatever good we do must be because we love God not because we think we can influence Him with our works. Our works do not impress God.

TAKE AWAY # 2. When God directs you to do something, do it. Follow His directions of when and how regardless of what your human senses are telling you.

TAKE AWAY #3. Remember the battle is the Lord's; don't get in the way and don't delay.

> Numbers 14:44-45 (NIV)
> 44 *Nevertheless, in their presumption, they went up toward the highest point in the hill country, though neither Moses nor the ark of the LORD's covenant moved from the camp.* 45 *Then the Amalekites and the Canaanites who lived in that hill country came down and attacked them and beat them down all the way to Hormah.*

In spite of the warning from Moses, they insisted on entering the Promised Land and the discipline they faced for unbelief had begun with defeat. The ten spies were right, in a way, they could not take the city. This was to be a gift from God; a gift is freely given not earned. They had insulted God, again. First, they didn't believe Moses warnings. Secondly, they tried to overcome in their own strength. Thirdly, they were headstrong and refused to take Godly advice. They did as they wanted to do regardless of the good advice they had been given. Their attack was more than repulsed – they were routed in battle, they panicked, broke ranks, and ran for their lives. They experienced a total devastating defeat. They tried to go it alone, and in their pride, they were really saying, "We don't need God." They were chased back into the wilderness to wander until everyone 20 years old, and older had died off.

TAKE AWAY # 4. When we Christians operate on our own wisdom, strength, and knowledge, the outcome of our actions will fall well short of our best intentions. God will not be glorified and will be angered by our desire to say, "I Did It My Way."

TAKE AWAY # 5. We Christians can learn a very valuable lesson if we have eyes to see and a mind that is teachable. When a major decision is being thought out, consult your heavenly Father to determine whether it is prudent for you now, and if so, how it should be done.

THE SECOND "NO WATER SITUATION" IT'S THE SAME TEST, AGAIN

NUMBERS 20:1-4

We will face our "no whatever" test, how will we respond?

After that faithless generation had died off, the next generation of Israelites returned to the same place where their fathers failed their "no water" test. They would face the exact same trial. Would this generation, when tested, REMEMBER how God had always provided everything that they needed? Would they REMEMBER what happened when their fathers forgot God's blessings and revolted against Moses and God's leadership? Or would they be like their fathers, and become overwhelmed by their physical senses? Which would be more real to them: what they could see and feel at that moment, or would they REMEMBER God's faithfulness to provide for their needs as they had continually experienced all of their lives? How would they respond? God's grace and provisions are all they had ever known; every need had been provided. Would they REMEMBER God's faithfulness or would they believe only what they could physically see and experience rule their actions? As we grow spiritually, we trust God more and more. If we can see the problem as God sees it, our perspective will change.

This happened over two thousand years ago and is recorded for our benefit. Will we learn from it and benefit from its lesson? We all will face "no water" situations; if not right now, just wait, ones on the way. Will it be no money? Will it be chaos in the streets of your city? Will it be the loss of your mate, your child? Will it be sickness? Will it be a disappointment? Everyone will face problems and tests. Every problem has a purpose just as it did for the Israelites. There is a reason for the test/problem. Will you trust God? God has given us His Word. It contains over 7,000 promises for believers. They are there for us to use whenever we need them. God's character stands behind every one of them. But it is up to us to know them, to write them on our hearts and to REMEMBER them. When we do, they are available to be applied. When God says it, that settles it! When God put them in writing, He wanted us to know and apply them!

1 Peter 1:25a (NIV)

25a *But the word of the Lord endures forever.*

God cannot go back on His Word. We have the promises of the Almighty God; we should make sure that none go unclaimed.

The faith of the Israelites was tested with a "no water" situation; likewise, our faith will be tested through stress and pressure. These tests are for our benefit; we must learn to lean on our heavenly Father and wait for His solution. As we demonstrate our trust in Him to deliver us, we become more mature.

If you're on easy street right now and having a mountaintop experience, Praise God. Even when everything is going well, REMEMBER there are problems even in prosperity. When things are going smoothly, we tend to be proud. Religious thinking is prevalent today in that we still believe as Job's three friends did. God blesses us because we are righteous and He punishes us when we do wrong. Pride can lead us to think we're being blessed by God as a reward or pride may lead us to believe that God had nothing to do with our circumstance. We can fall into the "I did it my way" trap. I've never heard anyone say God is testing me with all these blessings.

Proverbs 16:18 (NIV)
18 *Pride goes before destruction, a haughty spirit before a fall.*

Proverbs 6:16-19 (NIV)
16 *There are six things the LORD hates, seven that are detestable to him:* 17 *haughty eyes, a lying tongue, hands that shed innocent blood,* 18 *a heart that devises wicked schemes, feet that are quick to rush into evil,* 19 *a false witness who pours out lies and a person who stirs up conflict in the community.*

Just around the next curve or just over the knoll in the road may be a test of another kind…one that is not so pleasant.

My best advice is to adopt the Boy Scout motto "Be Prepared" by making it a habit to always REMEMBER how God has blessed you in the past and be aware of how He is blessing you in the present. When the storm strikes, you must know what to do if you're going to survive. So why not read your Bible like the prospector scratches in the ground looking for gold? Pay attention and search for those nuggets of gold that are the promises of our God and do it diligently. When you find one, pick it up or mark it in your Bible, repeat it, committed to memory, and own it, for it belongs to you and it's worth remembering. It's more important to know the promises, really know them down deep in your soul, than to know their addresses so you can find them when you need them.

For instance, it's better to know and REMEMBER "If I confess (agree with God) that I have sinned (name it), He is faithful and just to cleanse me from all unrighteousness (what I'm confessing and even sins I don't realize I've committed)" than to remember it's address is 1 John 1:9. To remember both would be fantastic.

Remember that prosperity doesn't last forever, and adversity is sure to come into our lives at some time. Yet even in suffering and under pressure, we can possess the same joy and the same peace and blessings that we had in prosperity. Continuous faith no matter what the circumstances, reveals the stability and faith surpasses understanding. If we remain stable during adversity, we will be comforted, and those who observe us will want what we have. Then our light will shine like a bolt of lightning in the darkness.

Numbers 20:2-3 (NIV)

> 2 *Now there was no water for the community, and the people gathered in opposition to Moses and Aaron.* 3 *They quarreled with Moses and said, "If only we had died when our brothers fell dead before the LORD!"*

It seems more than reasonable that this generation had been well schooled on what had happened to their father's generation. I believe that we can be assured that Moses and others were teaching this new generation the "no water lessons." How a lack of faith in the face of everything God had done, cost their parent's generation their time in the Promised Land. How their bull-headed self-righteous belief that they could take the "promised land in their own strength without God compounded the problem because so many were killed as they were repealed and rioted. They must have been instructed on how their parent's failure caused them to be in the wilderness rather than the land of plenty. Even so, this is a common complaint. "I wish I were dead," and "no one has had it as rough as I do," and "Lord let me die." Here they go again gripping and complaining, failing to REMEMBER God's provisions. If not corrected they will enter a downward spiral from which they may not be able to recover.

Numbers 20:4-5 (NIV)

> 4 *Why did you bring the LORD's community into this wilderness, that we and our livestock should die here?* 5 *Why did you bring us up out of Egypt to this terrible place? It has no grain or fig s, grapevines or pomegranates. And there is no water to drink!*

This generation has never seen or experienced the things that happened in Egypt. The only thing it knows about Egypt is what their parents and members of the previous generation had told them. They must have been told about the hard times in Egypt, but who wants to remember the hard times. Only in one's mind can those really hard times be less hard than just wandering in the wilderness. Really! They had no cares at all. God was providing everything they needed, even a dietary miracle food supplement. God was always with them. In Egypt their parents were slaves, they worked until the work killed them, and they saw the wealth of the Egyptian's, but that was out of their reach. They didn't even have hope. Now they're blaming Moses for their perceived problems.

Down they go into an ever-tightening spiral. In aviation jargon, it's known as a death spiral. In life, you may have experienced a situation that goes out of control, and nothing you do corrects the problem. The more you do, the worse it gets. It seems to have a life of its own and must run its course before it can be corrected. It appears that the Israelites are in that kind of situation, but it's not true. It wouldn't have taken much, just to start REMEMBERING how God had always taken care of them and then speaking up to remind the others. But that was not to happen, and they really failed their "no water" test just as their fathers had. They should have REMEMBERED God's constant provisions for them and used the command and promise that we have in:

1 Thessalonians 5:18 (NIV)

18*Give thanks in all circumstances; for this is God's will for you in Christ Jesus.*

"Foul," you shout, "they didn't have the New Testament." Okay, but we do, and this is written for us. So here are some Old Testament scriptures that apply. "Foul," you shout again, "they didn't have those either." Maybe that's so, maybe not. The human author of these books is Moses, their leader. It's unlikely that he started writing until he led them out of Egypt, and he was their leader until he died. Therefore, he had to be writing the first five books of the Bible while he was leading them. Even if they didn't have the text, the relationship that Moses had with God should have been an inspiration to the people. Plus, God had provided for these people their entire lives, always supernaturally. They, like we, should always REMEMBER and give thanks to God for His many blessings.

Exodus 15:2 (NIV)

2 *The LORD is my strength and my defense; he has become my salvation. He is my God, and I will praise him, my father's God, and I will exalt him.*

Genesis 14:20 (NIV)

[20] *And praise be to God Most High, who delivered your enemies into your hand*

The congregation knew the story of their parent's failure to trust God at the first "no water" test. One would think that they would recognize that they were being set up for a second chance, but they didn't.

Forty years before, Moses was instructed to strike the rock and when he did enough water sprang from the rock to quince the thirst of about 4 million people and all of their animals. That's a lot of water! That event must have been chronicled in their history for them to REMEMBER, but they were not focused on how God was providing for and protecting them, but they were focused only on what they could see, feel and taste.

Are we any different?

Numbers 20:6-8 (NIV)

[6] *Moses and Aaron went from the assembly to the entrance to the tent of meeting and fell facedown, and the glory of the* LORD *appeared to them.*[7] *The* LORD *said to Moses,* [8] *"Take the staff, and you and your brother Aaron gather the assembly together. Speak to that rock before their eyes, and it will pour out its water. You will bring water out of the rock for the community so they and their livestock can drink."*

The test for this new generation would be the same test their fathers had failed. The place and the rock would be the same, but Moses and Arron had a different set of instructions. They were told to speak to the rock, and it would provide water. In a fit of anger, Moses admonished the people. "Listen you rebels! Must we bring you water from this rock? Then he struck the rock, and no water came, so he hit the rock again, even though Moses and Arron had disobeyed, God delivered the water, that's grace! Then God took them aside and privately told them, they would never enter the promised land. That's a harsh punishment but did they through a pity party? No, they didn't. They took their medicine and continued to serve.

Aaron had long before failed in his leadership responsibilities. While Moses was on the Mount receiving the commandments from God, Aaron gave into the pressure from the people and built a golden calve and even led the people in its worship. He was the leader but subjected himself to the desires of the masses instead of exercising his God-given responsibilities.

Now Moses and Aaron went to the meeting tent to pray in private about what to do. That was good and proper. God answered their prayer with simple, clear instructions, to take the staff, gather all of the people, and speak to the rock; and the promise that when they did the water will pour out. But they didn't follow the instructions, and that failure lead to their disqualification to entering the Promised Land. Just 16 verses later God passes Arron's leadership position to Arron's son Eleazar on Mount Hor for all to see and Arron dies without seeing the promised land. Moses will continue to lead the people right up to the edge of the promised land, he will be allowed to see it but will be denied entry into it.

Caleb and Joshua and the children under the age of 20 years were the only ones from two generations that were allowed to enter the Promised Land, and that was because they continuously lived their lives on positive volition towards God's leadership, having always REMEMBERED God's provisions and blessings in the times of testing.

TAKE AWAY #1: If we don't learn the lesson from our experience that God wants us to learn, He will bring us back to the same place until we have learned it.

TAKE AWAY #2: It's not to our advantage to move forward unprepared and unequipped.

TAKE AWAY #3: It's wise to ask for and follow God's leadership in all things.

The human author of Hebrews, probably Paul, gives the New Testament believers the application of the Old Testament verses.

> Hebrews 3:11 NIV—Warning Against Unbelief
> [7] *So, as the Holy Spirit says: "Today, if you hear His voice,* [8] *do not harden your hearts as you did in the rebellion, during the time of testing in the wilderness,* [9] *where your ancestors tested and tried Me, though for forty years they saw what I did.* [10] *That is why I was angry with that generation; I said, 'Their hearts are always going astray, and they have not known My ways.'* [11] *So I declared on oath in My anger, 'They shall never enter my rest.'"*

"Today" is in the continuous tense, which means it is just as pertinent today as it was the day it was written. Konia Greek, the language of the New Testament, can isolate a word and perpetuate forever. "Today" is structured to convey that thought, as in "If you hear His voice ..." His voice is in the Bible. It's the commands, the promises, the parables, and the historical accounts of events that are recorded for our benefit.

He tells us:

Hebrews 3:8-10 Paraphrased

[8]*Do not harden your hearts (become angry with God) when adversity faces you. Learn from the past and learn from these Israelites. If you don't trust Me, after all, I've done for you I will be very angry, and you will not enter my rest.*

Isaiah 41:10 (NIV)

[10]So do *not fear, for I am with you; do not be dismayed, for I am your God. I will strengthen you and help you; I will uphold you with my righteous right hand.*

Today we would say learn from those who have gone before you, don't make the same mistakes. Trust me in this. Learn from the past or be doomed to repeat it. Those who don't learn from the past are bound to make the same mistakes. Will you hear Him when He speaks to you?

F.E.A.R. is False Evidence Appearing Real!!!!

365 times the Bible tells us to fear not. Do not be afraid.

The secular world declares that reality is determined by one of two basic systems of human perception:

1. Rationalism is perception through reason and deductive thought. That is being able to come to a decision, and that we are born with innate ideas. Rationalism also includes perception through emotions.
2. Empiricism is perception through the senses, touch, sight, smell, feel, and taste. Perception is through experience, and there are no innate ideas.

Actually, there is a third system of Perception.

3. Faith—The evidence of things unseen. Faith is the exclusive gateway to spiritual matters.

What is more real to you? Are your emotions and reason more real than what the Bible says? Is what you perceive through your physical senses more real than what you perceive through faith? If so, you have really missed the boat. What the Bible says about any subject is actually more real than what we can sense through our senses, or our feelings, or our emotions, or our ability to reason it out.

Here are a few more personal promises to those who choose to trust God when the elephant charges.

Proverbs 3:5 (AKJV)
5*Trust in the Lord with all your heart: and lean not unto your own understanding. In all your ways acknowledge Him, and He will direct your paths."*

Psalm 37:4 (KJV)
4*Delight yourself also in the Lord; and He will give you the desires of your heart. Commit your way unto the Lord, trust also in Him; and He shall bring it to pass.*

1 Peter 5:7 (KJV)
7*Casting all your care upon Him, for He cares for you.*

Hebrews 3:8 (NIV)
8*Do not harden your hearts as you did in the rebellion, during the time of testing in the wilderness.*

Psalm 55:22 (KJV)
22*Cast your burden upon the Lord, and He will sustain you; He will never suffer the righteous to be moved.*

God, through His Word in the third chapter of Hebrews, is saying to us, that in the past God gave His people promises, then He demonstrated His faithfulness, then He put them in a place of and time of testing, and said, "Will you trust Me, or won't you?" They failed. God is saying to us today, "Are you going to fail like they did, or are you going to trust me?" You have trusted Me for the most important thing, your salvation; will you trust Me for the everyday needs of your life, will you trust Me when everything seems to be falling apart? Will you trust me for that?

Hear His warning! "Harden NOT your hearts as in the day of the rebellion in the day of testing in the wilderness, when your fathers tested Me, proved Me, and saw My works for 40 years."

It's more than interesting that from God's viewpoint He saw their griping and complaining and unbelief as testing Him. And His patience was tested beyond what He was willing to allow. He is God, and they were not, just as we are not. He is the Sovereign Being of the Universe, and they were His children. They (we) cannot be allowed to show disrespect and a lack of gratitude any more than we can allow our children to show those traits. The sooner we learn that lesson, the more blessed we will be.

Hebrews 3:10 (NIV)

10 *That is why I was angry with that generation; I said, "Their hearts (minds) are always going astray, and they have not known My ways."*

Not only did they fail to trust Him and claim His promises in faith, but the Holy Spirit says, "They didn't even know His ways. After all of those years of proving His faithfulness, they still didn't trust Him."

Hebrews 3:11 (NASB)

11 *I swore (the solemn, divine oath) in my wrath, they shall not enter my rest.*

God is declaring a solemn oath and promise that because that generation did not REMEMBER the many miraculous ways He protected and guided them, and because they failed to REMEMBER His faithfulness in providing their freedom, provisions and the promises He had given all along their journey Caleb and Joshua were the only two of that entire generation that didn't die in the wilderness. This is serious business. The Holy Spirit through the Apostle Paul has written this letter to the Christians of his day but what he says still applies to you and me today. There is a place of peace and safety for us today, but if we don't use it, we'll lose it. We can imitate the unbelievers, or we can have the peace that surpasses all understanding when the elephant charges.

Hebrews 3:12 (NIV)

> [12]*See to it, brothers and sisters, (this includes believers today) that none of you has a sinful, unbelieving heart (it is evil to refuse to believe the promises God has given us) that turns away from the living God" (literally, keep standing off from God, or pushing God away).*

It is possible for people who possess eternal salvation, to standoff from God in time? Who in their right mind wants to intentionally provoke the God of the universe who saved them from the pit of hell? We do it without a second thought. If we are facing a "no water" situation, if it seems nothing is going right, if we're losing control and we're upset, if we're focusing on the problem, we are standing off from God or pushing him away. All the while he is waiting to bless us. But He will not bless us until we trust Him through faith.

Exodus 14:13 (NLT)

> [13] *Don't be afraid. Just stand still and watch the LORD rescue you today…*

Isaiah 40:31 (ESV)
*31 They that wait upon (keep on trusting) the Lord
shall exchange their strength for His strength. They
shall mount up with wings as eagles; they shall run
and not be weary; they shall walk and not faint.*

To wait means to keep trusting every moment. No matter how bad it may look don't stop trusting God.

The strength of the Christian life is to continue to stand still and wait on God.

HIS REST IS AVAILABLE TO US

Hebrews 4:1-7 (NIV)
*1Therefore, since the promise of entering his rest
still stands, let us be careful that none of you be
found to have fallen short of it. 2For we also have
had the good news proclaimed to us, just as they
did; but the message they heard was of no value to
them, because they did not share the faith of those
who obeyed. 3Now we who have believed enter that
rest, just as God has said, "So I declared on oath in
My anger, 'They shall never enter My rest." And
yet his works have been finished since the creation
of the world. 4For somewhere He has spoken about
the seventh day in these words: "On the seventh
day God rested from all His works." 5And again
in the passage above He says, "They shall never
enter My rest." 6Therefore, since it still remains
for some to enter that rest, and since those who for-
merly had the good news proclaimed to them did
not go in because of their disobedience, 7God again
set a certain day, calling it "Today." This he did
when a long time later He spoke through David, as
in the passage already quoted: "Today, if you hear
His voice, do not harden your hearts."*

That's good news! The promise of entering His rest still stands for Christ followers today! God still offers His rest to any Christian who demonstrates his or her faith in God's fidelity. Every aspect of the essence of God is involved in His decision to make this incredible promise of peace available to any Christian who exercises faith when facing the trials of this life. God is the Sovereign power of the universe, and He is Omnipotent. He has the authority to give the protection of His rest and the power to back up His word.

We should live to claim the appropriate promises when our "no whatever" trial occurs. When our economic well-being is threatened, when our health or the health of a loved one is under attack, when we are abandoned or feel that we are all alone, frightened, and vulnerable we need to claim His promises and enter His rest.

Be sure that you benefit from the recorded history of those who failed to REMEMBER God's provisions and failed to act on their faith because of fear. Therefore, they were unable to enter into God's rest. Remember also those who retained their faith in their time of testing and entered God's rest. Let us always be alert to recognize immediately the temptation of unbelief when our test comes. God calls it disobedience when we believers fail to turn to God's promises in our time of testing.

EXAMPLES OF TRUSTING IN GOD

Example #1: Shadrach, Meshach, and Abednego—

Shadrach, Meshach, and Abednego and the fiery furnace is an accurate Biblical account of the faithfulness of these three men. The story has been taught in Churches to our children for as long as I can remember. It was not the first time their faith had been tested, and it would not be the last time, but it is a grand illustration of how the Christian Life should reflect one's faith in God. There was no wringing of hands or worry. They chose to trust God whatever the outcome would be.

Daniel 3:1-30 (NLT)

[1]King Nebuchadnezzar made an image of gold,
ninety feet tall and nine feet wide and set it up
on the plain of Dura in the province of Babylon.
[2]He then sent messages to the high officers, offi-
cials, governors, advisers, treasurers, judges, mag-
istrates, and all the provincial officials to come
to the dedication of the statue he had set up. [3]So
all these officials came and stood before the statue
King Nebuchadnezzar had set up. [4]Then a herald
shouted out, "People of all races and nations and
languages, listen to the king's command!" [5]When
you hear the sound of the horn, flute, zither, lyre,
harp, pipes, and other musical instruments, bow to
the ground to worship King Nebuchadnezzar's gold
statue. [6]Anyone who refuses to obey will immedi-
ately be thrown into a blazing furnace. [7]So at the
sound of the musical instruments, all the people,
whatever their race or nation or language, bowed
to the ground and worshiped the gold statue that
King Nebuchadnezzar had set up. [8]But some of the
astrologers went to the King and informed on the
Jews. [9]They said to King Nebuchadnezzar, "Long
live the king!" [10]You issued a decree requiring all
the people to bow down and worship the gold statue
when they hear the sound of the horn, flute, zither,
lyre, harp, pipes, and other musical instruments.
[11]That decree also states that those who refuse to
obey must be thrown into a blazing furnace. [12]But
there are some Jews – Shadrach, Meshach, and
Abednego – whom you have put in charge of the
province of Babylon. They pay no attention to
you, Your Majesty. They refuse to serve your gods
and do not worship the gold statue you have set

up. 13Then Nebuchadnezzar flew into a rage and ordered that Shadrach, Meshach, and Abednego be brought before him. 14When they were brought in, Nebuchadnezzar said to them, "Is it true, Shadrach, Meshach, and Abednego, that you refuse to serve my gods or to worship the gold statue I have set up? 15. I will give you one more chance to bow down and worship the statue I have made when you hear the sound of the musical instruments. But if you refuse, you will be thrown immediately into the blazing furnace. And then what god will be able to rescue you from my power?"

Nebuchadnezzar was very fond of these young men. They, along with Daniel, were prime examples of his leadership. He had been tricked into decreeing that whoever refused to bow to the statue would be thrown into the fiery furnace. He had spoken and because of pride could not rescind his order, even though he apparently didn't want to execute them. So, he pleads with them and gives them one more chance. This was entirely outside of his nature and unheard of, but he was proud of them. It's astonishing how pride can cause us to do things we really don't want to do. Nebuchadnezzar wants to save face and get the boys off. He wants it both ways, so his grand plan is to give them one more chance to do as he has decreed. That's far more than he would do for anyone else. Their answer astounds him. Not one of them faltered. They were steadfast in their response. They would not bend!

Hebrews 4:16-18 (NIV)

16 Shadrach, Meshach, and Abednego replied, "O Nebuchadnezzar, we do not need to defend ourselves before you. 17 If we are thrown into the blazing furnace, the God whom we serve is able to save us. He will rescue us from your power, Your Majesty. 18 But even if he doesn't, we want to make it clear to you, Your Majesty, that we will never serve your gods or worship the gold statue you have set up."

They were firm in their faith that their God could deliver them from his power and the furnace. They knew that God could, but if He didn't, they chose to be faithful to God, to obey God and refused to put no other god before Him. This was one of His Appointments, and they passed the test by standing tall and trusting their God. They were willing to wait and see God's deliverance. We know the rest of the story, but they didn't. They would not bow even when everything they saw and heard meant they would be burned to death! Outstanding courage, yes, because they believed God more than anything. This was faith in action.

Hebrews 4:19-20 (NIV)

[19]*Nebuchadnezzar was so furious with Shadrach, Meshach, and Abednego that his face became distorted with rage. He commanded that the furnace be heated seven times hotter than usual.* [20] *Then he ordered some of the strongest men of his army to bind Shadrach, Meshach, and Abednego and throw them into the blazing furnace.*

The story points out that the king ordered some of the strongest men in his army to tie them up. He must have thought that they would bolt and try to escape. They would not have struggled at all. It would have been more in their character to march into the furnace on their own at the king's orders, but they were denied that show of faith.

Hebrews 4:21-25 (NIV)

[21]*So they tied them up and threw them into the furnace, fully dressed in their pants, turbans, robes, and other garments.* [22]*And because the king, in his anger, had demanded such a hot fire in the furnace, the flames killed the soldiers as they threw the three*

men in. [23]So Shadrach, Meshach, and Abednego, securely tied, fell into the roaring flames. [24]But suddenly, Nebuchadnezzar jumped up in amazement and exclaimed to his advisers, "Didn't we tie up three men and throw them into the furnace?" They replied, "Yes, Your Majesty, we certainly did."[25]"-Look!" Nebuchadnezzar shouted. "I see four men, unbound, walking around in the fire unharmed! And the fourth looks like the Son of God!"

The fire could not consume them! The fourth man was the revealed member of the Godhead, Jesus the Christ. Scholars argue over how would Nebuchadnezzar know the Son of God or in fact, how would the ancient Jewish scholars know the doctrines of the Son of God? They miss the point. God, the Holy Spirit, was the actual author of the Holy Scriptures, and He knew!

Hebrews 4:26-29 (NIV)

[26]Then Nebuchadnezzar came as close as he could to the door of the flaming furnace and shouted: "Shadrach, Meshach, and Abednego, servants of the Most High God, come out! Come here!" So Shadrach, Meshach, and Abednego stepped out of the fire. [27]Then the high officers, officials, governors, and advisers crowded around them and saw that the fire had not touched them. Not a hair on their heads was singed, and their clothing was not scorched. They didn't even smell of smoke! [28]Then Nebuchadnezzar said, "Praise to the God of Shadrach, Meshach, and Abednego! He sent his angel to rescue his servants who trusted in him. They defied the king's command and were willing to die rather than serve or worship any god except their own God. [29] Therefore, I make this decree: If any people, whatever their race or nation or language, speak a word against the God of Shadrach, Meshach, and Abednego, they will be

torn limb from limb, and their houses will be turned into heaps of rubble. There is no other God who can rescue like this!"

No matter what your circumstance, no matter what your life has been, God can rescue you. He wants it so much that He sent His Son to die for you so that if you will agree with God that you need to be saved and acknowledge that Jesus died for you and defeated death to ascend to heaven and now at God's right hand, you too can be rescued.

Hebrews 4:30 (NIV)

30 *Then the King promoted Shadrach, Meshach, and Abednego to even higher positions in the province of Babylon.*

Example # 2: The Theban Roman Legion

In AD 286, an incredible heroic display of Christian faith occurred in an unlikely setting. An entire Roman Legion was comprised of 6,666 men, every one of them a Christian. Its officers, noncommissioned officers, and enlisted men were all strong born-again believers. Their core beliefs would be tested beyond anything we could imagine today, but some of us are being tested just as severely. They would make history and provide an example of how Christians should respond to tyranny and temptation. Regardless of the probable outcome, they exhibited a marvelous display of the Faith Factor Life. History records that not even one failed his faith test.

This legion was called the Theban Legion because the men were Egyptian Christian Copts who had been recruited from and stationed in Thebes, which is in Upper Egypt. They were good men and good soldiers who, even under arms, did not forget to render to God the things of God and to Caesar the things of Caesar. They served the Emperor and God in an exemplary way until the day came when they had to make a choice to either serve God or serve the world. To a man, each chose to follow what Jesus had done.

The Legion was quartered in the East until Maximinus II Daia ordered them and other Imperial units to march to Gaul and put down an uprising of the Gauls. It was the custom of the Romans to move troops from extreme parts of the empire to avoid the problem of Roman-trained soldiers participating in uprisings to free their native lands.

It's interesting that the people accepted Christianity so rapidly that the Romans had to exercise a series of persecutions in an attempt to suppress the growth of Christianity because it openly defied the divinity of the Emperor. The Roman edict of A.D. 202 decreed that Christian conversion should be stopped at all costs. Citizens were forced to carry at all times a certificate issued by the local authorities testifying that they had offered sacrifices to the Roman gods. Those who refuse to conform were tortured with unprecedented ferocity. Some were beheaded, others were thrown to the lions, and others were burned alive. All were subjected to innovative and veracious torture techniques regardless of age or sex. This reign of terror for the Christian Church was from A.D. 284 - A.D. 305, twenty-one long years. Amazing, isn't it, that today they the Coptic Christians still remain in Egypt and other Eastern countries, yet the Rome Empire is the one that was destroyed?

The area around Thebes had also enjoyed a reputation for it's strong, almost fanatical, Christianity. The first monks in the Christian tradition, known as "The Desert Fathers," contained a majority of Thebans. Theban Christians celebrate many martyrs who had refused to yield their faith during the many persecutions in the first century of the church.

Landing near Rome, The Theban Legion marched through northern Italy, passed through the Alps, and moved across the St. Bernard Pass into Gaul. After the revolt was quelled, they camped near the present-day town of St. Maurice, was named to honor Maurice the Commander of the Theban Legion. This small and ancient Swiss town is on the highway that leads from Geneva to Rome. This town was known in the Roman times as "Aguanum," and was an important communications center. The Theban Legion, under the command of Maurice with his Lieutenants Candid and Exuperius, served Rome well. After the successful completion of their mission, Maximinus II ordered a general sacrifice to the gods of Rome. The whole army was to join; they were also commanded to take the oath of allegiance and swear at the same time to assist in the total annihilation of the Christians in Gaul and destroy any evidence that they had even existed.

Alarmed and dismayed at these orders, every soldier of the Theban Legion absolutely refused either to sacrifice to the Roman gods or to take part in their prescribed action of total and complete annihilation. Their commander sent a letter requesting that the orders be rescinded. This so enraged Maximinus II that he ordered the Legion to be decimated, that is, every tenth man was to be killed by the sword. The names of the 666 soldiers were written on paper and placed in the caps of the centurions; they were destined to perish as examples. Their commitment to Christ was so great that they embraced their comrades, who encouraged them and even envied their fate. The Theban Legion was of great value to Maximinus II, or maybe he was more than a little concerned that they might revolt against him, so he appealed to the survivors to do as he had commanded and to "have no confidence in either their number (now 6,000) nor their weapons." In other words, he implied, *don't think you can fight your way out of my decision.*

The survivors persisted in declaring that they were Christians and again resolutely refused to sacrifice to pagan gods or to take part in the destruction of any sign that Christianity had ever existed in Gaul. Maximinus II became enraged, and the butchery began again; the blood of another 600 was required. This second decimation did not alter the determination of those who remained. The soldiers who remained preserved their fortitude and stood fast to their principles and faith.

At the advice of their officers, they drew up a loyal but brave response to the Emperor.

"Emperor, we are your soldiers but also the soldiers of the true God. We owe you military service and obedience, but we cannot renounce Him who is our Creator and Master, and also yours even though you reject Him. In all things which are not against His law, we most willingly obey you, as we have done hitherto. We readily oppose your enemies whoever they are, but we cannot stain our hands with the blood of innocent people. We had taken an oath to God before we took one to you, you cannot place any confidence in our second oath if we violate the other. You commanded us to execute Christians, behold we are such. We confess God the Father the Creator of all things and His son Jesus Christ, God. We have seen our comrades slain with the sword; we do not weep for them but rather rejoice at their honor. Neither this nor any other provocations have tempted us to revolt. Behold, we have arms in our hands, but we do not resist because we would rather die innocent than live by any sin."

This, it might have been presumed, would have softened the Emperor, but it had the opposite effect. Enraged at their perseverance and unanimity, he commanded that the whole Legion be put to death.

The troops sent to execute this order came to the Thebes Legion, drew their swords and began the slaughter. Even though the Thebans loved life, they chose death over dishonoring their God. They never resisted in any way. Putting aside their weapons, they offered their necks to the executioners.

Neither their numbers nor the strength of their arms tempted them to uphold the justice of their cause by force.

They kept just one thought in their minds—that they were bearing witness to Jesus who was led to death without protest, and who, like a lamb, opened not his mouth; but that now, they themselves, sheep in the Lord's flock, were to be massacred as if by raging wolfs.

When the time came they, although heavily armed and being well trained in the school of the soldier, could have put up a good fight, destroying many of their attackers. But they did not. Every man of them was cut to pieces with swords. All were executed no one tried to escape on 22nd day of September in the year A.D. 286.

I could find no record of how these selfless acts of love, bravery, and devotion to their God affected those who were ordered to be the executioners, or how it affected Maximinus II after the heat-of-the-moment decision had destroyed one of his finest Legions, except that the record of their actions has been preserved through the ages.

Interestingly, one record reveals that 24 years after the Theban Legion was welcomed into heaven, on the very day, the 22nd of September, A.D. 310, Maximinus II was commanded to commit suicide at the orders of Emperor Constantine, his grandson. Another report states that he died a miserable death, blind and suffering in August A.D. 313 in Tarsus.

Constantine was the first Emperor to claim conversion to Christianity. Under Constantine's rule, Christianity and Rome flourished. Later the Roman Empire was torn apart from the inside out because of the rotting decay of greed, and self-indulgence. Rome was defeated because it was corrupt and had lost its moral courage. An elite class developed and stripped away the rights and benefits of being a

Roman citizen. High healthcare costs and an army that was supplemented by mercenaries because the citizens were not required to serve. Justice was corrupted. Sound familiar? The grandeur of Rome that once was had diminished and has never been even close to what it once was.

Example #3: MARTIN LUTHER REFUSES TO RECANT

On October 31, 1517, Martin Luther nailed the "95 Theses" to the door of the Castle Church in Worms, Germany. The doctrine was also sent to a Bishop and an Archbishop to protest "indulgences" being sold by the Catholic Church and some basic doctrines that could not be reconciled to what the Bible said.

Martin Luther was born in 1483, became a Monk in 1505, and earned a doctorate degree in theology in 1512. As an instructor in Bible, he became convinced through the study of the Holy Scriptures that:

- The Bible was and is the sole source of religious authority.
- The church is the body of a believer priests.
- Every believer is a priest (the priesthood of believers).
- Salvation is obtainable only by faith in Jesus as Messiah.
- The church cannot mediate faith.

When the Emperor and the church officials received the "95 Theses," they were outraged and summoned Luther to the Castle Church in Worms to discuss his differences with the church. His trip began April 2, and he arrived on April 26. The Emperor and the church officials expected Luther to recant his theses. A lot of pressure had been focused on him to ensure that would happen. His books were placed on a table in front of him. He was asked if these were his works and if he wanted to recant. Luther knew that if he did not recant he would face excommunication and/or death, so he asked to delay his response until the next morning.

What would you do? That night as you pondered your fight, where would your mind take you?

Luther's response will exemplify the faith that we are instructed to live by. Christians have been challenged to live by faith and not by sight. We have identified this lifestyle as "living by faith." Living by faith is letting go and letting God. As long as we hold on and wrestle with a situation, He will not. When we let go, He can pick it up. In our weakness, His strength is glorified.

Legend has it that Luther meditated on Psalms 46 that night, and what is known as "Martin Luther's Hymn: A Mighty Fortress is our God. He focused on God's power and nature, not on his problem. He was at complete peace, even though (humanly speaking) the circumstances demanded that he be depressed, discouraged, full of regret, full of doubt and self-pity.

The next morning Luther gave his response.

"Unless I am convinced by the Scriptures and plain reason—I do not accept the authority of the Pope's and councils; for they have contradicted each other. My conscience is captive to the word of God. I cannot and will not recant anything, but to go against conscience is neither right nor safe. Here I stand, I cannot do otherwise. God help me. Amen."

Although they wanted to execute him, they couldn't because Luther had a 21-day safe conduct pass, so he was dismissed and not arrested. When Luther and the princes who supported him left Worms, the Emperor imposed an Imperial Act declaring Luther, an outlaw. This meant that he could be killed without the threat of punishment. On the trip home,

Elector Frederick the Wise of Saxton allowed Luther to be kidnapped. This guaranteed Luther's safety and let him disappear. While a fugitive he translated the Bible from Latin into German, the language of the people.

What can we learn from these real-life stories?

- God has a plan and a purpose for your life.
- Life may not be easy, especially for the believer.
- If you are in His plan, you will be protected until the work is completed.
- There is no better place to be than in the center of His will.
- God is God, and we are not, so let go in faith and let God control your fate.

CHAPTER TWENTY-ONE

Prayer Our Communications Provision

"We have to pray if we are going to be God's people."

- David Jeremiah

"You learn to pray by praying."

- Jack Hibbs

It has been said that an army moves on its stomach. That means that a well-fed army has a high degree of morale and is strong, efficient, and effective. Therefore, it advances toward the goal and is not deterred by any distractions the enemy may attempt. The statement has great merit, but good communications are far more critical. The Mechanized Infantry has but one standing order: shoot, move and communicate. All three capabilities are vital to its mission, but communication is the key. When a unit has no communication with its higher command, and its adjacent units it is cut off from its command and support elements; it's on its own and in danger of annihilation or capture. It is useless to its higher command because the maneuver element of its mission can't be used to strengthen the defense or move to exploit the enemy's weakness, or in any way provide the flexibility needed on a rapidly changing battlefield.

For lack of information, the South lost a battle that never should have been fought. General Lee desperately needed the information that Jeb Stuart's Calvary should have provided. Its primary purpose was to be General Lee's eyes and ears but was distracted from its primary function of providing combat intelligence to raiding and skirmish attempts. Stuart had been ordered to protect the right flank of the Army of Northern Virginia but became so detached that Stuart didn't even know where his commander was. By the time he arrived at Gettysburg, the second day of the three-day battle was nearly over. Other officers say that General Stuart was severely reprimanded and ordered to occupy his original position. Poor communications more than anything led to the Battle of Gettysburg. Had General Lee known what General Stuart should have been able to provide (the enemy disbursement of troops and the strength of their position), he would not have engaged, and there would not have been a battle at Gettysburg.

We also become very vulnerable to our arch enemies, our own sin nature, the rulers of the darkness of this world, and spiritual wickedness in high places when we fail to maintain good communications with our Commander-in-Chief, our heavenly Father.

But be not disheartened, for God has a variety of ways He can communicate with His children. He does this through His Word, friends, and family, and He has provided a grace method for us to communicate with Him. Prayer is the Christian's communication system connecting us to our heavenly Father, the Supreme Commander of the Universe.

Prayer is far superior to anything that man has been able to create. Immediately the Christian is in communication with his or her heavenly Father. All we need to do is speak His name, and we are connected.

Even when we are out of fellowship and out of communication, our Father has provided a way for us to reconnect and regain our friendship, and thus be in a position for our prayers to be heard. He really does always answer our prayers, but maybe not always the way we want them answered. His answer can be yes, no, or not now. He may answer our desire, but not our petition. He may answer our petition, but not our desire. What we ask for may not be to our advantage, and our heavenly Father's desire is always about blessing us, even when we are under His discipline.

I remember that every time my Dad took me to the woodshed he would say, "This is going to hurt me more than it will hurt you." I didn't believe that, not even for one second. It didn't seem possible then because he could really provide strong positive motivation to do what was right in a way that I would long remember. But when I became a dad, his actions and motives became abundantly clear, and I discovered that dad was hurting too. Sure, some of what my dad dished out was punitive, but mostly it was meant to correct the path I was on. At its core, it was intended to bless me.

The believer must know how to pray. This cannot be stressed enough. Prayer is the most vital and essential operating asset that the Christian possesses. When the preponderance of our prayers are asking the genie in the bottle for all the stuff we want, we miss the mark. God is not our genie in a bottle.

Prayer is such an essential part of being the Christian God wants us to be, that hundreds of books have been written about it. There are many training aids or methods that have been taught to help us learn how to and remember how to pray. One of my favorites uses the fingers of praying hands as an outline.

The THUMBS are closest to and point to your heart. Pray for those closest to your heart; members of your family and close friends.

The INDEX finger is the pointing finger. Pray for the teachers and instructors that are preparing you and improving your skills and knowledge.

The MIDDLE finger is the predominate finger. Pray for all those who have accepted the responsibility of positions of authority in local, state, and federal government, as well as law enforcement and military service.

The RING finger is the weakest finger. Pray for those in need. The homeless, the hungry, those who have fallen on hard times whether by unfortunate circumstances, or those who have just given up, folded up their wings, and just sat down.

The PINKIE or little finger is the least of all the fingers and represents you. Lastly, pray for your own needs and desires.

BASIC PRINCIPLES OF PRAYER

I. Prayer Is Having A Conversation With Our Heavenly Father

Prayers should be easy. They should be simple. It's nothing more than conversing with our heavenly Father. Let that sink in for just a moment. It's not only talking; it's also listening. So how is it that believers, in general, are so inept? I believe it's because we've never been taught, or never learned how to pray.

When we were younger, we watched and listened to our elders pray. In my youth, their prayers were filled with the thundering language of the King James Bible—words like "thou," "wilt," "thee," "hast," and so on. It was just unnatural speech. I do not for a moment question the sincerity or the effectiveness of those prayers; it just seemed strange for those people to be speaking perfectly good ordinary Southern American one moment, and the next moment to be speaking 16th century English as if it was a special prayer language. There is no unique prayer language. Pray the way you talk.

II. Prayer Is For Believers Only

Of all that I've said, this is the one that will get me in trouble with the worldly, so you can imagine how important it is. If God is not your Father, He has no responsibility to even hear your voice. If you are not a child of God the Father, you can't even gain entrance into the throne room. His children can, however, at any time, run into the throne room, call out "Abba," which means Daddy, climb into His lap, and stay there as long as you want. When we do that, we absolutely delight His heart. If you are not one of His, there is no relationship, and prayer is not a bona fide function.

Proverbs 1:24-32; Micha 3:2-4; John 9:31; Psalms 18:40-41; Zachariah 7:11-13; Isaiah 59:2; Isaiah 1:15; Jeremiah 14:10-12; Jeremiah 11:11-14; Ezekiel 8:15-18; John 1:12

If you are a believer and out of fellowship, in a stall, all He wants to hear from you is the "Stall Recovery technique." You've come to your senses and agreed that you have sinned reconnecting the broken connection.

There is only one exception, and that is the unbeliever's prayer for salvation. That prayer breaks the family barrier, and all of heaven hears it and rejoices. The unbeliever is transformed and becomes a member of God's family. The very moment a lost soul agrees with God that he is a sinner and needs a savior, asks for forgiveness, acknowledges and accepts the gift that Jesus gave on the cross, and turns to God he becomes a child of God. As he speaks, his prayer is immediately heard by the Father. There are no protocols or barriers of any kind.

All prayer is directed to the Father in the name of the Son and the power of The Holy Spirit. We should never direct our prayers or praise to Jesus or to the Holy Spirit.

Hebrews 7:25 says that Jesus is praying for us. Romans 8: 26-27 says that the Holy Spirit is praying for us and helping us pray. Therefore, we should do as they do and pray only to the Father, never to Jesus nor the Holy Spirit.

Matthew 6:9 (NIV)

9 *This, then, is how you should pray: 'Our Father in heaven, hallowed be your name…'*

2 Thessalonians 1:12 (NIV)

12 *We pray this so that the name of our Lord Jesus may be glorified in you, and you in Him, according to the grace of our God and the Lord Jesus Christ.*

Ephesians 6:18 (NIV)

18 *and pray in (the power of) the Spirit on all occasions with all kinds of prayers and requests. With this in mind, be alert and always keep on praying for all of the Lord's people.*

Hebrews 7:25 (NIV)

25 *Therefore he is able to save completely those who come to God through Him because He always lives to intercede for them.*

Romans 8:26-27 (NIV)

26 *In the same way, the Spirit helps us in our weakness. We do not know what we ought to pray for,*

> *but the Spirit Himself intercedes for us through wordless groans. [27] And He who searches our hearts knows the mind of the Spirit because the Spirit intercedes for God's people in accordance with the will of God.*

Long prayers should be reserved for private prayers.

Public prayers are generally for something specific. Pray for that particular thing and that thing only. Matthew 6:7 (NIV) states, "And when you pray, do not keep on babbling like pagans, for they think they will be heard because of their many words."

There are four types of private prayer.

1. Confession

According to Psalm 66:18 (NIV), "If I had cherished sin in my heart, the Lord would not have listened" to be effective, all prayer must begin with confession. By claiming the promise of 1 John1:9 and staying current and up to date, we can master the concept of 1 Thessalonians 5:17, which is "Pray without ceasing." When we are in fellowship with our heavenly Father, our eyes are opened to the many blessing that He sends our way, and we know the true source of them. The more aware we are, the more thankful we are.

When we are not positioned to see God's blessing, we are likely to say we were just lucky. Now I've planted a little reminder in your head. The next time you say, "I was lucky," let that automatically remind you that you were not lucky; you were blessed by one of God's interventions.

2. Thanksgiving

1 Thessalonians 5:18 (NIV)

> [18] *give thanks in all circumstances; for this is God's will for you in Christ Jesus.*

Ephesians 5:20 (NIV)

> [20] *always giving thanks to God the Father for everything, in the name of our Lord Jesus Christ.*

Note we are told to give thanks in ALL things, not just the "good things," but the "bad things" also. It is important to remember the spiritual as well as the material things. So what things are you thankful for right now?

3. Intercession

Intercessory prayer is simply praying for others. "Others" fall in one of two categories; believers and the unbelievers.

Ephesians 6:18 (NIV)

> [18] *And pray in the Spirit on all occasions with all kinds of prayers and requests. With this in mind, be alert and always keep on praying for all of the Lord's people.*

An easy way to accomplish this is to stop everything and pray when prayer is requested. This simple action may shock the person making the request, but you will also see the relief on his or her face. Secondly, make a list of known needs and pray specifically for each person and their need on your list until the prayer is answered. If the list grows too long to pray for each person, divide the list in half or quarters or a specific group on a given day of the week. Pray for your friends every day. Pray for your family members. Pray for missionaries and evangelists. Pray for your pastor.

Matthew 5:44 (NIV)

> [44] *But I tell you, love your enemies and pray for those who persecute you.*

Luke 6:28 (NIV)

[28] *bless those who curse you, pray for those who mistreat you.*

Instead of retaliation, put these matters in the hand of God. Take refuge in His place of rest and let the Lord do the fighting for you. The battle is the Lord's. This is the grace response.

Prayer for the salvation of the lost is usually to bring the lost to a place of God consciousness. Let happen what must in order for the lost to accept His gift of salvation and everlasting life on earth and in heaven.

When you hear a fire truck or ambulance siren shrieking by and realize it's not coming for you, send a prayer to heaven for the victims as well as the rescuers.

4. Petition

Petition is simply praying for our own needs. Although I've listed it last, it isn't necessarily the least important. If we want to bless God's heart, pray for Knowledge (knowing what is true and right and what to do) and wisdom (judgment in action, knowledge plus acute mental discernment and insight, soundness of judgment) for whatever situation we face. Pray that our actions and responses will glorify Him. Ask for His protection. Thank Him for safe travel, and when we return home to find there has been no disaster or vandalism, thank Him. There are many things we can thank Him for, and they are all appropriate.

Inappropriate things to ask for are those things that are already provided. For instance, "Fill me with the Holy Spirit." The moment you became a Christian, you received all of the Holy Spirit that you ever get, none of Him was held back. We may not give Him full access to our being, or we may lock Him off from some areas of our life, but He's all there. When we sin, the Holy Spirit is grieved, but He doesn't leave us. We have 1 John 1:9 to regain the fellowship lost and this prayer is always heard.

There are several reasons why prayers are not heard.

1.) Failure to confess sin—

Psalm 66:18 (NIV)

18 *If I had cherished sin in my heart, the Lord would not have listened.*

2.) Lack of Faith—Mark 11:24; Matthew 21:22; Matthew 18:19
3.) Selfishness—James 4:2,3
4.) Lack of compassion—Proverbs 21:13
5.) Lack of Domestic Tranquility—1 Peter 3:7
6.) Pride—Job 35: 12, 13
7.) Failure to comply with Divine Will—1 John: 5:14
8.) Lack of Obedience—1 John 3:12.
9.) Not being controlled by the Holy Spirit—Ephesians 6:18

God doesn't answer prayer because we deserve or earn it. Prayer is answered because of who and what God is, never because of who and what we are. Prayer is a marvelous grace provision (an essential Operating Asset) provided to the children of God.

Prayer is a powerful asset. It is available for the believer to use. Use it!! Use it often and stay connected. It will rock you!! John 9:31; Micha 3:2-4; Psalms 18:40-41; Isaiah 59:2; Isaiah 1:15; Jeremiah 14:10-12; and 11: 11-14; Proverbs 1:24-28; Zachariah 7:11:13; Ezekiel 8:15-18; John 1:12

The disciples had watched Jesus go off and pray, and they had watched Him do miraculous and supernatural healings and blessings. They had seen and heard Him outwit the Scribes and Pharisees and others who continually tried to trap Him by putting Him in what they thought would be untenable positions, regardless of His answer.

Luke and Matthew both give us an account of the disciples asking Jesus how to pray. Luke 11:1 tells us that one of the disciples asked Jesus to "teach us to pray," and in verse 2 Jesus gives the same prayer that we find in Matthew 6:9-13. This is incorrectly known as "The Lord's Prayer." A better title is "The Disciple's Prayer." Our Lord could not pray this prayer. He had no sins that needed to be forgiven. This is instruction on how to pray, so we will spend some time with our Lord's instructions.

Matthew 6:5 NIV

5 *And when you pray, don't be like the hypocrites, for they love to pray standing in the synagogues and on the street comers to be seen by others. Truly I tell you, they have received their reward in full.*

Prayers that are directed to people's ears are not prayers. They are self-promotion or propaganda or attempts to sell a point of view.

Matthew 6:6a NIV

6 *But when you pray, go into your room, close the door*

This means we should find a quiet, private place where we will not be disturbed or distracted, and we can speak honestly about whatever is on our minds without the fear of hurting someone or equipping others to hurt us. In that quiet, private place we don't have to wear a mask; we can be the authentic persons that we are.

Matthew 6:6b NIV

6b *and pray to your Father, who is unseen. Then your Father, who sees what is done in secret, will reward you.*

We are instructed to direct our prayers to the Father. This is Jesus speaking, and He says to direct your prayers to the Father, not to Jesus, and not to the Holy Spirit. We should never direct our prayers to Jesus or to the Holy Spirit. We glorify Jesus when we do as He says, and we dishonor Him when we direct our prayers to the Holy Spirit or to Him.

Matthew 6:7-8 NIV

> [7] *And when you pray, do not keep on babbling like pagans, for they think they will be heard because of their many words.* [8] *Do not be like them, for your Father knows what you need before you ask him.*

Our prayers should be short and direct. Continual babbling does not impress our Father. Besides, if you forget something and later remember it, you can go right back to the throne room and add another prayer as many times as you wish. Paul tells us to pray without ceasing, and that means to be in a continual state of worship.

Toney Evans defines prayer as, "the earthly ones giving the heavenly permission to supernaturally intervene in earthly happenings."

A good many of us know the "Disciple's Prayer" by heart and can recite it at any given moment, but that is not the intent of Jesus's instruction. It is, in fact, an outline of how we should pray. Dr. John MacArthur says this prayer is a skeleton, and we are to add the flesh to it to make it personal and meaningful.

Matthew 6:9a (NIV)

> [9] *This, then, is how you should pray: Our Father in heaven, hallowed be your name*

Note that "hallowed" means that His name is holy, sacred, blessed, greatly revered or respected.

Matthew 6:10-11 (NIV)

[10] *Your kingdom come (to earth) so that Your will be done, on earth just as it is in heaven.* [11] *Give us today our daily bread*

This means that we acknowledge that He is our provision for everything, even our meals.

Matthew 6:12 (NIV)

[12a] *And forgive us our debts (sins)*

Name those sins. In so doing, we have judged ourselves and are in agreement with God. When we are in agreement, we are back in fellowship.

[12b] *as we also have forgiven our debtors.*

I want to forgive those who do all manner of evil against me and ask God help me do that. If I chose not to forgive them, the Father is not obligated to forgive me.

Matthew 6:13 (NIV)

[13] *And lead us not into temptation (help me be alert to the tempter's ways and to move toward you and away from their snares, traps, and pathways) but deliver (save, protect) us from the evil one."*

Note that some Greek copies add "For the kingdom and the power and the glory belong to you forever and ever. Amen."

Matthew 6:14-15 (NIV)

[14] *For if you forgive other people when they sin against you, your heavenly Father will also forgive you.* [15] *But if you do not forgive others their sins, your Father will not forgive your sins.*

Verse 14 is a promise from the lips of Jesus and is so important that it is stated both positively and negatively so we cannot miss its meaning. As you pray, speak plainly and let your desires be known, but subject them to the Father's will.

Matthew 26:39 (NIV)

39 Going a little farther, he fell with his face to the ground and prayed, "My Father, if it is possible, may this cup be taken from me. Yet not as I will, but as you will."

Jesus models for us another aspect of positive prayer. Pray your heart's desires, open up and ask or say whatever you want, but be sure and subject your desire to His will. Jesus shows us that we should consider those around us who are always watching and listening to see what we will say and how we will react. Therefore, we should always respond and speak in a way that glorifies our heavenly Father.

John 11:38-44 (NIV)

38 Jesus, once more deeply moved, came to the tomb. It was a cave with a stone laid across the entrance.
39 "Take away the stone," he said. "But Lord," said Martha, the sister of the dead man, "by this time there is a bad odor, for he has been there four days."
40 Then Jesus said, "Did I not tell you that if you believe, you will see the glory of God?" 41 So they took away the stone. Then Jesus looked up and said, "Father, I thank you that you have heard me. 42 I knew that you always hear me, but I said this for the benefit of the people standing here, that they may believe that you sent me." 43 When he had said this, Jesus called in a loud voice, "Lazarus, come out!" 44 The dead man came out, his hands and feet wrapped with strips of linen and a cloth around his face. Jesus said to them, "Take off the grave clothes and let him go."

Jesus knew that the Father always hears the prayer of the believer and had heard it even before it had been prayed. The purpose of His prayer and the following miracle was that the people would know that Jesus was sent by God. We are invited—no, *commanded*—to pray for the same reason, so that we may know and believe that Jesus was sent by God the Father. Failure to pray robs us of the privilege of participating in the miracle or may, in the worst case, result in the miracle being lost.

These are only four of the many Operating Assets that God has provided. They all are important, but to me, these four are extremely important if we are to live the life God has directed us to live while we remain on special duty in His service. He has provided a communication system that reaches into His heart; a Stall Recovery promise that restores our lost relationship; and the key to our relationship with Him—the Trust Factor. We have His Love letter that tells His Story.

CHAPTER TWENTY-TWO

HISTORY—His Story

Time has been seamlessly divided into sections of unequal durations to demonstrate how God interacts differently with mankind at different times. Doing so is called the study of Dispensations. It is the study of history before there was time, during all of time, and things to come as foretold in the Bible. Put another way it is the study of "His Story" (history).

Some say time can be divided into three dispensations: 1.) the Gentile Age, 2.) the Jewish Age, and 3.) the Christian Age. Some say there are seven divisions, some say there are nine, still others identify as many as 37 divisions, and each stand firmly by their own definition. It's easy to see why there is some confusion regarding the study of dispensations, so much so that I was strongly urged not to include this chapter. But I'm going to anyway because my studies on the subject cleared up many Biblical mysteries and concerns for me.

It is my intention to provide enough information to help you understand "His Story." So here we go. This study of "His Story" will be divided into six sections of time:

1. Eternity Past,
2. The Gentile Age

3. The Jewish Age
4. The Church Age
5. The One Thousand Year Reign of Christ
6. Eternity Future.

God is eternal. He exists outside of time. He has always and will always exist. God is timeless. His abode has always been a place where time does not exist. There was an era when there was no time – Eternity Past. There will be a time in the future when there is no time – Eternity Future. Time will not end when the earth ceases to exist. The term "time" indicates a beginning and an ending. The complete period called time is bracketed by Eternity Past on its left and Eternity Future on its right. Time will be subdivided into four unequal periods of time. It's important to also note that God, who is outside of time, will intervene in time as He desires. At the same time, God lives in the soul of every believer. He is never so far away as to be called near.

God inserted time into eternity

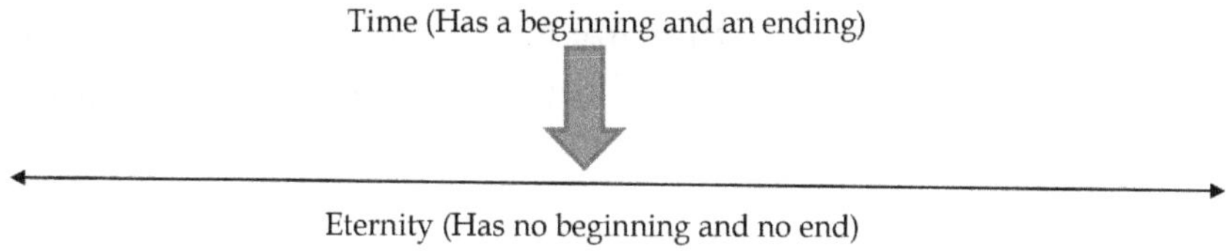

We know very little about the Eternity Past and Eternity Future periods, but we do know some things. In the period called time, we find the history of man and how God has always related to His creation. God has sovereignly chosen to deal with man differently in each category of time, but His truths have been constant throughout history.

Things that we should learn from the study of His story (history) are:

1. This is God's world, and we are stewards charged with its care. The Earth does not belong to us. We can ruin parts of it, but we can't destroy it. Destruction of the earth will only happen as He has preordained it to happen and when its purpose is completed. God has proven that He is very capable of intervening when it pleases Him. Therefore, He would intervene to preserve the prophetic promises He has made regarding any future event.
2. God the Creator gave man the freedom of choice. It's called volition. We can respond positively to Him and His authority, or we can choose to ignore or disobey Him. There will be consequences, good and bad, based on our response.
3. God is the same today, tomorrow, and forever. His promises endure through all ages.
4. God interacts with man differently in each dispensation.
5. How we respond to God's leadership alone determines who we become.
6. Our total existence is not limited to our life time or the life time of the earth.
7. Throughout all of Eternity Past, throughout all of time, and throughout all of Eternity Future, God has and will always be in control.

ETERNITY PAST

THE BEGINNING – There is no beginning date. God has always been. You can draw the timeline as far back into the past as you want, but you won't ever get to a beginning.

THE ENDING – Although Eternity Past didn't have a beginning, it does have an ending, and the ending was the day Adam was created. Some might say that's not right, the end of eternity past was recorded in Genesis 1:1 the first day God created the heavens and the earth, so that should be the beginning of time and the end of Eternity Past. Adam was created on the sixth 24-hour day. That's fine; I won't argue that point. But I chose to start with Adam because he was the first person and time was created for people. God created many things before Genesis 1:1. The Universe and Angels are two. Additionally, the planet, the plants, the ocean, the animals, fish, and birds don't know or care about our timetables. They have their own so, stay with me, okay?

EVENTS & CHARACTERISTICS OF ETERNITY PAST

a. God Rules. God has always existed and has always ruled.
b. Angels were created and serve God. Psalm 148:2-5; Colossians 1:16-17
c. There are three types of Angels: Cherubim, Seraphim, and Archangels. Each has its own purpose and function, but that's the subject of another book.
d. The Universe was created by Jesus, who spoke it into existence. That was the real "Big Bang." Scientists are still trying to discover how and why it happened. We have the answer: God did it and wrote it down in His word so that we would know. God spoke the Earth into existence. Out of nothing He created it. Then He told us how He did it in the first chapter of Genesis and in the book of Job. God's verbal joust with Job over the how's and what's of creation left Job speechless, and he questioned his circumstance no more. Other jewels about creation are sprinkled throughout the Bible.
e. God created the earth.
f. At some point Lucifer, the most beautiful, the most articulate angel and the guardian of the Throne Room, challenged God.

Isaiah 14:12-14 (ASV)

12 *How art thou fallen from heaven, O day-star, son of the morning! How you are cut down to the*

> *ground, you who laid the nations low!* [13] *And you said in your heart, (1) I will ascend into heaven, (2) I will exalt my throne above the stars of God; and (3) I will sit upon the mount of congregation, in the uttermost parts of the north;* [14] *(4) I will ascend above the heights of the clouds; (5) I will make myself like the Most High.*

To help us understand the struggle we face, the Bible has preserved Satan's five "I will" statements that, in effect, threw down the gauntlet to God. It is Satan's manifesto to overthrow God and take over the Kingdom. Satan's coup d'état failed. Satan and the rebellious angels were thrown out of heaven. The final nail was driven into Satan's plans when Jesus defeated spiritual death by living a sinless life and while on the cross with His sacrificial death, and physical death when the grave could not hold Him. The stone was rolled back not to let Jesus out, but to show the world of His day and throughout history that the tomb was empty.

Revelation 12:3-4 (NIV)

> [3] *then another sign appeared in heaven: an enormous red dragon with seven heads and ten horns and seven crowns on its heads.* [4] *Its tail swept a third of the stars out of the sky and flung them to the earth. The dragon stood in front of the woman who was about to give birth so that it might devour her child the moment he was born.*

Satan is the great red dragon. His rebellion is the tail that swept down a third of the stars (angels that believed Satan rather than God and joined in the rebellion) as God's forces consolidated their victory. No one knows how long it took God to put down this rebellion but when the victory was won one-third of all the angels were cast out of heaven. Satan shouts, "Your decision is not fair! Your judgment is too harsh! How could a good God do such a mean-spirited thing? We don't deserve such hash treatment! An undisclosed number of fallen angels ended up on earth. Do you suppose that they could be the celestial aliens that some say came from other planets? They would have been superior to humans in every way. They could have built the pyramids for their own evil purposes. Fast forward into the Jewish Age at the Virgin Birth of the son of God, the dragon stood in front of the woman (Mary) to devour the baby Jesus. It was Satan, through King Herod, who had all the male children two years old or younger slain. But God is on His Throne, and He is in control. An angel was sent to warn Joseph. Joseph chose to believe God rather than anything that he could see or reason. He immediately, without any hesitation, gathered his family, picked up whatever belongings he could and escaped to Egypt. It would have been easy to think the visiting angel was a bad dream, or perhaps blame the dream of bad food. It would have been easy to believe the angel and delay the departure until he could get his affairs in order or be sensible and take time to plan out and equip for the trip. But Joseph was in tune with God and recognized the warning for what it was – and they immediately departed.

THE GENTILE AGE (Genesis 1-11)

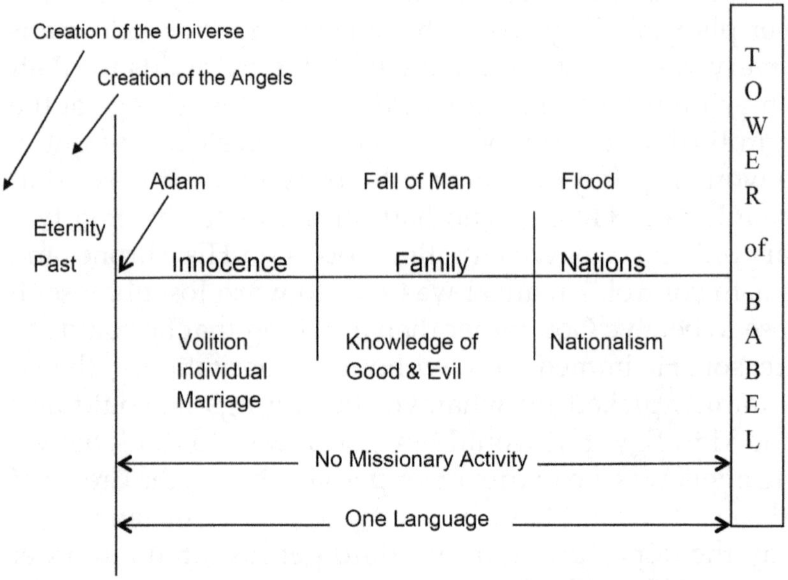

THE BEGINNING—The Gentile Age began when God created Adam.

2. THE END—The Gentile Age ended with the destruction of the first United Nations building the Tower of Babel.

The Gentile Age has been divided into three parts:

A. The Age of Innocence

Adam was given specific instructions by God and followed those instructions perfectly. He operated positively to them (Genesis 1:28-3:22). In Genesis 2:16-17, God introduced volition into the relationship by giving Adam choice.

> *"You may eat freely from any tree, but of the tree of good and evil you shall not eat, for on the day that you eat its fruit you will surely die."*

God had created the angels with volition and man was created a little lower than the angels, but man was also given the gift of volition (choice). He could obey or not obey. He could love or not love; it would be man's choice.

When Adam and Eve did eat the fruit from the tree of good and evil, they did not immediately die physically, so God had not spoken of physical death. They did, however, immediately die spiritually. Their human spirits, which gave them the ability to understand the spiritual phenomenon, resided in their souls but were now dead and shriveled up. They were not functional. A nature to sin, the "sin nature" had been absent in them, and now it indwelled them. They were, for the first time, but not the last time, spiritually separated from God. The consequences were devastating.

The Bible teaches that Adam's "sin nature" is passed down through Adam's seed to all of us. It's interesting that while they were in this state of separation from God, neither Adam nor Eve thought to go looking for God, or even to call out His name. So, God initiated the move and went looking for them. It wasn't that He didn't know where they were or even what they had done, but He simply wanted to re-establish fellowship with them. When fellowship was re-established the "Human Spirit" was reactivated, it was born again. Being the first humans, Adam and Eve were unique. They are not born, they were created; we were born with a major difference. At birth, our "human spirit" is inactive, but our "Sin Nature" is very much active. That's the reverse of the way Adam and Eve were created. Their human spirit was very active, and there was no "Sin Nature."

The good news is that God is still seeking out the lost sheep as he did with Adam and Eve. The power to understand thoroughly the good news of the Gospel message is a gift from the Holy Spirit. It is He who calls the lost to a relationship with God, not we humans. Because it pleases God, He uses man to present the Gospel. All we need to do is be available; He will use us to accomplish His desires. Unbelievers are free to say no to the call, but if we say yes, the "Human Spirit" is permanently activated. Now there is a tug-a-war going on in our minds between the "Human Spirit" and the "Sin Nature."

The Holy Spirit seeks us out though we are covered in sin. Then He entices us into that lifesaving and everlasting relationship. He does this because He loves us and has a purpose for our lives.

B. Age of Knowledge of Good and Evil

Gen. 3:23-8:20 is the Age of Conscience or The Age of Knowledge of Good and Evil. The knowledge of good and evil could not keep humanity from doing evil. It might have restrained the sinful nature of some men if the act would have violated their set of norms and standards. I'm sure you know someone who is humanly good regardless of their relationship with Jesus Christ. Some of the best people in the world are unbelievers. They have a sweet, loving and respectful nature, and some are even trying to earn a relationship with God. Likewise, some of the worst people in the world are believers who are out of fellowship with Jesus Christ. They're like a boat in a storm with a broken anchor chain; they are being violently carried along by the winds and currents. They are so close to being in a safe harbor, but at the same time so close to being smashed against the rocks.

C. The Age of Nationalism

Gen. 8:21-11:32 establishes that God's purpose for nationalism is for the protection of the Gospel. If the whole world were ruled by one evil king, the entire world would suffer because of the absence of the "Good News." Custodial care of the "Good News" has resided in many nations—Israel, Rome, Spain, England, and currently the United States. There are other nations back in history that have had and lost this awesome responsibility, but my purpose is to give you an idea of the use of nationalism, not to provide you with a complete list of nations.

3. Key Events & Characteristics of the Gentile Age

There was a time span of 1,657 years from the creation of Adam until God told Noah to leave the ark and 2,000 years until the Tower of Babel was destroyed.

a. God created Adam in His image and Adam was given dominion over the Earth. Then He created Eve, and His creation was perfect.
b. There was one language - everyone spoke the same language.
c. There was one race, the Gentiles.
d. The foundation for the protection of civilization was laid in early in Genesis: Marriage (Genesis 2:21-25), Family (Genesis 4:1,2), Volition (Genesis 2:16,17), and Nationalism (Genesis 11:8-9). They were attacked almost immediately. The attack on Marriage and Family are explained in Genesis 6:1-4. The attack on Volition is covered in Genesis chapter 3. The attack on Nationalism is in Genesis 11:9. The battle rages today to create a one world society. This is not biblical nor is it good. The Antichrist will try to accomplish it during the tribulation, but it will fail. We will have a one world society only when Jesus Christ sits on the throne during His thousand-year reign on Earth.
e. The fall of man occurred.
f. The first murder occurred when Cain killed his brother Abel.
g. There was no specified missionary agency. Every believer was responsible for sharing the Gospel.
h. Family Priesthood was established in Genesis 13:3 and Job 1:5.
i. The Flood occurred.

j. Salvation was through faith (believing God), not by works. It will be the same throughout all of history.
k. God revealed Himself in dreams, visions, and direct contact. There was no written Word.
l. The people made bricks and began to build the Tower of Babel. Their efforts revealed the same sin that caused Lucifer to revolt against the sovereignty of God—pride!

C. The Jewish Age (Genesis 12 through the Gospels)

Many Languages – One Nation – Specialized Priesthood

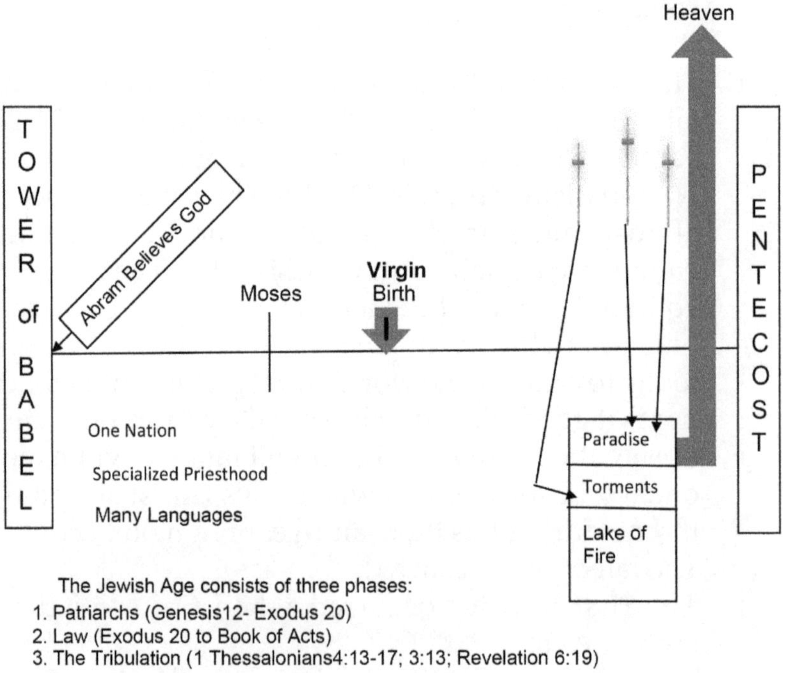

1. THE BEGINNING: The Call of Abram (later known as Abraham)

Genesis 12:1-4

[1] Now the Lord said to Abram, "Go from your country and your kindred and your father's house to the land that I will show you. [2] And I will make of you a great nation, and I will bless you and make your name great so that you will be a blessing. [3] I will bless those who bless you, and him who dishonors you I will curse, and in you, all the families of the earth shall be blessed." [4] So Abram went, as the Lord had told him, and Lot went with him. Abram was seventy-five years old when he departed from Haran.

Genesis 12:1 is God's command. Genesis 12:2-3 are God's promises. Genesis 12:4 records the beginning of The Jewish Age when Abram believed God and gathered up everything and left to go he knew not where. What remarkable faith Abram displayed!

Abram believed in and followed God's leadership. That belief was so strong that he did as God said and it was credited to him for Righteousness. He was a Believer from God's viewpoint. Abram grabbed God's hand and was snatched out of the slave market just as we are today. Abram, who was a gentile, became the first Jew, and he was a believing Jew. His faith saved him. We read in Genesis 17:5 that God renamed Abram, now referring to him as Abraham and promising he would be the father of many nations.

The Jewish Age can be divided into three separate and distinct phases.

A. The AGE OF THE PATRIARCHS: Genesis 12 through Exodus 20 covers the time from Abraham to Moses.

B. The AGE OF THE LAW: Exodus 20 to the Book of Acts covers the time from Moses through the ascension of Jesus.

C. THE TRIBULATION is a time span of seven years. The Jewish Age ends at the Second Advent when Christ returns. He will come as the conquering King that the Israelites have always expected.

2. THE END OF THE JEWISH AGE

The Jewish Age will end when the Messiah comes as the King of Kings and Lord of Lords, defeating all of the world's Armed Forces that are amassed against Israel at the valley of Megiddo. This is known as the battle of Armageddon. The Messiah is the Lord Jesus Christ. The Battle of Armageddon will not be the end of the world as some say, but it will be the final war between human governments and God (Daniel 2:44). The Messiah, Jesus Christ, will obliterate His enemies. Satan will be defeated and will be cast into the abyss for a thousand years.

Key Characteristics of the Jewish Age:

a. There are many languages.
b. There is a Specialized Priesthood (Leviticus; Hebrews 7:5).
c. God created and chose the Jewish Nation to be His people, and has blessed, disciplined, protected, and will continue to protect His special people up to and including the final judgment. Some advocate that the church replaced the Jewish nation, but that claim cannot be validated in the Bible. In fact, the Bible specifically states that the Church is a spliced-in branch, and therefore this understanding is not valid.
d. God used many nations to achieve His purposes, but Israel is His chosen nation.

e. There is a specific missionary agency—the regenerate Jews. Keeping the Law could not save anyone then, and it cannot save anyone now. It is impossible to keep the Law. Its sole purpose was to point to the way to salvation, which was, and still is, to believe God. Salvation is more than just academically knowing about Jesus. It is a grace gift when we believed God as strongly as Abraham did. At the age of 75 and set in his ways, Abraham submitted all that he had and left his comfort zone, to follow God's leadership without knowing where he was going. That's the relationship God wants with us, one that exemplifies total trust, regardless of what others may say or we may tend to think.

f. There were many races of people.

g. Spirituality: The mechanics of confession of sin were given in Leviticus 5:14-19, which explains how a sinner can regain his relationship with God (recognize that you have sinned, confess that sin, name it, ask for forgiveness, and be willing to pay the consequences of that sin). Jesus satisfied our debt with His life's blood and death, purchasing our freedom from sin. Being spirituality means living in faith (Romans 4:17-22; Hebrews 11).

h. Salvation was through faith—believing Jesus Christ rather than doing good works or keeping the Law (Genesis15:6; Galatians 2:16).

i. The virgin birth of Jesus establishes that He is the unique person of the universe. Jesus was fully God and fully human. Jesus could not have an earthly father. He had to be free from the inherited sin nature that any earthly father would've passed on to Him. He could have a human mother. That mother had to be a virgin. That is to say; she could not have had sex with any man. It mattered to God that she be pure. Some scholars say the word virgin could only mean young woman, and that may be so, but they lack the understanding of the importance of Jesus being absolutely clean at birth, and then that He lived a sinless life to be qualified and acceptable as our substitute. Jesus' enemies tried to execute Him, but Jesus died to pay for your sins and mine. God the Father looks at believers and does not see their sins. He only sees Jesus.

j. Jesus died on the cross, not because of the cruelty of the Romans, and they certainly were cruel, but because He willingly died on our behalf. Jesus could have called down legions of angels to save Him from the suffering and the cross, but He didn't because the cross was the purpose of His humanity. In the Old Testament, we learn that the blood of an innocent, spotless lamb was required as payment for sins. Jesus was that lamb in the New Testament. He is the fulfillment of God the Father's plan. One day Jesus will return as the Lion of Judah, but not before the cross. He died first and will return at a time appointed by God. Satan offered Jesus the kingdoms of the world without having to suffer the indignity of the cross. It was a legitimate offer that Jesus rejected for our sakes. When suffering comes our way, we complain.

k. Jesus and the forgiven thief went to Paradise. Jesus was the first fruit—the pathfinder. The saints who had died before Jesus were in paradise waiting for Him to lead them to heaven.

l. The sealed tomb was blasted open by the angels so all could see that Jesus had risen. The soldiers who were eyewitnesses reported exactly what happened. Under normal circumstances, they would have been executed, but they were paid and protected by the religious leaders to say they were asleep.

m. Our adversary, Satan, has had almost 2,000 years to prove the resurrection of Jesus to be a lie. But he can't do it because Jesus' resurrection is true and legally provable. It actually occurred.

1 Corinthians 15:6 states that there were over 500 witnesses who saw Jesus alive after the crucifixion and burial. During the first 40 days after the resurrection, Jesus appeared to 12 groups of people numbering from 1 to 500.

n. The day of Pentecost interrupted the Jewish Age for an undetermined number of years; it was the opening parenthesis to the beginning of the Church Age.

D. THE CHURCH AGE (Acts through the Epistles to Revelation 4)

~The Church Age~

Only God knows how long the Church will last. He is patient, waiting for the last person to accept Jesus as his Lord and Savior.

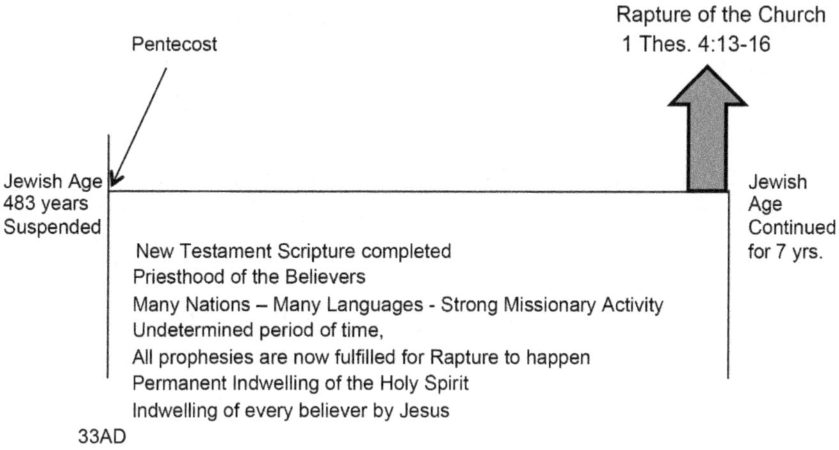

Jesus Christ, the Gospel, and The Church Age are the mysteries spoken of in many Bible verses. It pleases God to allow ordinary humans to participate in the salvation of others. We are positioned to share the Gospel and to be His loving hands and feet. All Christ Followers have been provided a set of Operation Assets, and each of us is divinely and specially gifted to complete our ordained purpose in life. To our human eyes our purpose may seem minuscule or great or anywhere in between, but in God's eyes, we each have a very crucial purpose in His kingdom. The Christian's calling is to always respond positively to His leadership and authority.

THE BEGINNING

The Church Age is a parenthesis inserted into the Jewish Age. It begins at Pentecost. Pentecost means 50 and occurred on the fiftieth day after the Sunday of Passover week (Exodus 34:22). In the New Testament, the Holy Spirit descended upon the Apostles. There was wind, tongues of fire, and people of all nationalities understood in their own language what was being said.

Notice the miracles done for the benefit of the eleven disciples (Acts 2:38; Luke 24:49; Luke 10:20). They are emboldened and gifted by the Holy Spirit. They spoke in their natural language, yet everyone heard what was spoken in their own language. Notice also Peter's bold sermon now that the Holy Spirit is permanently in him. Peter is caught up in the moment and God the Holy Spirit is using Peter's vocabulary and knowledge to deliver God's message to the people.

I know some pastors and teachers who have planned to say and teach one thing, but the Holy Spirit took over and delivered an entirely different and extraordinary message.

The beginning of the church is so spectacular, so unique, and so vital that I have included the complete record as it is recorded in Acts chapter 2.

> Acts 2 (NIV)—The Holy Spirit Comes at Pentecost
> 1 *When the day of Pentecost came, they were all together in one place.* 2 *Suddenly a sound like the blowing of a violent wind came from heaven and filled the whole house where they were sitting.* 3 *They saw*

> *what seemed to be tongues of fire that separated and came to rest on each of them. 4 All of them were filled with the Holy Spirit and began to speak in other tongues (languages) as the Spirit enabled them. 5 Now there were staying in Jerusalem God-fearing Jews from every nation under heaven. 6 When they heard this sound, a crowd came together in bewilderment, because each one heard their own language being spoken. 7 Utterly amazed, they asked: "Aren't all these who are speaking Galileans? 8 Then how is it that each of us hears them in our native language? 9 Parthians, Medes and Elamites; residents of Mesopotamia, Judea and Cappadocia, Pontus and Asia, 10 Phrygia and Pamphylia, Egypt and the parts of Libya near Cyrene; visitors from Rome 11 (both Jews and converts to Judaism); Cretans and Arabs – we hear them declaring the wonders of God in our own tongues!" 12 Amazed and perplexed, they asked one another, "What does this mean?" 13 Some, however, made fun of them and said, "They have had too much wine."*

Peter, who was the only one brave enough during the trials of Jesus to remain close, was also too afraid to acknowledge that he was with Jesus when a small girl identified him. Peter followed the procession to the Place of the Skull – Golgotha. He stood at a safe distance, taking advantage of the crowd and shadows to be anonymous as he watched Jesus being crucified. Peter was so much like the 21st century Christian. But now he is different and filled with the Holy Spirit. Peter addresses the crowd:

> *14 Then Peter stood up with the Eleven, raised his voice and addressed the crowd: "Fellow Jews and all of you who live in Jerusalem, let me explain this to you; listen carefully to what I say. 15 These people are not drunk, as you suppose. It's only nine in*

the morning! [16] No, this is what was spoken by the prophet Joel: [17] "'In the last days, God says, I will pour out my Spirit on all people. Your sons and daughters will prophesy, your young men will see visions, your old men will dream dreams. [18] Even on my servants, both men and women, I will pour out my Spirit in those days, and they will prophesy. [19] I will show wonders in the heavens above and signs on the earth below, blood and fire and billows of smoke. 20 The sun will be turned to darkness and the moon to blood before the coming of the great and glorious day of the Lord. [21] And everyone who calls on the name of the Lord will be saved.' [22] "Fellow Israelites, listen to this: Jesus of Nazareth was a man accredited by God to you by miracles, wonders, and signs, which God did among you through Him, as you yourselves know. [23] This man was handed over to you by God's deliberate plan and foreknowledge; and you, with the help of wicked men, put Him to death by nailing him to the cross. [24] But God raised him from the dead, freeing Him from the agony of death because it was impossible for death to keep its hold on Him. [25] David said about Him: "'I saw the Lord always before me. Because He is at my right hand, I will not be shaken. [26] Therefore my heart is glad, and my tongue rejoices; my body also will rest in hope, [27] because You will not abandon me to the realm of the dead, You will not let Your holy one see decay. [28] You have made known to me the paths of life; You will fill me with joy in your presence.' [29] "Fellow Israelites, I can tell you confidently that the patriarch David died and was buried and his tomb is here to this day. [30] But he was a prophet and knew that God had promised him on oath that he would place one of his descendants on his throne. [31] Seeing what was to come, he spoke of the resurrection of the Messiah, that he was not abandoned to the realm of the dead, nor did his body see decay. [32] *God has raised this Jesus to life, and we are all witnesses of it.* [33] *Exalted to the right hand of God, He has received from the Father the promised Holy Spirit and has poured out what you now see and hear.* [34] *For David did not ascend to heaven, and yet he said, "'The Lord said to my Lord: "Sit at my right hand* [35] *until I make Your enemies a footstool for Your feet."'* [36] *"Therefore let all Israel be assured of this: God has made this Jesus, whom you crucified, both Lord and Messiah."* [37] *When the people heard this, they were cut to the heart and said to Peter and the other apostles, "Brothers, what shall we do?"* [38] *Peter replied, "Repent and be baptized, every one of you, in the name of Jesus Christ for the forgiveness of your sins. And you will receive the gift of the Holy Spirit.* [39] *The promise is for you and your children and for all who are far off – for all whom the Lord our God will call."* [40] *With many other words, he warned them; and he pleaded with them, "Save yourselves from this corrupt generation."* [41] *Those who accepted his message were baptized, and about three thousand were added to their number that day.*

2. THE END

The Church Age will end with the Rapture of the church. This is not the Second Advent. It is not when Messiah Jesus will come and set up His earthly kingdom. Jesus, with a mighty roar, will call His bride to the wedding feast. Jesus will meet His bride, the Church, in the clouds. The world will be left void of believers except for 144,000 Christian Jews, 12,000 from each of the 12 tribes of Israel, and the two witnesses. Their purpose will be to evangelize those who are left behind.

There will be a time when any chance for men to be saved will be cut off, but it's not yet that time. However, today in the Church age, if you are not a believer your time to accept Jesus may be cut off before death, or in God's grace, it may come at death. A natural death would give the lost soul the maximum amount of time to be saved. With so much on the line, no one should delay making that momentous decision to follow Jesus.

At the end event of the Church Age, the Rapture is described in 1 Thessalonians 4:13-18 (NIV). Paul is writing to the Thessalonians to clear up points of doctrine that they had learned. Knowing that the rapture would occur, they were concerned about their friends and family members who had died. Paul writes not only to instruct but to comfort them and us regarding things that are to come:

> 13 *Brothers and sisters, we do not want you to be uninformed about those who sleep in death so that you do not grieve like the rest of mankind, who have no hope.* 14 *We believe that Jesus died and rose again, and so we believe that God will bring with Jesus those who have fallen asleep (died) in Him (believers).* 15 *According to the Lord's word, we tell you that we who are still alive, who are left until the coming of the Lord, will certainly not precede those who have fallen asleep (those who have preceded us in death are not asleep they are with Jesus now).* 16 *For the Lord, himself will come down from heaven, with a loud command, with the voice of the archangel and with the trumpet call of God, and the dead in Christ will rise first (their bodies will be summoned up and miraculously made whole again).*
> 17 *After that, we who are still alive and are left will be caught up together with them in the clouds to meet the Lord in the air. And so we will be with the Lord forever.* 18 *Therefore encourage (comfort) one another with these words.*

This is not the end of the world as some perceive but it is the end of the Church Age. Verse 14 indicates that those Saints who had died before Jesus did not go to heaven but went to a place called Paradise. It was a wonderful place as reported in the story of Lazarus the beggar and the rich man in Luke 16:19-31. Paul says that Jesus went to Paradise and gathered those saints with Him, and then He took them to heaven. Jesus was the first fruit and the pathfinder; no one could enter heaven before Him.

Abraham's Bosom or Paradise was the place that had been prepared for the saints whose death had preceded Jesus. A Heaven like place that they enjoyed as they waited for Jesus to take them to Heaven. It was not Heaven. Paradise is empty now and has no reason or function anymore, so it's doors have been closed, locked, and it is out of business. It no longer exists. When a believer dies, he is immediately in heaven.

Those from the beginning of human history up to and including the present day who remained among the "lost" at death go to a place of suffering called Torments, it's a terrible place of suffering. Hell (the lake of fire) is their final destination after the Great White Throne judgment of Revelation 20:14-15. Revelation 20:10 says that Satan will be chained in the Abyss for 1,000 years. The Abyss is another place of suffering. Released to test the volition of the people he incites a revolt hat God handily destroys and Satan is thrown in to the Lake of Fire forever. Revelation 19:20 tells us that the Beast and the false prophet were cast into the Lake of Fire 1,000 years earlier at the conclusion of the Battle of Armageddon.

No one in their right mind would want to go to Hell, and they don't have to. All they need to do is to acknowledge that Jesus is now Lord of their lives and put Him on the Throne of their lives instead saying, "I'll do it my way."

After the crucifixion of Jesus, when a Christian dies the soul is immediately in "the twinkling of an eye" in God's presence, but the bodies remain buried, cremated or disposed of in some other way. The Holy Spirit through Paul is saying in this passage that the bodies of all who have died before the rapture will be reunited with their souls at the Rapture. Each in his own order, the dead in Christ will rise first, and then those who are alive will rise to meet Jesus in the air. The bodies of the sailors who were buried at sea and have entirely decayed, or soldiers who were mutilated by the ravages of war, or a civilian who has been buried for thousands of years—all will in an instant be put back together not as it was before, but with a new and better body, one suited for life in heaven, not on earth.

Paul says this will be a "parade of the saint's bodies." Notice, in this procession there is order. The Old Testament saints will be first, followed by the New Testament saints. Like divisions of soldiers passing in review, those who have died, each in their own division, and finally those who are alive when the Rapture occurs, will pass in review before their commanding officer, Jesus Christ. They will be caught up, and body and soul will be reunited. Today the body is a life support system that supports life on the planet earth, much like a space suit supports life in outer space, or a deep sea diver wearing a diver's suit to sustain life under the sea's surface. Our bodies will be modified to accommodate a new environment. We will be recognizable, but different. This is not the end of the world. It is the end of the Church Age. The world will continue for seven more years to fulfill the Jewish Age, plus the thousand-year reign of Jesus on earth and before the concluding business of the Great White Throne Judgement of all of the unbelievers.

3. Key Events & Characteristics of the Church Age

Jesus is said to be seated at the right hand of God but is not so far away from us to be called near. He is closer than near.

a. The Holy Spirit now permanently indwells the believer.
b. There is worldwide missionary activity.
c. The Royal Priesthood of the believer is evident. Every believer is a priest and can enter the presence of God (1 Peter 2:5-9). We don't need anyone to intercede for us. Jesus is our advocate (Galatians 3 26-28; Hebrews 7:28-8:13).
d. Christians are the body of Christ (Colossians 1:18).
e. Christians are the bride of Christ (Ephesians 5:25-27; 2 Corinthians 11:2; Revelation 21:2; Revelation 19:7-9).
f. We are not under the Law, but grace (Romans 6:14).
g. Salvation is by believing God, not doing good works. Good works are proof of our salvation. But understand that the "lost" can also do good works, so good works are not the way to salvation.
h. There will be wars and rumors of war (Matthew 24:6-7).
i. The poor will be with us always (Matthew 26:11a).

Scripture tells us that the Church Age will continue until the last soul who will accept Jesus as Savior and Lord has done so. We also know that all prophecy pertaining to the rapture of the Church has already been fulfilled. There is no unfulfilled prophesy that must be filled. The rapture can occur at any time. Only after the rapture of the church will the last seven years of the Jewish Age begin.

THE TRIBULATION PERIOD ~ THE JEWISH AGE—continued—

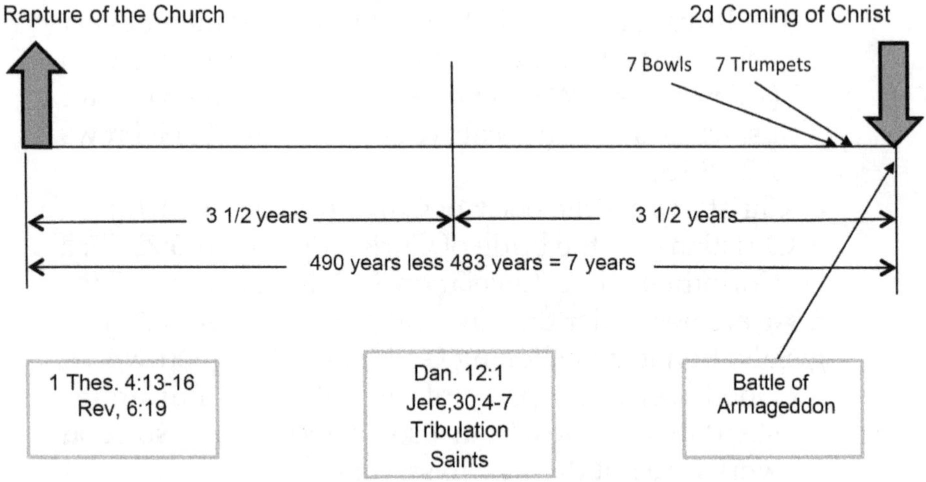

THE BEGINNING

What can I say about the Tribulation period? It's going to be the worst of times, and you don't want to be on Earth during that time. The good news is you don't have to be. Believers will not be around when the Tribulation Period begins. We will be raptured, and only unbelievers will be left. It's your choice.

If you look around and discover there are no Christians anywhere, it's too late to escape. You're in the Tribulation. The good news is that you still can accept Christ as your Savior and avoid the final judgment of the spiritually dead. They will receive the mark of the beast on the outside and will be full of dead men's bones on the inside. You'll be tempted to take the Mark of the beast, but if you're brave and do not, you will not be able to conduct commerce and will eventually be martyred. BUT great will be your reward, for you will reign with Christ for 1,000 years (Revelation 20:4) and have an everlasting life as one of God's children in heaven.

The Rapture of the Church closes the parenthesis, and the Jewish Age resumes the last seven years of the 490 years that Gabriel promised Daniel 483 years had been completed prior to the Church Age. The last seven years begin. When these last seven years are completed, the Messiah will come to reign for 1,000 years on Earth as the Angel Gabriel promised Daniel.

Now without the influence of the Church, without the presence of Christians to counter the power of Satan and his demons, the world quickly descends into chaos. There will be a great need for someone to step up and re-establish order. People will be willing to give up all of their independence to regain that lost order. A gentile Politician out of the east will prove to be very effective and provide what appears to be exceptional leadership. He will continue to gain more and more power and will climb the ladder to become the world leader very rapidly. His objective is to create and head a one world government. He is the antichrist. This gentile political leader will appear as an outstanding problem solver, saying he wants to establish world peace. Now, what could be wrong with that? Isn't it the answer to everyone's prayers? They should know that a snowball has a better chance of existing in hell than world peace being accomplished until Christ reigns on earth.

The antichrist will solve the problem between the Muslin nations and Israel with diplomacy. He will sign a 7-year treaty with Israel to "protect" Israel from all who would harm her. The Tribulation begins when the agreement is signed. But it will be broken by the Antichrist halfway through its term. So, three and one-half years into the tribulation period devastating events begin to happen.

Daniel 9:27 (NIV)

27 He will confirm a covenant with many for one 'seven.' (seven years) In the middle of the 'seven' (31/2 years) he will put an end to sacrifice and offering. And at the temple, he will set up an abomination (an idol of himself, some say he will sit on the throne in the holy of holies and proclaim that he is god) that causes desolation, until the end that is decreed is poured out on him.

One of the last things that happen in the first half of this age is that the Antichrist kills the "two witnesses" (Revelation 11:7-13). This will be allowed so they can dramatically complete their mission. Everyone who would be saved has been saved. There will be worldwide celebrations and happiness now that the two witnesses are dead. Their dead bodies will be displayed on worldwide TV as they lie on the street for three and a half days. Then, with the world watching, God will bring them both back to life. They will stand up on their feet and then ascend to heaven. Every corner of the earth will be terrorized by what they will have witnessed. When we see God do great things, praise should follow, but their hearts were so hardened that they experienced nothing but terror.

Daniel 9:20-23 (NIV)—The Seventy "Sevens"

20 While I was speaking and praying, confessing my sin and the sin of my people Israel and making my request to the Lord my God for his holy hill - 21 while I was still in prayer, Gabriel, the man I had seen in the earlier vision, came to me in swift flight about the time of the evening sacrifice. 22 He instructed me and said to me, "Daniel, I have now come to give you insight and understanding. 23 As soon as you began to pray, a word went out, which I have come to tell you, for you are highly esteemed.

Daniel was a devoted man of faith; he proved his trust in God when he steadfastly defied the King's edict that only the king, would be worshiped. It was of no consequence to Daniel that he would be thrown into the fiery furnace, Daniel was determined to obey God and worship God only. He didn't get that faith from taking an attitude of "I'll just make the best of a bad situation." He was a man of God and studied God's word diligently. He REMEMBERED how God had provided and protected him throughout his lifetime. He was taken into captivity as a young man, and in his 60s as he is studying Jeremiah 25, understood and believed that his people would be in captivity for 70 years. Daniel concluded that there are only a few years left until they will be free. He had misinterpreted what he read and expected that at the end of his 70-year captivity, the Messiah would come. This was a gross miscalculation, and God would not let it stand. God sent the angel, Gabriel, to explain what will happen to the Jews before the Messiah comes. Daniel has recorded for us in Daniel 9:24-27 what Gabriel told him. Gabriel says in effect, "Daniel you have misunderstood. It will not be 70 years, but 70 times 7." Then he breaks down the 490 years into 3 groups. First there will be 7 sevens or 49 years, then immediately following there will be the second period of 62 sevens or 434 years, and finally 1 sevens or 7 years, but this period will not immediately follow the second period.

This visit was not shocking to Daniel, he writes of it in a matter-of-fact way. We can understand why when we remember the relationship Daniel and God had. He was not killed nor wounded when Israel was conquered but was taken to the King's house where he grew to be Nebuchadnezzar's primary advisor. He became the ruler of Babylon and chief over all the Wise Men. He had seen his friends Shadrach, Meshach, and Abednego delivered from the fiery furnace, and he had been delivered from the Lion's den by the Hand of God. Throughout his lifetime he had faithfully deflected any praise from himself to his God. Daniel daily communed with God through prayer, and God continually blessed him as he served three kings, Nebuchadnezzar, Belshazzar the Chaldean and Darius the Mede. Isn't it interesting that God wanted Daniel to understand what he was studying so much that he dispatched the Archangel Gabriel to explain it?

Daniel 9:24-26 (NIV)

24 *Seventy 'sevens' (70x7= 490 years) are decreed for your people and your holy city to finish transgression, to put an end to sin, to atone for wickedness, to bring in everlasting righteousness, to seal up vision and prophecy and to anoint the Most Holy Place.* 25 *Know and understand this: From the time the word goes out to restore and rebuild Jerusalem until the Anointed One, the ruler, comes, there will be seven 'sevens,'(49 years) and sixty-two 'sevens.'(434 years) It will be rebuilt with streets and a trench, but in times of trouble.* 26 *After the sixty-two 'sevens,' the Anointed One will be put to death and will have nothing.*

The first 49 years begins with a decree to rebuild Jerusalem and ends when the project is wholly rebuilt with walls, streets, and even a moat. This whole project is completed during troubled times. The second block of time, 434 years, immediately follows the first block for a total of 483 years. The third block of seven years would not immediately follow the second block.

Verse 26 says the Messiah shall be cut off and shall have nothing. The Hebrew word for "cut off" means to be killed. The implication is that He wouldn't just be killed, but He would die a penal death by execution. The Hebrew expression translated "and shall have nothing" has two meanings, one emphasizing Messiah's state of "complete death." It can also be translated "but not for Himself." The meaning would then be that He died for others rather than himself, a substitutional death. The latter is more consistent with what the prophets had to say about the Messiah's death (Isaiah 53:1-12).

Messiah was executed as a criminal, died, and was buried as recorded in Daniel during the 62 sevens (434 years), and very close (about 50 days) to the end of the period.

The Roman Legions will come and destroy the city and the sanctuary. The end will come like a flood: war will continue until the end, and desolations have been decreed.

The city and the Temple that had been rebuilt would now be destroyed. So sometime after Messiah was executed, Jerusalem and the Temple would be destroyed again. This happened in AD 70 when the Roman legions destroyed the city as Jesus had prophesied. "Not one stone would be left on another."

Mark 13:1-2 (NIV)

> 1 *As Jesus was leaving the temple, one of his disciples said to him, "Look, Teacher! What massive stones! What magnificent buildings!"* 2 *"Do you see all these great buildings?" replied Jesus. "Not one stone here will be left on another; everyone will be thrown down."*

Matthew 24:1-35 (NIV)

> 1 *Jesus left the temple and was walking away when his disciples came up to him to call his attention to it's buildings.* 2 *"Do you see all these things?" he asked. "Truly I tell you, not one stone here will be left on another; everyone will be thrown down."*

Luke 21:5-6 (NIV)

> 5 *Some of his disciples were remarking about how the temple was adorned with beautiful stones and*

with gifts dedicated to God. But Jesus said, [6] "As for what you see here, the time will come when not one stone will be left on another; every one of them will be thrown down."

It happened fast and furiously, much like how a flood overtakes and entirely destroys. Therefore, Messiah was executed sometime before 70 AD. The next verse skips a whole lot of years, and there is no way to calculate how many because it omits the entire Church Age. We are living in the Church Age, and there is no known prophecy foretelling how long it will last. We know when it starts and how it ends, but we don't know how long it will last. Daniel 27 picks up at the beginning of the last seven years of the Jewish Age—the Tribulation period.

Daniel 9:27 (NIV)

[27] He (the antichrist) will confirm a covenant with many (Israel and other nations who want to go to war against Israel) for one "seven." In the middle of the "seven," he will put an end to sacrifice and offering. And at the temple, he will set up an abomination that causes desolation until the end that is decreed is poured out on him.

Verse 27 concerns the last seven years that will complete the 490 years that Daniel describes. 483 years into this timetable, the Church Age is inserted for an undetermined amount of time. Nearly 2,000 years ago the disciples asked Jesus when these last times would come. His response was, "Only God the Father knows."

Some of the disciples were still puzzled. After all, they had been so impressed with the Temple, but now the prediction was that it would be utterly destroyed, so they came to Jesus for clarification.

Matthew 24:3 (NIV)

[3] As Jesus was sitting on the Mount of Olives, the disciples (Peter, James, John, and Andrew) came to him privately. "Tell us," they said, "when will this happen, and what will be the sign of your coming and of the end of the age?"

They asked three questions: 1. When will the Temple be destroyed? 2. What will be the sign of your coming? 3. What will be the sign of the end of the age?

Jesus answers all three questions, but not in the order they were asked. He answered the last question first, the second question next, and the first question last.

Question 3. What will be the sign of the end of the age?

Matthew 24:4-14 (NIV)

[4] Jesus answered: "Watch out that no one deceives you. [5] For many will come in my name, claiming, 'I am the Messiah,' and will deceive many. [6] You will hear of wars and rumors of wars but see to it that you are not alarmed. Such things must happen, but the end is still to come. [7] Nation will rise against nation, and kingdom against kingdom. There will be famines and earthquakes in various places. [8] All these are the beginning of birth pains. [9] "Then you will be handed over to be persecuted and put to death, and you will be hated by all nations because of Me. [10] At that time many will turn away from the faith and will betray and hate each other, [11] and many false prophets will appear and deceive many people. [12] Because of the increase of wickedness, the love of most will grow cold, [13] but the one who stands firm to the end will be saved. [14] And this Gospel of the kingdom will be preached in the whole

world as a testimony to all nations, and then the end will come."

Question 2. What will be the sign of Christ's coming? These questions were answered during the last ten years of the Jewish Age. The answer to question 2 is for the Tribulation Saints and addresses an event that is still in the future.

Matthew 24:15-21 NIV

15 So when you see standing in the holy place 'the abomination that causes desolation, spoken of through the prophet Daniel – let the reader understand – 16 then let those who are in Judea flee to the mountains. 17 Let no one on the housetop go down to take anything out of the house. 18 Let no one in the field go back to get their cloak.19 How dreadful it will be in those days for pregnant women and nursing mothers! 20 Pray that your flight will not take place in winter or on the Sabbath. 21 For then there will be great distress, unequaled from the beginning of the world until now – and never to be equaled again (go immediately, do not hesitate, run for your lives and get to the safe place God has prepared for you).

How would they know where to run to unless the Lord supernaturally leads them? All they need to do is recognize what is happening, and start running. No matter what directions they begin to run He will override it to correct their course to get them to the prepared place of safety.

Matthew 24:22-26 NIV

22 If those days had not been cut short, no one would survive, but for the sake of the elect those days will be shortened. 23 At that time if anyone says to you, 'Look, here is the Messiah!' or, 'There he is!' do not believe it. 24 For false messiahs and false prophets will appear and perform great signs and wonders to deceive, if possible, even the elect. [25] *See, I have told you ahead of time.* [26] *"So if anyone tells you, 'There he is, out in the wilderness,' do not go out; or, 'Here he is, in the inner rooms,' do not believe it.*

Jesus was in effect saying: do not believe them because when I return it will not be in secret, everyone will know.

Matthew 24:27-35 NIV

[27] *For as lightning that comes from the east is visible even in the west, so will be the coming of the Son of Man.* [28] *Wherever there is a carcass, there the vultures will gather.* [29] *Immediately after the distress of those days 'the sun will be darkened, and the moon will not give its light; the stars will fall from the sky, and the heavenly bodies will be shaken.'* [30] *Then will appear the sign of the Son of Man in heaven. And then all the peoples of the earth will mourn when they see the Son of Man coming on the clouds of heaven, with power and great glory.* [31] *And he will send his angels with a loud trumpet call, and they will gather his elect from the four winds, from one end of the heavens to the other.* [32] *Now learn this lesson from the fig tree: As soon as its twigs get tender and its leaves come out, you know that summer is near.* [33] *Even so, when you see all these things, you know that It is near, right at the door.* [34] *Truly I tell you, this generation (not the generation of the disciples but the generation of the tribulation) will certainly not pass away until all these things have happened.* [35] *Heaven and earth will pass away, (this will happen at the end of the 1,000-year reign of Christ on earth) but my words will never pass away.*

Question 3. When will these things happen?

Matthew 24:36 NIV

[36] *But about that day or hour no one knows, not even the angels in heaven, nor the Son, but only the Father.*

2. THE LAST HALF OF THE TRIBULATION PERIOD

The abomination at the midpoint of the Age causes God to respond with unrelenting punishment. Anytime God punishes, the intent is to bless, and God will bless many as they seek Him. God will systematically destroy what He has always provided. It's like a man saying he can create life. First, you spread a little DNA onto a Petri dish, and God says, "Wait just one minute, make your own DNA."

Revelation 16:1-16 tells us about the pouring out of The Seven Bowls of God's Wrath.

1st bowl – Will be directed at those who had the mark of the beast and worshiped him. It will cause ugly festering sores.

2nd bowl – Will turn the sea into blood, killing every living thing in the sea.

3rd bowl – Will turn the rivers and springs into blood.

4th bowl – Will be poured out on the sun, perhaps destroying the ozone, so that the people will be seared and scorched.

We all know firsthand how much a little sunburn can hurt. That does not come close to comparing to how these people will suffer. These bowls were intended to bring the people back to the true God. They display His restrained power. But the people cursed God for causing their troubles. So, the bowls will continue to be poured out.

These judgments are not retaliatory; they are an act of love. God knows what is waiting for them after the Great White Throne judgment, and His love will go to any extreme to protect us from His Perfect Justice and Righteousness. He wants desperately to bring the people to the point that they recognize and acknowledge that God is God, and we are not, and for us to turn to Him. God will have done everything He could, short of violating man's volition, so much so that even those who do not accept His free gift of salvation will have to confess that His judgment on them is fair.

5th bowl – The bowl of darkness will be poured out on the throne of the beast. The throne will be thought of as the seat of ultimate enlightenment and pleasure. There will be utter darkness (absence of any trace of light). Total darkness is the absence of light. There will be a complete failure of electrical power sources, the absence of the Sun, Moon, and stars. There will be no source of light what-so-ever, even battery powered lights and cell phones will fail, and the people will bite their tongues in the anguish of it.

Someone has described hell as being in utter darkness without any functioning senses other than the pain of sounds, touch, and smell, and the inability to communicate. In other words, complete "aloneness." The people will refuse to repent for what they have done.

6th bowl – The river was seen as the source of the city's wealth. The commerce of many kinds will come to an end. Evil spirits will come out of the mouths of the dragon, the beast, and the false prophet. They will go to the heads of the nations of the world and gathered their armies for war. They will join forces at Armageddon.

7th bowl – Flashes of lightning, rumblings, and rolling thunder will precede the worse earthquake in all of history. 100-pound hailstones will fall on people. Yet the people will curse God, not repent.

Afterward, the seven trumpets will begin.

The first, second and third trumpets:

Revelation 8:7-12

7 *The first angel sounded his trumpet, and there*
came hail and fire mixed with blood, and it was
hurled down on the earth. A third of the earth was
burned up, a third of the trees were burned up, and
all the green grass was burned up.
8 *The second angel sounded his trumpet, and some-*
thing like a huge mountain, all ablaze, was thrown
into the sea. A third of the sea turned into blood, 9 *a*
third of the living creatures in the sea died, and a
third of the ships were destroyed.
10 *The third angel sounded his trumpet, and a great*
star, blazing like a torch, fell from the sky on a third
*of the rivers and on the springs of water -*11 *the name*
of the star is Wormwood. A third of the waters
turned bitter, and many people died from the waters
that had become bitter.

The fourth trumpet:

12 *The fourth angel sounded his trumpet, and a third*
of the sun was struck, a third of the moon, and a
third of the stars, so that a third of them turned
dark. A third of the day was without light, and also
a third of the night.

The days and nights will be shortened by four hours each. The shortened day will affect the crops, and with one third of the moon darkened, the ocean's tides will also be affected. Everything that happens until now has really been terrifying. The world seems as if it is being destroyed. People are dying and suffering wishing they were dead, but now even worse things are foretold.

The fifth trumpet:

Revelation 9:1-4 (NIV)

[1]The fifth angel sounded his trumpet, and I saw a star that had fallen from the sky to the earth. The star was given the key to the shaft of the Abyss. [2]When he opened the Abyss; smoke rose from it like the smoke from a gigantic furnace. The sun and sky were darkened by the smoke from the Abyss. [3]And out of the smoke locusts came down on the earth and were given power like that of scorpions of the earth. [4]They were told not to harm the grass of the earth or any plant or tree, but only those people who did not have the seal of God on their foreheads."

People will be saved during the Tribulation Age, and they will be given a mark or seal on their foreheads. It is not hard to surmise that this "seal" will be visible only to other Tribulation Saints and instruments of God such as these locusts. Otherwise, they would be easily identified by the satanic forces that rule.

Revelation 9:5-21 (NIV)

[5]They were not allowed to kill them but only to torture them for five months. And the agony they suffered was like that of the sting of a scorpion when it strikes. [6]During those days people will seek death but will not find it; they will long to die, but death will elude them. [7]The locusts looked like horses prepared for battle. On their heads, they wore something like crowns of gold, and their faces resembled human faces. [8] Their hair was like women's hair, and their teeth were like lions' teeth· [9] They had breastplates like breastplates of iron, and the sound of their wings was like the thundering of many horses and chariots rushing into battle. [10] They had tails with stingers, like scorpions, and in their

tails, they had power to torment people for five months. [11] *They had as king over them the angel of the Abyss, whose name in Hebrew is Abaddon and in Greek is Apollyon (that is, Destroyer).* [12] *The first woe is past; two other woes are yet to come.*

The sixth trumpet:

[13] *The sixth angel sounded his trumpet, and I heard a voice coming from the four horns of the golden altar that is before God.* [14] *It said to the sixth angel who had the trumpet, "Release the four angels who are bound at the great river Euphrates."* [15] *And the four angels who had been kept ready for this very hour and day and month and year were released to kill a third of mankind.* [16] *The number of the mounted troops was twice ten thousand times ten thousand. I heard their number (200,000,000).* [17] *The horses and riders I saw in my vision looked like this: Their breastplates were fiery red, dark blue, and yellow as sulfur. The heads of the horses resembled the heads of lions, and out of their mouths came fire, smoke, and sulfur.* [18] *A third of mankind was killed by the three plagues of fire, smoke, and sulfur that came out of their mouths.* [19] *The power of the horses was in their mouths and in their tails; for their tails were like snakes, having heads with which they inflict injury.* [20] *The rest of mankind who were not killed by these plagues still did not repent of the work of their hands; they did not stop worshiping demons, and idols of gold, silver, bronze, stone, and wood – idols that cannot see or hear or walk.* [21] *Nor did they repent of their murders, their magic or, their sexual immorality or their thefts.*

It would seem that those left alive would realize that the unnatural calamities they have survived were supernatural and that they would have fallen on their faces recognizing that God Almighty was the source of their problems and surmised that since they survived, it was all for their benefit to bring them back into His Presence. But their calluses were too thick, and they just continued in their sinful lifestyle. Now a member of the Godhead, Jesus, Himself, will come just as He has always been expected, to set up His Righteous Kingdom.

The Seventh Trumpet:

Revelation 11:15 (NIV)

[15] The seventh angel sounded his trumpet, and there were loud voices in heaven, which said: "The kingdom of the world has become the kingdom of our Lord and of his Messiah, and he will reign forever and ever."

3. THE ENDING

All of the armies of the world are gathered to destroy Israel. Jesus comes back riding a white horse. This is the way the Israelites have always believed He would come. They missed the First Advent, but everyone will recognize the Second Advent. The Lord's bride will be with Him dresses in white robes. White seems strange for a battle, you may say. But the bride is not there to fight but rather to witness. The battle is the Lord's. The beast and the false prophet will be captured and thrown into the fiery lake. Jesus the Christ, the Messiah, will utterly destroy the armies that are gathered with the Words that He speaks.

Revelation 20:1-3 (NIV)

[1]And I saw an Angel coming down out of heaven the key to the abyss and holding in his hand a great chain. [2] He seized the Dragon that ancient serpent, who is the devil, or Satan and bound him for 1,000

years. [3] he threw him into the abyss and locked and sealed it over him, to keep him from deceiving the nation's anymore until the thousand years were ended.

4. EVENTS & CHARACTERISTICS OF THE TRIBULATION

a. The void caused by the rapture of the church will cause bewilderment and dismay by their loved ones.
b. Disasters will occur immediately. Pilotless airplanes fall from the sky, ships will run aground, and buses, trucks, and cars all crash because their drivers are gone.
c. The law enforcement agencies are diminished by the lack of Christians who are no longer there to respond. Lawlessness of all kinds will break out all over the world. There will be a worldwide calamity.
d. The Antichrist will make a 7-year treaty with Israel
e. At its midpoint (3 ½ years) he will break the treaty.
f. 144,000 believing Jews and the two witnesses will witness to a godless world.
g. The Antichrist will kill the two witnesses, and they will be left where they fell as the world watches and gloats.
h. After 3 ½ days, God will bring them back to life. They will stand up and then ascend into the heavens as the world gasps and is terrified.
i. God will dispense the seven bowls, and the people will curse God rather than embrace Him.
j. God will dispense the seven trumpets, and the people will continue to curse God.
k. The world's armies will gather at the Valley of Megiddo to destroy Israel.
l. The Lord Jesus Christ will return to earth this time, just as the Jews have always expected that He would come. He will come as the King of Kings and Lord of Lords and will destroy the world's Armed Forces and set up His kingdom on earth.

F. THE THOUSAND YEAR EARTHY REIGN OF JESUS

Revelation 20:4-6 (NIV)

4 I saw thrones on which were seated those who had been given authority to judge. And I saw the souls of those who had been beheaded because of their testimony about Jesus and because of the word of God. They had not worshiped the beast or its image and had not received its mark on their foreheads or their hands. They came to life and reigned with Christ a thousand years. 5 (The rest of the dead did not come to life until the thousand years were ended – the unbelievers). This is the first resurrection. 6 Blessed and holy are those who share in the first resurrection. The second death has no power over them, but they will be priests of God and of Christ and will reign with him for a thousand years.

THE BEGINNING

The Tribulation Period ends when Jesus defeats the armies of the world in the Valley of Megiddo in the battle of Armageddon, and He ushers in the beginning of His Millennium Reign on earth.

It is true that the word millennium does not appear in the Bible. However, in Revelation 20:4 the Bible states plainly that when Christ comes, He will reign on earth for 1,000 years. Millennium is the Latin word meaning 1,000. Therefore, it is entirely correct to say either the millennial reign or the 1,000-year reign.

2. THE END

As the Millennial Reign concludes, Satan will be set free to test the volition of the people who have populated the world for 1,000 years in a perfect environment with perfect justice without war. Satan will find world leaders who are greedy for power and will lead his final rebellion against the righteous. God will destroy this pagan army with fire from heaven. Then the old heavens and old earth will pass away, but there will be a new heaven and a new earth.

I think it is fitting to tell you that there are people who read Revelation 20:1-7 and cannot comprehend it, and therefore they do not believe it. They quote Scripture that is irrelevant and meaningless to this discussion, so be careful if you decide to do additional research on the subject. Pray for discernment and wisdom before you get started. If you search the web regarding the thousand-year reign of Christ, there are many articles written by people with different views than what I am about to present, but by far the majority of Biblical scholars agree that the premillennial interpretation of history is the most accurate and sound. You also need to know that there are three primary views as they pertain to the second coming of Christ. All three are very different, and each is held by Christians. None are damnable.

1. The Amillennialist view is that the 1,000 years reign of Jesus on earth is not literal, but a symbolic number. They believe the symbolic 1,000 years reign has already begun and is identical to the Church age. They think that Christ's reign during the millennium is spiritual in nature and at the end of the Church age Christ will return in final judgment to establish a permanent reign in the new heaven and new earth. They would prefer to be called now-millennials or realized millennials. This view sets no event or conditions that must take place before Christ returns. They believe the return of Christ is imminent; they confused the second coming of Christ with the rapture when Christ meets His bride the Church in the air. This view was introduced by Augustine in the fourth century and was dominate for a thousand years. Their understanding leaves

numerous promises that God has made to His people and the covenant with David unfulfilled. They and many unfulfilled prophesies that must come to pass before Christ will return requires a literal kingdom on earth. The Temple must be rebuilt, for one. The Amillennialist makes no provision for the rapture of the saints.

2. The Postmillennialist view was held by many during the nineteenth century. There are a few who still call themselves Postmillennialist today, and they believe that the church's influence will continue to make the earth a better and better place, and that through its aggressive evangelism and missions activities the world would be won to Christ. Jesus would reign in the hearts of Christians and the world so thoroughly, that it would last one thousand years. Then the Second Coming would take place. From the events of the War Between the States (inaccurately known as the Civil War) throughout American history up to and including this current time, the Postmillennial view has not been viewed favorably. Civilization is declining, not improving. The church is becoming irrelevant in the eyes of man. Fear in the Church and the Christian heart has neutralized our effectiveness. Of course, at this writing, the world's history is not complete. But for the postmillennial view to dominate Christian thinking again, the church will have to supernaturally reverse its decline. This view was at its zenith prior to 1860. I knew a postmillennial pastor who said he believed the rapture of the church would be one soul at a time as that believer died. But that is not the way Paul describes the grandeur of the rapture. This preacher only preached from the four Gospels, and the deacons believed the Bible was "full of errors."
3. The Premillennialists interpret the subject texts much the same as the Christians from the New Testament

times up to Augustine. They believe that the Church Age is the mystery and that it is inserted into the Jewish Age at Pentecost and the church will be raptured out of this world without warning. One of God's attributes is truth. When he speaks on a subject, what he says will happen, and does happen. God has made many promises in the Old Testament and New Testament about the establishment of an earthly Kingdom. These will be discussed as we continue the study.

From the very beginning History (His-Story) has been moving towards the Millennium Reign of Jesus, the Christ on earth. So how will this unique time be different from how it has always been, or from what we have known?

To find the answer, let's start with the Bible in the Book of Revelation chapter 20. This is one of the most controversial chapters in the Bible because of preconceived bias and beliefs. But to me, it quite simply lays out what will happen in a way that is easily understandable.

Revelation 20:1-2 (NIV) – The Thousand Years
1 *And I saw an angel coming down out of heaven, having the key to the Abyss and holding in his hand a great chain.* 2 *He seized the dragon, that ancient serpent, who is the devil, or Satan, and bound him for a thousand years.*

This is an angel with authority. It is not Jesus. He comes out of heaven with the key to the bottomless Abyss and a great chain. Satan will be bound and cast into the Abyss for a thousand years. Satan was once the most beautiful and most eloquent angel in God's Kingdom. He was the guardian of the Throne room. He had great power and authority, but now he is seized, subdued, chained, and cast into a place he didn't want to go. The Abyss is not the Lake of Fire that is reserved for the last judgment. Notice how completely the Bible reveals Satan's many identities. He is the dragon of the tribulation, the ancient serpent that deceived Eve, the devil and Satan. From the beginning of time up until this time, Satan roamed the earth like a lion looking for anyone he could devour (1Peter 5:8). Now he is bound up and shut off so he will have no influence.

Revelation 20:3

> 3 *He threw him into the Abyss and locked and sealed it over him, to keep him from deceiving the nations anymore until the 1,000 years were ended. After that, he must be set free for a short time.*

John sees this saga unfold, and when he writes about it, in his mind, it has already happened. When we read about the events of Eternal Future, we need to remember that they are true. They will happen just as we have been told. There is nothing gentle about Satan's capture. He will be thrown into the Abyss, and the door will be locked and sealed to ensure he will not get free until the 1,000 years had ended. This most eloquent being will be shut up, shut out, and shut down; there will be none of his influence until the reign of Jesus is completed.

The ensuing 1,000 years will be so wonderful. So why must Satan ever be set free?

The end of the tribulation comes at the battle of Armageddon. Jesus completely and utterly destroys the unbelieving forces that oppose Him. With all of the unbelievers dead and the birds feasting on their carcasses, is there anyone left to enter the millennial reign of Christ? Well, yes there is. Remember, the tribulation Saints were warned to run to the mountains to a place of safety that God had prepared for them. The only survivors of the tribulation are those Saints who made it into His protecting arms, their hiding place. These Saints are the ones who will enter into the millennial reign of Christ. I believe that the Saints will live for the entire 1,000 years. They will have children, and their children will have children. All these children and grandchildren will have to be taught the biblical principles that God has established for all of us. They will all still have a "sin nature." They will also have volition. They will have the same choice we have and the opportunity to accept Christ as their Lord and Savior, or not.

Jesus will reign over the entire world from His throne in Jerusalem. He will govern with one fist of velvet and one fist of steel. There will be no opposition to Jesus's rule. His reign will be one of righteousness; there will be swift and perfect justice, and unbounded love. There will be some crime during this period, but I would imagine it would be minimal. The people will still have a rebellious nature because the "sin nature" is still a part of their soul. No matter how compliant they are, their nature to sin will have to be dealt with. Some of these people will be good citizens and do as they're told. They celebrate Christmas, they go to church, and they stand and bow their heads, but do not pray. Their lips are silent, and their minds are empty of His presence because they do not know Him. They open their mouths to sing praises, but their hearts are empty of His love, so the songs are meaningless. They know the believer's vocabulary but don't have what the believers have—Jesus in their hearts. Satan will be loosed as prophesied. The purpose will be to test the volition of those who inhabit the world during the millennial reign. The people of this age will go through a refining and purification process. Those that are sludge will be judged with all of the unbelievers from the past ages by their works not their sins. It will not matter how good they might be if they don't have Jesus they will be short of the mark and will be found guilty. They will bow their knee and confess that Jesus is Lord, but it will be too late.

The Millennium period will prove that even under the best circumstances, a thousand years of safety, prosperity, health, long life, and peace the wickedness of an unrepentant and unredeemed heart cannot be changed.

Revelation 20:4

4 I saw thrones on which were seated those who had been given authority to judge. And I saw the souls of those who had been beheaded because of their testimony about Jesus and because of the word of God. They had not worshiped the beast or its image and had not received its mark on their foreheads or their hands. They came to life and reigned with Christ a thousand years.

The Tribulation Saints Will Reign With Christ During The 1,000 Years

Revelation 20:5

5 The rest of the dead did not come to life until the thousand years were ended.

In review, the souls of the Old and New Testament saints who died before Jesus were excitedly waiting in Paradise for Jesus and went to heaven with Him. The souls of the saints who died after Jesus were, in an instant, in the presence of the Lord in heaven. The bodies of both groups of believers will be summonsed, made new and suitable for their new environment, and reunited with their souls. Those believers who are still alive at the end of the Church Age will be snatched up body and soul. The bodies of the martyred Tribulation Saints will be united with their souls and will sit on thrones and reign with Christ for 1,000 years. The second death has no power over these.

Who are not accounted for? Oh yes, it's the unbelievers, the lost, the pagans, and the rebels who have continually rejected

Jesus. Their souls are still in Hades being tormented, and their bodies in their graves. They are the rest of the dead. Their day is coming, but not until the end of the 1,000 years. They will have their day in front of the Great White Throne.

Revelation 20:6

6 *Blessed and holy are those who share in the first resurrection. The second death has no power over them, but they will be priests of God and of Christ and will reign with him for a thousand years.*

The second death is reserved for the unbelievers. Throughout all of history, the only ones who do not die are the surviving tribulation saints. The dead Saints experience the first resurrection. The second death has no power over them. Only the unbelievers will be judged, and that judgment is based on their works, and then they will experience the second death.

The Judgment of Satan

Revelation 20:7-8

7 *When the thousand years are over, Satan will be released from his prison* 8 *and will go out to deceive the nations in the four corners of the earth – Gog and Magog – and to gather them for battle. In number, they are like the sand on the seashore.*

There is a lot of discussion over who Gog and Magog are, and I don't know or much care. They have lived under the rule of Jesus Christ and are evil. They are consumed with their lust for power. And have ascended into leadership positions over a population that is as numerous as sands on the seashore. The term refers to an overwhelming significant force that opposes God. The millennium Christians could not survive the ruthless attack of the well-armed savages. Satan is free to entice them with the idea that they can defeat God. How stupid can anyone be? But they believe

Satan, probably because theirs is a rebellious nature and off they go to do battle.

Revelation 20:9

> [9] *They marched across the breadth of the earth and surrounded the camp of God's people, the city he loves. But fire came down from heaven and devoured them.*

They've come from all over the world and surround God's people in Jerusalem. This situation reminds me of the United States Army Ranger who said, "Now they've got us surrounded, they're right where we want them, God help them!" That is a fitting description of what's about to happen to them. Fire came down from heaven and devoured them. God is our champion and defender. He preemptively attacks and utterly destroys them.

Revelation 20:10

> [10] *And the devil, who deceived them, was thrown into the lake of burning sulfur, where the beast and the false prophet had been thrown. They will be tormented day and night forever and ever.*

Now the devil is thrown into the lake of fire to be tormented day and night, but the fire will not consume him. One of the "scholars" commented in his writing that fire did not affect the devil. But the Bible says right here that he will be tormented day and night forever. Guess who's wrong! Anytime you see or hear something that disagrees with the Bible, know that the Bible is correct and what you are seeing or hearing is wrong and dangerous. That's an excellent reason to know what the Bible teaches.

The Judgment of the Dead

Revelation 20:11-12

[11] Then I saw a great white throne and Him (Jesus the Christ) who was seated on it. The earth and the heavens fled from His presence, and there was no place for them. [12] And I saw the dead, great and small, standing before the throne.

Who are the dead? Well, it's not the believers, because all the believers of all time are with Jesus. The dead are those that were spiritually dead because they rejected Jesus. Now they stand before Jesus the Christ to be judged. Those who were great in their day and those who were not, all stand before the throne.

Another book was opened, which is the Book of Life. The dead were judged according to what they had done as recorded in the books. The sea gave up the dead and death, and Hades gave up the dead that was in them, and each person was judged according to what he or she had done.

Revelation 20:14-15

[14] Then death and Hades were thrown into the lake of fire. The lake of fire is the second death. [15] Anyone whose name was not found written in the book of life was thrown into the lake of fire.

As the unbeliever stands before the judge, the books will be opened, and another book which is the Book of Life will be opened. I submit to you that the Book of Life is a book that lists the name of every person who has ever been born.

John 3:16-17

[16]God so loved the world that He gave His only Son so that whoever believed in Him would not perish but have everlasting life. [17]God did not send His Son into the world to condemn it but to save it."

Although all provisions had been made, even to the recording of our names in the Book of Life, those people who died without receiving the Righteousness of God, by accepting the work Jesus had offered, had their names blotted out of the Book of Life.

As the Clerk of the Court searches alphabetically for the name of the person standing before him, Charles S. Smith XXII, he comes to the name and sees that it has been blotted out or lined out. Since his name has been removed from the Book of Life, he will be judged based on his deeds. On his DEEDS not on his sins! Did you get that? Jesus was judged for our sins, all of them, and was found guilty!

That's how I believe it will be, but some disagree. They think that the moment we accept Jesus as our Lord and Savior, our names are written in the Book of Life. I like what I believe, but the point is the unbeliever's name will not be found in the book. The Clerk of the Court then goes to the Books of Deeds. He opens the Books of Deeds and once again searches alphabetically for the name. "Here it is," he says as he shows it to the accused. He confirms that the one standing before him is actually Charles S. Smith, XXII. Once that is established, the defendant is amazed to find that during his lifetime he had done 1,754,251 good deeds. The judge asks him, "Is this a complete list? Is anything left out?" Charles has to admit that he had no idea he had done so many good deeds and that it is complete and correct.

Charles will not be judged for his sins. That would be double jeopardy since Jesus has already paid the penalty for all of Charles' sins. Due to God's Righteousness and perfect Justice, those sins cannot be mentioned in this court. Based on the evidence that Charles does not have the Righteousness of God credited to his account (he did not accept the gift Jesus offered), his list of good deeds, no matter how long it is, or how great the good deeds were, comes up short of God's Righteousness, and Charles is condemned to the Lake of Fire.

Charles will kneel and confess that God's judgment is fair and just.

My lifespan is not the beginning or end of time, and neither is yours. There are forces at play that are far beyond you and me. The majority of believers do not understand how blessed we really are, and that is unfortunate because, without even a basic understanding of what Jesus has done for us, and how well we have been equipped to represent Him, we will be poorly prepared to defend against the assaults of the devil and his demons.

The Holy Spirit through Peter is telling us that the most important thing we can learn is to see as God sees. It may seem to us that nothing changes, but we must get in an operational mode so we will stop, think, and remember. It is vital that we, to the best of our ability, see as God sees. We are reminded in these verses that things are not as they seem.

> 2 Peter 3:1-10 (NIV)—The Day of the Lord
> 1 *Dear friends, this is now my second letter to you. I have written both of them as reminders to stimulate you to wholesome thinking.* 2 *I want you to recall the words spoken in the past by the holy prophets and the command given by our Lord and Savior through your apostles.*

It is essential that we Christians REMEMBER whose we are and that He is on His throne. Nothing happens that has not first been sifted through His fingers. What we see and hear are not as real as Almighty God, and we are His children. If we are in His will and doing the purpose He has called us to do; nothing will happen to keep us from completing that purpose. On the other hand, if we are not pursuing His mission for our life, He may remove us from this earth to make room for someone else to complete our objective. If we are in a life-or-death situation, we should be bold and not shrink from our witness. Remember, Jesus has defeated death, and if we die, we will be face to face with our Lord in much better place—a place we would not leave to come back for any reason.

> *3 Above all, you must understand that in the last day's scoffers will come, scoffing and following their own evil desires.*

Remember this is not Peter speaking as much as it is the Holy Spirit, who is giving us Jesus' warning and advanced notice of what will happen. "Above all" could be "Most importantly." You must understand that scoffers will come, mocking us and following their own evil desires.

> *4 They will say, "Where is this 'coming' he promised? Ever since our ancestors died, everything goes on as it has since the beginning of creation." 5 But they deliberately forget that long ago by God's word the heavens came into being and the earth was formed out of water and by water. 6 By these waters also the world of that time was deluged and destroyed. 7 By the same word, the present heavens and earth are reserved for fire, being kept for the Day of Judgment and destruction of the ungodly. 8 But do not forget this one thing, dear friends: With the Lord, a day is like a thousand years, and a thousand years are like a day. 9 The Lord is not slow in keeping his promise, as some understand slowness. Instead, he is patient with you, not wanting anyone to perish, but everyone to come to repentance. 10 But the day of the Lord will come like a thief.*

We are most likely to think of a thief coming at night, cloaked in darkness and being stealthy, but that's not what this is saying. In the days the Scriptures were written, thieves would come quickly and with overpowering force in light of day or the darkness of night. They would quickly take whatever they wanted. A great visual of this is the opening scene of the 1975 motion picture "The Wind and the Lion."

The heavens will disappear with a roar; the elements will be destroyed by fire, and the earth and everything that is done in it will be laid bare. This verse skips ahead to the end of the world. Further explanation is revealed below:

Revelation 21:1 (NIV)

> 1 *Then I saw "a new heaven and a new earth," for the first heaven and the first earth had passed away, and there was no longer any sea (separation).*

The first heaven and earth have passed away at God's command, and now we see a new heaven and a new earth. The sea has always represented separation, but there will be no separation. Jesus will be with us more than He has ever been.

What I want you to glean from these passages is precise and straightforward. Man will not destroy the earth! Man will not blow up the world in a Nuclear War. He will not destroy the world with global warming, nor will he be capable of killing the ecological system that sustains life on earth. How can I so boldly make such a statement? These seem to be treasonous statements or at least those of a raving maniac, but I've read the Bible, and I know how it all ends. This world will come to its end, but it will be God who is the destroyer, and not man. The world will not be destroyed until all of the events you have just read have been accomplished.

3. Events and Characteristics of the Millennial Reign of Christ
   a. For 1,000 years there will be a perfect environment (Isaiah 11:1-9).
   b. 1,000 years reign Israel is restored. In 1948 the nation of Israel was re-established, and its people began to resettle there. The countries that surround Israel have fought continuously to destroy it just as they

did in the Old Testament days. It appears that this is the beginning of the fulfillment of God's prophecy. When Christ returns to earth, He will again regather Jews that are still scattered all over the earth (Isaiah 35:3-10; Ezekiel 20:34).

c. There will be a maximum number of believers. They will be ecstatic as they worship God (Joel 2:28-29).
d. There will be no religion. Religion is man's efforts to please God through his own efforts, and thereby gain salvation. It's never been about what man can do for God, but always, from the very beginning, it's been about what God has done for man. To have a perfect environment, there can be no religion.
e. There will be perfect world government through Jesus Christ. There will still be nations, but universal rule will emanate from Jerusalem (Psalms 72; Isaiah 11:1-5; Zachariah 14:9).
f. Satan will be cast into the Abyss, and it will be securely locked and sealed so that there will be a 1,000 year without his influence.
g. Universal Peace will exist for the first time since the fall for man (Psalms. 46:9; Hosea 2:18; Micah 4:3).

Isaiah 2:4 NIV

4 He will judge between the nations and will settle disputes for many peoples. They will beat their swords into plowshares and their spears into pruning hooks. Nation will not take up sword against nation, nor will they train for war anymore.

h. Salvation. Just as it has always been, salvation will be by faith in Jesus Christ. The children of those saints who entered the Millennium will have to exercise positive volition toward Jesus, just as their parents did if they are going to be saved. Sadly, some will not.
i. Satan will be released to lead a rebellion and test the volition of those who have lived during the 1,000

years of perfect times. A vast army will gather, and God will destroy it with a breath of fire.

j. Satan will be thrown into the lake of fire to suffer day and night for ever.
k. The Great White Throne Judgment of the unbelievers.
l. The earth is destroyed as God removes His governing forces that provide it's stability.
m. A New heaven and New Earth appears.

Revelation 21:1-5 (PHILLIPS)

21 [1-4] *Then I saw a new Heaven and a new earth, for the first Heaven and the first earth had disappeared, and the sea was no more. I saw the holy city, the new Jerusalem, descending from God out of Heaven, prepared as a bride dressed in beauty for her husband. Then I heard a great voice from the throne crying, "See! The home of God is with men, and he will live among them. They shall be his people, and God himself shall be with them and will wipe away every tear from their eyes. Death shall be no more, and never again shall there be sorrow or crying or pain. For all those former things are past and gone."* [5] *Then he who is seated upon the throne said, "See, I am making all thing new!" And he added, "Write this down for my words are true and to be trusted!"*

Overview of His Story of the Times

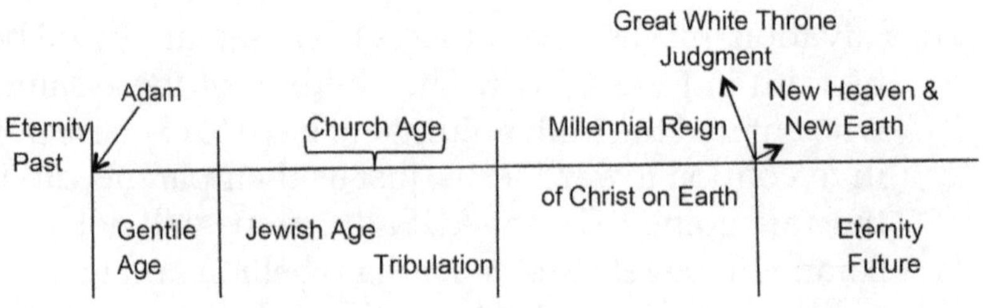

I've just scratched the surface of the history that we can know. There is so much more that God has revealed in His Word regarding His Story. You will uncover more ancient promises and prophecies if you become a miner and search the Scriptures for those "nuggets of gold" – the promises God has given you.

CONCLUSION

In the beginning, there was a reason *Light Up The Darkness* caught your eye. You opened it and perused its contents. There was something you saw that rang a bell, maybe for you, or for someone you love. Whatever the reason, perhaps you now have a better understanding of who God is and who we are in Christ.

God does really exist, and He is a loving God. He's not sitting in heaven waiting for us to make a mistake so He can zap us with some punitive tragedy. His desire is to always bless us. What He wants more than anything is to fellowship with us, to be the closest of friends. He loves us so much he recorded the very mind of Christ, and He continues to preserve it so we can know how and what He thinks. It is the ultimate authority on spiritual thinking. It is His love letter to humanity, The Bible.

You understand:

1. Christianity is not a religion, and Christians should not be trapped by religious thinking.
2. In our humanness, we feel a need to be in control, but that desire will only lead to doom, gloom, and despair. As Christians, we have a Champion who wants to fight our battles for us.

3. God has a master plan for our lives, and we have a purpose for being. -It is a mission impossible, but God has provided many powerful Operation Assets to assist the believer in accomplishing that purpose. The impossible is the realm in which God delights in operating.
4. You know Satan will use any tool available to implement Operation Neutralization and political correctness to defeat your efforts.
5. To embrace the importance of REMEMBERING how God has blessed and continues to bless you.
6. God has from the beginning and continues to intervene in history.
7. History is HisStory. We are told God created the world and He will ultimately destroy it. He has told us when and how. Therefore, you know that man will not.
8. You can be free from that worry. In fact, you should be free to live a worry-free life by trusting Him.

We have so much to be thankful for, and we know it. It should be easy for us to REMEMBER at least some of what He has done for us. We should be grateful, but we have a hard time REMEMBERING. That's not good because it is fundamental to the problem resolution process of any problem the believer will ever face. REMEMBER!!

REMEMBER as you face your problems, the most significant problem in your life has been solved. It was settled at Calvary's Cross some 2,000 years ago. Before there was you, God knew you and made provisions for you.

II Corinthians 5:21 (NIV)

21 *God made Him who had no sin to be sin for us so that in Him we might become the righteousness of God.*

Jesus Christ solved the sin problem completely once and for all, for every sin that you have ever committed or will ever commit. When you trusted the Son of God, when you received Him as your Lord and Savior, the Justice and Righteousness of God's character were satisfied, and your sins past, present, and future were forgiven and were blotted out. God has forgotten them. It is as if they never happened as far as God is concerned. Now you must forget them. Know that your adversary, Satan, will try to remind you of how terrible and vile you are. Consider the source and dismiss the allegation. Yes, that was you, but God has forgiven that, you are a new creation now.

Refuse to let that hang around your neck like a millstone. You entered into a relationship with God for eternity as well as in time.

Christians understand that accepting Jesus as their Lord and Savior means they have an everlasting life with their Savior, and we try to live our lives as God says we should live them. But we don't have a good and complete understanding of how God wants us to have a temporal relationship with Him. Our Lord wants to fellowship with us in "real" time, in the normalcy of our everyday life. God the Father very much wants a relationship with you moment by moment, every day. He wants to stroll with you in the cool of the evening and talk with you as the early morning dew falls. He really desires to be your constant companion. You can honor Him and represent Him best by realizing that as long as you are still alive, God has a purpose for your life. You have a reason for being. You are to always, regardless of the circumstances, glorify Him and fulfill your responsibilities as His ambassador.

365 time God speaking through the Bible tells us not to worry. It say's fear not. Fear is an acrostic for False Evidence Appearing Real. There are over 7,000 promises recorded in

God's Word for us to use as we need them. Why not become a prospector for them? When you find them mark them and remember them. We should be the happiest people in the world to smile and laugh more. People will wonder what you know, and you may get the opportunity to tell them.

Matthew 28:19-20

> [19]*Everywhere you go make disciples, baptize them in the name of the Father and the Son and the Holy Spirit, and teach them to obey everything I have commanded you.* [20]*And for sure I will be with you always to the very end.*

CPSIA information can be obtained
at www.ICGtesting.com
Printed in the USA
LVHW05s2347070518
576390LV00001B/176/P

9 781545 623978